INSIDE
TEAM SKY

Also by David Walsh:

Seven Deadly Sins

INSIDE
TEAM SKY
DAVID WALSH

**SIMON &
SCHUSTER**

London · New York · Sydney · Toronto · New Delhi

A CBS COMPANY

First published in Great Britain by Simon & Schuster UK Ltd, 2013
A CBS COMPANY

Copyright © 2013 by DW Publications Limited

1 3 5 7 9 10 8 6 4 2

Simon & Schuster UK Ltd
1st Floor
222 Gray's Inn Road
London WC1X 8HB

www.simonandschuster.co.uk

Simon & Schuster Australia, Sydney
Simon & Schuster India, New Delhi

A CIP catalogue record for this book is available
from the British Library

All photographs © Getty Images

Hardback ISBN: 978-1-47113-331-2
Trade paperback ISBN: 978-1-47113-332-9
eBook ISBN: 978-1-47113-334-3

Typeset in the UK by M Rules
Printed and bound by CPI Group (UK) Ltd, Croydon, CR0 4YY

For Jess, John and little Rory.

Team Sky characters

Staff:

Sir David 'Dave' Brailsford
Conductor of the orchestra that is Team Sky, Dave Brailsford is Team Principal. Brailsford's Midas touch extends both to Team Sky – seeing Wiggins ride to 2012 Tour de France victory – and his role as performance director of British Cycling, leading Team GB to unrivalled cycling success including eight gold medals at the London 2012 Olympic Games.

Rod Ellingworth
After a short spell as a pro, Rod found his real talent was coaching. Now Performance Manager within the team and another of the British Cycling *émigrés*, Ellingworth has brought a generation of successful British road racers through his U23 Academy.

Tim Kerrison
Head of Performance Support, Kerrison is the sports scientist of the group. Coming from huge successes with the Australian swimming team, his arsenal includes a deep knowledge of the

science but it comes with a humanity that allows him to be both man and genius to his athletic charges.

Alan Farrell
At the beginning of 2012, Alan Farrell was just a doctor with a passion for cycling; now he is Lead Doctor in the most successful pro team in the world. Covering all three Grand Tours in his first year, Alan was thrown in at the deep end but like a boy who'd run away with the circus, he was in his element.

Mario Pafundi
Hailing from Southern Italy, Mario Pafundi is Lead Carer. He brings his infectious Italian charm to everything he touches, including aching legs, sleepy hotel staff, colleagues at the dinner table. And because of how he's lived his life, he sleeps on seven pillows.

Gary Blem
South African Gary Blem is Lead Mechanic. Humble and down to earth, Gary is a master of his craft and a dealer in respect and fairness. 'Froomey,' he says, 'is a Kenyan and African.'

2013 Tour de France riders:

Chris Froome, 28
Chris Froome leads the team into the 2013 Tour de France. A poly-national if ever there was one, this summer Chris flies the Team Sky flag, and he intends to plant it at the top of every mountain.

Richie Porte, 28

Richie is Tasmanian, a talented climber and comes into the Tour in the midst of an impressive season of racing including a win at Paris–Nice. What he lacks in height he makes up for in 'small man attitude'.

Geraint 'G' Thomas MBE, 27

Flitting between track and road, this Welshman is no stranger to success. With Olympic gold in both Beijing and London in the team pursuit, G goes into the Tour hoping to show that in today's Tour you can see tomorrow's champion.

Kanstantsin 'Kosta' Siutsou, 30

Siutsou is a reliable engine from Belarus, useful for taking the strain for long sections of the stage. After leaving the 2012 Tour early due to a broken leg, Kosta has been eyeing up 2013 from a long way out.

Vasil 'Kiry' Kiryienka, 32

The second big Belarusian engine, Kiryienka is known for putting himself on the ropes to preserve his team leader's legs. Easily the most stylish rider in the team.

Peter Kennaugh MBE, 24

Born on the Isle of Man, Pete Kennaugh is the youngest of the team and rides his first Tour de France in 2013. Not one to cower at big events, Kennaugh's mettle earned him a gold medal at the London 2012 Games.

Edvald Boasson Hagen, 26

The only Norwegian in the squad is also the only rider to have made it to every Team Sky Tour de France in the right colours. So classy is Eddy that everyone wonders why he doesn't win more.

David López, 32

This Spanish *domestique* is a new recruit for Team Sky after signing him at the end of the 2012 season from Movistar. Because Froome prefers to room with his friend Porte, López will be given the one single room available to the riders at the team hotels.

Ian Stannard, 26

The third big engine of the group, this time of a British stripe. Sporting some of the biggest pistons in the peloton, 2013 will be Stannard's first ever Tour de France.

CHAPTER ONE

"Butterfly, don't flutter by, stay a little while with me."

Danyel Gérard, 'Butterfly'

It is Thursday afternoon, 27 July, two days before the start of the Tour de France, 110 years after the first staging of this pilgrimage. Back then it was men and bikes, now the cyclists are just part of the commercial juggernaut that follows the money and takes over part of Western Europe every July. For the start of this year's race, the Tour has set up camp on the island of Corsica.

For me this Tour is the beginning of the end of an odyssey with Team Sky. Eight months before, team boss Dave Brailsford had said, 'Come and live with us, spend as much time as you like. Look wherever you want, ask whatever questions you want.' It started in Malaga at the end of January, a week there. Then there was a second training-camp week in Tenerife, a few more days in Malaga, two days in Nice, two weeks at the Giro d'Italia and now, the Tour.

At the small airport in Figari, Marko Dzalo waits for me. It is the fourth time Sky has sent someone to pick me up. Always the designated driver is there before I land and the greeting is friendly and businesslike.

'How was your trip?'

'Yeah good. All well with the team?'

'Think so.'

It takes about twenty minutes to reach the hotel just outside Porto-Vecchio. Dzalo is a *soigneur* with Team Sky. Officially, the team prefers that he and the brotherhood of *soigneurs* are called 'carers'. Superficially this distinction is nothing – '*soigneur*' is the French word for 'one who cares for' – why should it matter that Sky has chosen to go with the English version?

But it does matter. They prefer 'carers' because traditionally *soigneurs* have been carriers and providers of doping products and central to the culture that Brailsford, performance manager Rod Ellingworth and head of performance Tim Kerrison despise. First you change the name, then the habits. To their own *soigneurs* they are saying, 'We employ you to care for the riders. Nothing more.'

To the rest of the peloton there is a message that some on the receiving end will chose to see as a two-fingered salute. Like Sky is saying, 'We are not like you.'

Among themselves Sky's rank and file staffers refer to the carers as 'swannies', which isn't exactly a toeing of the party line.

Dzalo and I got to know each other during the Giro d'Italia earlier in the summer. One short conversation stayed with me. We'd stayed at a hotel in Tarvisio, an Italian town close to the borders with Slovenia and Austria, and he had tweeted about his home country, the beautiful mountains he could see from the Italian side and the sign that said '12 kilometres to Slovenia'.

Next morning he was loading suitcases onto the truck when he said, 'You know my home town is just over that mountain. I could be there in no time.'

'Does it make you want to drop everything and just go?' I ask.

'No,' he said. 'I left home to work in this sport. This is my life, where I now belong.'

He was sure about the road he'd taken, no interest in turning back. This struck a chord because I'd encountered the same sense of purpose a lot in Team Sky. It is common for people in this sport to fall in love with the milieu and their lives on the road. A lot of the Sky people don't feel like that, but they do like the environment around their team: the good organisation, the intelligent approach to preparation, the behaviour demanded of both riders and staff.

Though they often complain about having to work longer hours than any other team, even on the worst days they don't speak of wanting to leave. Not many of the drifters who move from team to team stop off at Sky.

'Room two-one-two, second floor,' says Mario Pafundi as I pull my bag across the hotel car park. For two years running Pafundi has received the Team Sky staff award for 'Happiest Ant of the Year'. Head *soigneur* – or 'lead carer' – and an important character on the team. Bright, conscientious, Italian Mario has charm and good looks but nothing compares to the trick he runs with the room numbers.

Sky bring a team of nine riders and twenty-two support

staff to the Tour de France and it is Mario who gets to the hotel early and assigns riders and staff to the available rooms. He then takes all of the suitcases to their respective rooms and, over lunch, he sits down with the room list in front of him and memorises it. So when riders and staff arrive at the hotel they will quickly find Mario, who's never far away, and he will give them their room number.

Sometimes the key will be in the room, often it's at reception. Mario's efforts mean no one has to check in. '*Deux cent douze, s'il vous plaît,*' and on you go.

From 212 I look down on the car park in front of the hotel and admire the matter-of-fact cycling people go about their work. Bikes are checked, cars washed and, because I haven't seen some of these guys for five weeks, I wander down their way.

'Did you see last night's game, Spain and Italy?' David Fernandez, the mechanic asks.

'No,' I admit.

'Spain won seven-six on penalties, Jesus Navas got the winning penalty, the one who's going to Manchester City.'

There is general agreement that the mechanics and *soigneurs* work longer hours than everyone else in the team. For the mechanics, the Tour is a particular challenge as the riders all get new bikes for the race and they have to be set up exactly how each guy wants it.

For the Tour each rider has three road bikes and two time trial bikes, except Chris Froome and Richie Porte who have three road, two time trial and one other bike that is especially light and the one they will use in the mountains. That's forty-seven bikes and regardless of which mechanic gets a bike ready and passes it fit for racing, lead mechanic Gary Blem will then examine it and give it the second and final 'Okay.'

It is 7.30 on this beautiful Corsican evening when Brailsford returns from somewhere. Since I've been around the team he has been consistently friendly, helpful, at times disarmingly honest, and always interesting. The courtesies extended by the staff are in part a reflection of their respect for Brailsford. It was, after all, the boss's idea, so they all more or less bought into it.

We meet in the car park. Something's playing on his mind. There had been a press conference that afternoon and it hadn't passed smoothly. Now, a few hours later, he's gently shaking his head as if by doing so he can clear it.

'How did the press thing go?'

'It was all right, except for Paul's question.'

Paul Kimmage is one of my closest friends and three years previously he was in my exact position, all ready to travel with Team Sky on the Tour de France. The Kimmage/Team Sky marriage didn't survive the honeymoon. Kimmage's take on the divorce was straightforward. Brailsford had offered full access to the team but when he started to ask tough questions, they didn't like it.

Brailsford says he was deeply embarrassed by the way things turned out because he had given an undertaking that he couldn't honour. According to him, Kimmage rubbed people up the wrong way and they came to Brailsford with their objections. Part of the difficulty was that, while the team's policy precluded the employment of any rider or staff member with a doping past, not every rider or staff member was going to be comfortable with the kind of scrutiny that Kimmage wished to exercise.

Feeling that Kimmage's presence would negatively impact on the team performance, Brailsford withdrew the offer. Kimmage was furious. Their relationship never recovered.

'What did he ask you?'

'Towards the end, he asked a question about Eddie [Team Sky rider Edvald Boasson Hagen]. He said something like, "A few years ago Edvald was being spoken of as the next Eddy Merckx, why is he then not a contender here?" I expected Paul would ask a doping question and wasn't sure I'd heard correctly. So I repeated Paul's question back to him, saying "Are you asking why Edvald is not a contender here?" He said "Yes." He asked the question quietly but I still thought it was incredibly insulting to Edvald.

'He's a young guy, he's sitting there in front of hundreds of journalists and he's being made to look like he's some kind of failure. If the circumstances had been different, it would have been a fair question. Say Paul was interviewing me, one on one, or he was at a press conference where Tim Kerrison and I were being quizzed about the team performance, that question would have been fine.

'It's one we've discussed many times within the team. Eddie's a bit of a conundrum. He started really well within the team, then didn't progress as much as we expected but we feel like we're beginning to understand him better. Last year he didn't have a brilliant first half to the season, but rode really well at the Tour and finished second at the World Championships.

'This season it's been the same. Okay in the first half of the season but he's improved as he did last year and comes into this race on very good form. He's a very important member of the team and a really popular guy with the other riders. You could feel the other riders bristle when Paul asked that question because they would have felt it was disrespectful to Eddie. I thought it was too, and I just said, "You have your opinions and you're entitled to them and I have mine."

'In terms of world ranking points, Eddie is twelfth. He's a very good rider and I just wanted to lean over towards him when Paul asked that question and say, "Don't pay any attention to this, Eddie, this isn't about you, this is about this guy getting at me and getting at the team." In that setting, I thought it was a cheap shot and I can understand why the riders were pissed.'

I find myself in the unusual position of hearing about a small journalist/manager contretemps but from the point of view of the latter. Boasson Hagen thought the question slightly unfair but wasn't bothered by it. Laid back and ultra calm by nature, it would take more than that to ruffle his Norwegian feathers.

'After you gave Paul the answer about your opinion differing from his, I presume you then defended Edvald?' I say, suspecting that in his anger at Kimmage he'd not done this.

He looks at me silently, confirmation of what I'd imagined.

Through years of success with the Team GB track cycling team, and more recently with Team Sky, Brailsford regularly lauded the influence of forensic psychiatrist Steve Peters who worked with him and a high percentage of the athletes who passed through the GB system. One important Peters contribution was his 'chimp model' analysis, that both athletes' and managers' performances diminished when actions were inspired by the irrational side of their personalities. The 'chimp' is essentially an emotional machine that behaves independently of us. It is neither good nor bad. It competes with our 'computer', the logical and calculating side of our character, and if left to dominate can result in bad decision making. We are not responsible for the nature of our chimp but we are responsible for managing them. If you understand that part of your own brain, the part that reacts emotionally rather than logically, you will be more effective.

It is a concept that has been embraced by Team Sky's management, and within the team different individuals talk about the chimp and the need to keep it in its place. Brailsford is an avid believer, or at least he was until Kimmage asked that question. Then it was over to you, Mr Chimp, you tell Kimmage what you think of him.

In 2012 Dave Brailsford felt his chimp straining at the leash a lot of the time on the Tour. He was taken aback at the ferocity of the questioning his team faced on the doping issue and this year he had assumed that the issue would have faded away.

'Last year it seemed full on, and I had never been exposed to that level of aggression. I couldn't get my head around how unjust it was, and this time last year I felt just rotten. I felt terrible for Tim [Kerrison] who I had persuaded to come into this sport.'

Dave Brailsford is not often wrong, but on this assumption he was. Nothing had faded away. His antagonism towards Paul Kimmage's edgy but not particularly disrespectful question at the pre-race press conference showed his chimp had made the journey to Corsica. It is remarkable a man so bright can so easily lose his ability to be rational and do what is best for the team.

As the Tour unfolds there will be press conferences far more hostile than that opening salvo on the cruise ferry. And Brailsford knows he will have to do better.

By now Brailsford is sitting on the low shelf that runs across the back of the camper van, SKY 18. He senses he's made a bad start to his media performance at the Tour and though he barely shows the disappointment, it is there.

Rod Ellingworth, the team's performance manager, comes to where we're talking. Affable, enthusiastic, an outstanding planner. He has been for a walk and arrives with beads of sweat. Most mornings Brailsford and Kerrison, and general facilitator Dario Cioni will rise around six and be out on their bikes before seven. A former bike rider, Ellingworth has previously said he wouldn't be comfortable disappearing at that time in the morning, preferring instead to hang about, breakfasting with the carers and mechanics, available to anyone with a problem he can help solve.

Empathy comes easily to him and underpins his role within the team. A lot of the staff find it easy to relate to him, and him to them, and as well as his people skills he is a master planner. Quickly picking up on the fact that Brailsford isn't his usual self, Ellingworth makes a little small talk and soon carries on to the hotel.

Chris Haynes walks from the hotel, as quietly and as unobtrusively as he does most things in life. He is softy spoken, polite, gentle even, and you wonder how he was ever persuaded to head up Team Sky's media operation. His day job is in London with the ultra-successful *Sky Sports* television channels, where he is head of media and, though he consulted with and offered guidance to Team Sky, it was never more than an adjunct to his primary role.

Bradley Wiggins and a moment of breathtaking madness changed that. After the finish of the eighth stage of the 2012 Tour, Wiggins was asked in a press conference what he had to say to critics on Twitter who publicly accused him of doping. Perhaps the journalist asking the question didn't realise it, but this was one question guaranteed to evoke a vitriolic response from Wiggins.

Two months before he'd won the Tour de Romandie but soon after, while recovering with his family, he'd gone on Twitter and was sickened by what he read. A lot of people, mostly under the cover of their anonymous Twitter names, accused him of doping. For all the cool, Wiggins needs to be respected, even loved, and he couldn't just dismiss those accusing him as people who didn't know what they were talking about.

Instead he looked at himself as others were looking at him: dominant cyclist who wins time trials and occasional sprints, who stays with the best climbers in the mountains, yeah, he could see why there were suspicions. He thought it would be better if he didn't win his next race, the Dauphiné Libéré, as another victory would only make things worse. He worried what winning the Tour de France would do to his reputation. He told his wife Cath that he didn't want to win the Tour.

Shane Sutton, the mate and Team GB coach who wasn't afraid to stand up to him, told Wiggins to ignore the accusers. He said he wasn't able to do that. Tim Kerrison told him to accept that he was going to get this kind of criticism. He stopped checking Twitter, tried to put it out of his mind, but it lay there, in a quiet corner, waiting to be roused.

So the question comes at him like a grenade. He catches, pulls the pin, and flings it back into the crowd.

'I say they're just fucking wankers. I cannot be doing with people like that. It justifies their own bone-idleness because they can't ever imagine applying themselves to doing anything in their lives. It's easy for them to sit under a pseudonym on Twitter and write that sort of shit, rather than get off their arses in their own lives and apply themselves and work hard at something and achieve something. And that's ultimately it. Cunts.'

To get 'fucking', 'wankers', 'shit', 'arses' and 'cunts' in one answer must be a record, possibly even more rare than winning Paris–Nice, Tour de Romandie, Dauphiné Libéré, Tour de France, and an Olympic gold medal in the same season, as Wiggins did. You could rightly argue about how he expressed his frustration, but if he was clean, as he insisted he was, then it was easy to understand what drove him to say exactly what was on his mind, and in exactly the way he wanted to say it.

Back at BSkyB's headquarters, the corporate bosses may have empathised with the sentiments but they wouldn't have liked the expletives. Wiggins's targets could have been Sky subscribers! Chris Haynes was on the next plane to France. Wiggins once said, 'I'm not a well-trained corporate dream.' That much was apparent when he made the air turn blue in the small Swiss town of Porrentruy.

Haynes, though, is a paragon of reasonableness and it is difficult not to agree with most of what he says. Before he took his place in the front line at Team Sky there had been accusations of Team Sky trying to influence what was asked at press conferences. They'd ask journalists not to ask about such-and-such doping case because there was always the fear that Wiggins or Cavendish might react badly.

That desire to control the agenda irritated journalists and offered another reason to any journalist inclined to dislike the team. Of which there were plenty.

Haynes came with a more grown-up attitude, extolling the virtues of openness and encouraging the riders to see doping questions as inevitable and understandable. He reminded Wiggins that his knowledge of, and appreciation for, cycling's history was something that would endear him to fans of the sport, especially to continental Europeans. By the end Wiggins was in his element speaking with reporters, eloquent and utterly engaging, maybe even almost a 'well-trained corporate dream'.

The improvement changed Haynes's life, as he was seconded from BSkyB to Team Sky and he now divides his time between both. We ran together one morning during the Giro d'Italia, up a hill from our Italian hotel, round a few corners, then down a long straight road and past an unmanned border crossing and into Slovenia. Alas, we didn't have the stamina to reach Marko Dzalo's home town.

That morning Chris spoke a lot about his son who was about to go to his first Tottenham Hotspur game without an adult and Chris was both excited and nervous about this rite of passage experience. A few days before he had been speaking about his family and told me that although the boy was from his partner's previous relationship, he loved him as if he was his own son.

'Chris,' I said, 'what you mean is that you love him as *a son*, no qualification.'

A couple of days later we were talking again and he said there was something he wanted to say to me. 'You know what you said to me the other day?' I knew. 'That meant a lot to me. Thank you.'

Such sensibility hardly goes with the media manager's job but Haynes isn't your common-or-garden PR operator.

And when he came out of the Golfe Hotel in Porto-Vecchio, it was good to see him. We chatted for a bit; he then had to take a call, but when he came back a few minutes later he was excited. 'You know what's just happened?' he said. 'A beautiful butterfly came fluttering by, landed just there, and rose again and flew on. The butterfly was yellow-coloured, totally yellow.'

He saw it as an omen, this *papillon jaune*, a portent of good things to come.

The butterfly, which drops into Corsica on its journey from North Africa, is called Clouded Yellow.

CHAPTER TWO

'The best executive is the one who has sense enough to pick good men to do what he wants done, and self-restraint enough to keep from meddling with them while they do it.'

Theodore Roosevelt

On the evening before the Tour begins, a staff meeting is called for nine o'clock on the team bus. This is the team's fourth year and among the foot soldiers this gathering has taken on the status of the pre-Tour call to arms. By 8.55 most of the staff are in their places, the nine available seats filled, everyone else standing or sitting in the aisle. Excitement hangs in the air, tinged with apprehension for they know what they will have to do over the four weeks and whatever happens, it won't be easy.

At the front of the bus a digital clock with illuminated red numbers moves silently from 8.53 through 8.54 to 8.55 but in a team where everything is timed, it starts to draw attention.

'Who's not here?'

They search for the missing.

'He's gonna be late, gonna be in trouble,' someone says. There is laughter at the thought of imminent embarrassment.

Those who arrive in the nick of time are not jeered because they have cut it fine, but cheered because they are not actually late. At 8.59 everyone is present. Where's the fun in that? It's like we're in the Colosseum and the emperor has given everyone the thumbs-up.

The real emperor stands at the front of the bus. Forty-nine years of age, so neatly built his shaven head seems part of his DNA, clean-cut genetics. He smiles easily and is a natural communicator. People listen. His lucidity will carry him through this meeting. It was curious that in John Dower's beautifully made documentary about Bradley Wiggins' victory in the 2012 Tour, Brailsford claimed he didn't really have friends and was by nature a loner.

That's not the person he seems to rank-and-file Team Sky staff, all of whom are comfortable in his company and most of whom like him. He takes out his iPhone and asks if he can take a group photo of everyone on the bus. There is something vaguely flattering when the boss asks to photograph the staff and, immediately, people are listening. They look towards him, the digitally reproduced shutter sound is heard among the grins.

He then talks about the memories this photo might evoke in six months' time and what each individual will think when he looks at it. 'What you will want to say is that they were the best group of guys I ever worked with, as good as any team could have had. You also want to be able to say, "We were good together on that Tour, there wasn't another thing we could have done."'

Brailsford then speaks of his role and their importance. 'I am just the conductor of this orchestra, you are the guys who play the instruments and you were hand-picked for this job because you are the best at what you do.' What he doesn't say but everyone knows is that the road to this point could be paved with the bodies of those who were hired but just didn't fit in.

Team Sky isn't for everyone and Brailsford believes it's in all's interests if the ill-fitting are politely offered the opportunity to continue their careers elsewhere. Turnover of staff was high in the first three years, but the boss is now much closer to the back-up team he wants.

After identifying himself as the conductor of the orchestra, he then expresses one of the team's core values. He deliberately picks a senior staff member, operations manager Carsten Jeppesen, to make the point. 'If in our orchestra Carsten isn't playing his violin properly it is my responsibility to come along and say, "Look, Carsten, we need to have a chat."

'What I mustn't do is speak to Mario [Pafundi] and say, "You know what, Carsten's fucking this up," because then Mario might say, "Yeah, he's always fucking things up," and instead of my dealing with the problem we make it worse by talking to other people, who in turn talk to even more people.'

So, in this team, bitching about colleagues will not be tolerated. Every suggestion is coated with a sense of what seems entirely reasonable. 'We have come here without our wives, partners, children, and now for the next three weeks we have to make sure that we don't allow our personal lives to affect our jobs.'

During the course of the Tour different staff members will talk about how much harder they work in Team Sky than they have done in their previous teams and here, from the boss, is a warning about personal issues impinging upon their work with the team. Yet this isn't as uncompromising as it seems, for when Rod Ellingworth's little daughter gets sick in the first week, he is given the go-ahead to get himself home and take care of what matters.

Brailsford wants everyone to know that he believes they have helped get the team into a position to win its second consecutive Tour. 'We can look at what we've done and ask, "Could we have done more to this point?" I don't think we could have. The team is in good shape, we have good results this year and the nine guys we have chosen are all fit and well. But now we want to have a really good three weeks.'

He then gets into details that other teams mightn't see as important. 'Health is going to be a big issue. It is not a question of "if some of us get sick" but "when some of us get sick". So we take every precaution to ensure we don't help spread infection.

'It is common practice in France to shake the hand of the person you are meeting. If you can, avoid shaking hands. Smile, whatever, but try to cut down on the hand-shaking. And make sure to use the alcohol disinfectant. Before you eat, before you get on the bus, use it. We had an issue in the Giro with three riders sick, including Christian [Knees] and Bradley who sat alongside each other on the bus.'

He talks about security around the team. 'We have to be really vigilant about this, especially in relation to riders' food and drinks. If you see anybody, around the bus or any of our vehicles, who you're not sure about, don't let it pass. Ask him what he's doing, mention it to Rod or me. One guy contaminating one drink is all it would take to give us a big problem, so you've got to stay alert to the danger.'

The team doesn't shy away from expressions of self-belief. When he left the Garmin team to join Sky in 2009, Wiggins equated it to 'leaving Wigan [then a lowly Premier League football team] and joining Manchester United'. Once, in the car, Ellingworth complained about the team's arrogance in that first year, saying too much about what they would do before they had done anything.

'Like what Brad said about Manchester United and Wigan. You can't say that, although on that I do agree with Brad. We are Manchester United and they are Wigan.'

Brailsford was a shade more subtle in his closing message. 'If you all do your jobs, we have the best support team on this race and you guys will show that.'

He had spoken for about twenty minutes and then asked Ellingworth to run through some organisational and logistical issues. Ellingworth reminds everyone that just because they've got Tour de France stickers on the cars doesn't give anyone a licence to drive irresponsibly and the gendarmerie have told all the teams they won't tolerate it. (Brailsford had earlier reminded staff that anyone who drinks and then drives a vehicle will be fired, a rule that is non-negotiable.)

Lead mechanic Gary Blem asked Ellingworth to remind all drivers to fill their tanks at the end of the day so that those staff members who take care of the cars don't have to refuel them early the next morning. There was also a request to hand in the keys at the end of the day so that Neil MacDonald, the Jaguar mechanic in charge of the cars, can keep them all together.

Dave Brailsford then asked Tim Kerrison, head of performance support and the man most informed on the minutiae of the riders' form, to talk about what he expected from the team over the following three weeks. Kerrison is quietly spoken and thoughtful, a man who'd never claim to have invented hot water when all he'd done was stumble across a geyser. Deadpan tone and natural understatement lend weight to everything he says. Overall, the team were in very good shape. He spoke about some of the riders about whom there were worries. David López, who had been sick in the Critérium du Dauphiné, was fully recovered now, and Vasil Kiryienka, who seemed tired in the Dauphiné, was now back at his best.

Kerrison also spoke about how Pete Kennaugh had come through and was showing what the management always thought him capable of. He talked about the excellent form of Richie Porte and Chris Froome; he considered Porte was in the shape of his life and when he mentioned Froome he said Team Sky had by far the best rider in the race.

Kerrison delivers this verdict as if giving a weather report. Nicolas Portal, the young French *directeur sportif*, also spoke, as did Blem and Pafundi.

Towards the end, Brailsford spoke about the media and how it was better if he dealt with most of the enquiries. This would happen mostly by the bus and, though there would be occasions when it might be necessary for Tim and Rod to offer their opinions on things, and while it was appropriate for the *directeur sportif* to handle questions related to that day's race, most of the other stuff was best left to him.

Brailsford made the point that when journalists didn't get what they were looking for from him, they would go to Ellingworth or Kerrison trying to get what they actually wanted. Everyone needed to be aware of this and make sure there was as little leakage as possible. 'While we want to be open and transparent and polite at all times, we also want to stay in control of this.'

I'm sitting in the third seat on the left, listening and wondering if, unknown to myself, I am being controlled?

The meeting peters out which seems disappointing as it had been almost inspiring when Brailsford was in full flow. I'd wondered what he might do for a final flourish.

'I see you stand like greyhounds in the slips,
Straining upon the start. The game's afoot:
Follow your spirit, and upon this charge
Cry "God for Harry, England, and Saint George!"'

But this leader has come from the School of Dr Steve Peters and no need to rouse the chimps when a good night's rest is what everyone needs.

Seven months before, I'm sitting in the reception room at the Manchester velodrome waiting to meet Brailsford for the first time. Given what he has achieved with Team GB, it is strange that this is a first meeting, but my love for cycling had been destroyed by the Armstrong era and for six or seven years I'd given the sport a wide berth.

Only a couple of weeks have passed since the Texan was kicked out of cycling, and the whiff of scandal still hangs in the air. Brailsford wants to talk about the stuff I'd written along the way. 'What I can't imagine is how you dealt with the sense of alienation from a lot of the guys you were working alongside at the Tour de France,' he says. 'Many of them must have hated what you were doing?' That was, I say, the least of my problems.

We watch a group of children ride little bikes round the indoor BMX track, kids of four and five learning to be comfortable on a bike. This new facility has been built off the success of the track teams that Brailsford nurtured and though he doesn't claim any credit, he is due some.

Team Sky was conceived in this velodrome amid unanimous agreement that they would replicate their approach to track cycling on the road. Sports scientists would work with the riders, everything that the team would do on and off the bike would be thought through and evidence based, and there would be no doping.

He wants me to know where he's come from. 'I place a lot of trust and have a lot of confidence in Dr Steve Peters. We sat down and said, "Okay, well, our values and our beliefs, they are going to be unquestioned." It was very clear we are very anti-doping and that's how we're always going to be. If we couldn't do it that way, if it was impossible, then we'd stop. Winning is great but it's not about winning, it's the process that I like.

'How do you help somebody to improve? That's what we enjoy doing and we're thinking about it all the time.'

Depending upon your starting point this is either

admirable or PR fluff, and I am inclined to seeing it as the latter. But I would remember Brailsford's views on the process being more interesting than winning during the final stages of the 2013 Tour. Though Chris Froome had a healthy lead at that point there was still the 32km time trial from Embrun to Chorges and three tough Alpine stages to get through.

Rain was forecast and with two longish descents on the course, the time trial couldn't be regarded as a formality. Early that afternoon Brailsford retired to his room at the Hotel Les Bartavelles in Embrun to take an hour-long nap. More tired than he thought, he slept on and was woken by the France 2 commentary of the time trial, right at the point in the late afternoon when there was a spectacular crash.

'I was woken by the commentator screaming "*Chute, chute!*" Half awake, I thought it had to be Froomey. Then I saw it was the French rider Christophe Peraud who started the day ninth and was then out of the race.'

We talked about how he could sleep through an important moment in the race; he thought nothing of it. It wasn't his job to communicate with the team leader during the time trial. That was left to *directeur sportif* Nico Portal. If he had travelled in the car, he would have found it hard to stay quiet. In his management game, the conductor doesn't whisper advice to the violinist during the recital.

That afternoon in Manchester, Brailsford took me through his life. He left school at sixteen, determined to make something of his life but unsure about the direction. To get a qualification of some sort, he did an Ordinary National

Certificate (ONC) and then Higher National Certificate (HNC) in engineering. He felt those certs freed him to do what he wanted, which was to ride the Tour de France.

His dad worked every summer as an Alpine guide and when those engineering courses were done, he encouraged his son to come to France. Brailsford liked riding his bike and believed that with proper training, he might one day ride the Tour. He went to St Etienne, met people who saw him as you might see a stray dog and took him in. Long before the end of three years in France he realised he was never going to ride the Tour and would never be good enough to make his living from the sport.

'I guess the most I got out of the time in France was the fact that I became fluent in French.'

On his own, and with a lot of time, he used it to explore the worlds of physiology, sports science and training techniques. He wanted to find ways of making his training more efficient but he also discovered that no matter how intelligently and diligently he himself trained, it wasn't going to be enough to allow him to compete as a professional.

'I thought, "I've got to go back and work on my education." I came back, went to university to study sports science and psychology which was funny because I had hated school. But I couldn't wait to get back into education, loved every single minute of it, and went on to do an MBA because as well as the science of sport, I wanted to learn about the business side as well.'

We talk about the principles that underpinned the setting up of Team Sky. 'We had to be at the cutting edge of technology, and be up with the latest thinking in sports science, and ours was going to be a clean team. Our recruitment policy was simple: we would not hire any rider or staff who had tested positive or had any clear association with doping.

'It seemed to me the recruitment of doctors was key. We agreed not to take any doctor from cycling, and would hire doctors from outside cycling and work from there.'

I tell him that when it was revealed the team had employed Dr Geert Leinders from Rabobank, who was later shown to have been involved in doping, the question in my mind was, 'How could Brailsford have done that?'

'That's been a very humbling experience for me.'

Brailsford tells me the story of the June evening in 2004 when he and his pregnant partner Lisa were on a short break in Biarritz. He called David Millar who lived in Biarritz and was part of the Team GB track team. Unusually for him, Brailsford had allowed his professional relationship with Millar to also become personal. He and Millar were friends and that evening they decided to go to Millar's favourite restaurant, the Blue Cargo.

Intelligent and charming, Millar had just told an interesting anecdote about a long night partying with Lance Armstrong and two Aussies Matt White and Stuart O'Grady, when two men approached the table. 'David Millar?' The rider nodded, they flashed their police badges and asked him and Brailsford to come with them.

Outside, a third police officer waited. Millar was taken in the police car with two of the policemen, the third travelled with Brailsford and his partner in Millar's car. Heavily pregnant, Lisa didn't understand what was happening and was crying. Told to follow the car in front, Brailsford presumed they were going to Millar's apartment and knowing his way, he let the police car disappear. This infuriated the officer in the back seat of Brailsford's car who thought he had deliberately allowed the car in front to get away. The officer began punching the back of Lisa's seat which in turn infuriated Brailsford. He stopped the car. 'What the fuck are you doing?'

Not getting much by way of an apology, Brailsford drove on and Lisa was still deeply upset. After a stop at the Biarritz police station, they went to Millar's apartment, put Millar in one corner, Brailsford in the other, ransacked the place and found two used EPO syringes.

Brailsford was allowed take Lisa to a hotel before he reported back to the station for questioning. They grilled him for five hours, insisted he had to have known what Millar was doing and a female officer said, 'Your wife is pregnant and she's going to lose the baby because you're a fucking liar.' Brailsford said he didn't know what was going on.

A male officer showed him a little syringe, asked him what it was and when Brailsford said a syringe, it seemed only to make things worse.

'Of course it's a syringe, what kind of syringe is it?'

'It's a small syringe.'

Exasperated, the officers pointed to a word on the side of the syringe, Eprex.

'What's Eprex?'

'I don't know.'

'You must.'

'I don't.'

In the end they told him it was EPO and he had to have known what it was. Brailsford said the truth was that he didn't and what did they want from him. The truth, they said. 'That's what I'm giving you,' he replied. They convinced him they didn't accept a word he was saying.

Then, half an hour after the questions stopped, one of the officers returned to the interrogation room and politely told Brailsford they believed him. He couldn't believe what they'd put him through. 'You knew I had nothing to do with this,' he said. 'We weren't sure,' the officer replied.

He tells this story passionately, wanting me to understand he had been with Millar at the moment of his disgrace and that he had been treated like a criminal simply because he'd been in Millar's company.

Lisa wanted him to return home as soon as he could, advice reiterated by people back at British Cycling, but Brailsford stayed to support Millar who spent almost two days in prison before making a full confession in the 47th hour of a 48-hour detention.

When he was released from prison, Brailsford was waiting for him. They shared a bottle of wine and Millar told his friend and the boss of Team GB, for which he rode, the full extent of his doping. Brailsford listened but didn't judge, even though it emerged Millar had used drugs when riding for the GB team and by doing so jeopardised Brailsford's position and the entire programme.

After returning to Britain, Brailsford asked Steve Peters to go down to Biarritz and do what he could to help Millar through a difficult time. According to Millar, Brailsford paid for Peters's flight from his own pocket.

I listened without saying much.

Brailsford wasn't sure what I thought about Team Sky. Neither was I.

'Do you believe we're clean?' he asked.

'If you put a gun to my head and said, "Did Team Sky win the Tour de France clean?" I'd say, "Yes, I think they did win it clean." Then the trigger is pulled, I hear the click of an empty chamber and I think, "Phew, thank God I'm still around," because there would be a fair amount of relief. You see, I'm not sure. How can anybody be?'

'I know we are doing things correctly,' he said. 'I know we are clean.'

'If you are, why do you get so defensive when there are doping questions?'

'We don't get defensive,' he said.

'You do. Bradley's explosion at the Tour created the impression the team wasn't comfortable dealing with doping. Some journalists complained that the team was too controlling and occasionally tried to discourage journalists from asking about doping.'

'I'm sure we didn't do that,' he says.

'Certain journalists say you did, that they themselves were asked not to pursue a particular line at a Wiggins press conference for fear that it would upset the leader. And that was normally something to do with doping.'

I felt he didn't believe this had taken place, but it had.

He then changed tack. 'We have nothing to hide and if

you'd like to come and live with the team, you'd be more than welcome.'

'What do you mean, "live with the team"?'

'You would have complete access. Stay in the team hotel, eat with us. Travel with members of the team, speak to who you want to, go into the doctor's room, see who's coming in and out of the hotel. Literally, whatever you want to do.'

I hadn't expected anything like this and it put me in a slightly awkward position.

'You tried this before with my close friend Paul Kimmage and it didn't work.'

'I know,' he said. 'I was hugely embarrassed by what happened. I invited Paul to come with us on the 2010 Tour de France and then I had to withdraw the offer after the first few days. I found myself in an extremely difficult position, but a few of the staff didn't enjoy having Paul around. They found him intense and difficult to be around. We could have handled it better. He could have handled it better.'

'What do you think is the key to it working this time round?' I say.

'Paul came to a training camp for two or three days before the Tour; it wasn't enough. People didn't know him, weren't comfortable around him and I think he'd agree himself, he's not the easiest guy. If you're going to do this, you've got to come to our training camp at Mallorca in January. Spend a week with us there. Then you've got to spend a week with us in Tenerife, because it is regarded as the place teams supposedly go for doping. Come with us and see what we do there. Then come on the Giro and by the time the Tour comes round, you will know everyone and people will hopefully be

28

comfortable with your presence. And don't wait for us to ask you, you join up with us whenever you want.'

Leaving Manchester that evening, I knew the offer had to be accepted. How could you be a journalist and not want to travel inside the world number one cycling team?

CHAPTER THREE

'He has drawn back, only in order to have enough room for his leap.'

Friedrich Nietzsche, *Human, All Too Human*

If you are a Corsican separatist or if you just like a quiet life you had best swallow hard. The Tour de France is coming! The Tour de France is coming! Twelve hundred hotel rooms have already been annexed by teams and organisers. Half the population of the world are sleeping either in camper vans or on boats.

The Tour is celebrating its one hundredth edition by staying at home. The French have reclaimed their race – at least in the geographical sense. For the first time in a decade the peloton won't be straying outside French territory. It will be sunflowers, chateaux and blue skies all the way.

So you are Corsican and proud. Instead of swooning and falling in line you make an enormous banner, CORSICA IS NOT FRANCE, to welcome the visitors and you drape it across a bridge overlooking the route. A message to all who wonder about Corsicans' view of the motherland. But business is business, tourists are euros and you are out of step.

This is the moment to offer the world thousands of moving postcards from Corsica. That is what this deal is about: a three-week advertisement in which bike riders fill up the moments between the landscape portraits. This is the first Tour of the post-Lance era. It will be cleaner and at the beginning, here in Corsica, it will certainly be pretty.

So step up, Corsica. To make up for never having bothered to come here at any time in the last ninety-nine editions, Corsica is getting Le Grand Départ and two other stages. The island is rugged and beautiful but the roads are narrower, and when riders talk about the first three stages, the word carnage gets used a lot.

Team Sky arrive, like most other teams, on Wednesday. This is the start of a month living in each other's ears, dealing with each other under extreme pressure, a month of everybody being pushed to their professional limits.

It's life in the trenches, but Team Sky at least look like the best turned-out and best equipped army in the war. The bus is fit for the Dark Lord of Mordor, the uniforms and bikes uniquely in this era not festooned with the logos of dozens of companies. Restraint and good design pervade. The blue stripe, representing the thin line between success and failure, runs down everything from the back of the chef's whites to the team-issue iPhones.

The team are addicted to detail: pineapple juice to make water more drinkable; chemical weapons [alcohol disinfectant] deployed against germs; every bike checked and passed by two mechanics, working indoors to soft music in an air-conditioned truck which keeps the space at precisely 23 degrees. If it snows, rains or freezes, their colleagues on other teams are out in the elements fixing bikes, cursing the weather.

In the evening riders eat on their own, their dinner timed to start thirty or forty-five minutes before staff, so that the main men get a little privacy and the sense that though their days are hard, staff days are longer. Riders will eat food specially bought and prepared by their own chef, Søren Kristiansen. If any of this nutritious food is left over, provided the riders have left the dining room, Søren will invite the staff to help themselves. Otherwise it is hotel food.

Over dinner the second *directeur sportif,* Servais Knaven, will hand out the following day's plan. Sky's daily plan is produced by the performance manager Rod Ellingworth and is a work of art. It lists who will travel with whom from the hotel to the start, then who travels with whom from the start to the finish and, finally, how everyone gets from the finish to the hotel.

It can happen that a staffer will travel in three different vehicles for those three journeys and everything is underpinned by the need to make sure nothing encroaches upon the team performance. What never happens is someone stands around the team bus and vehicles at the end of a stage and asks who he is travelling with. Should that happen Ellingworth will say, 'Oh, did you not get the plan?' which might sound like a question but isn't.

The teams are presented to the public at a ceremony by the sea in Porto-Vecchio on Thursday. As the previous year's Tour de France winners, Team Sky are presented last. The team arrives like nine James Bonds atop a large white cruiser which cuts across the port. Some of the riders take photos of the scene ahead with their distinctive iPhones. Chris Froome stands to the side looking out to sea like Columbus who was born here, his Tintin profile peering towards either his destiny or a good spot for the spear fishing he enjoys so much.

When the boat hits Porto-Vecchio a ramp descends and the nine Team Sky riders roll down onto the dockside on their Pinarellos. When you were a gangly spotty teenager there was always a tall, smooth, blue-eyed and Brylcreemed boy who turned heads everywhere he went. Team Sky are that boy. Most of you hated him. He knew that but he didn't mind. You're only human.

This is my first time at the race since disillusionment caused me to hand in my little green accreditation badge in 2004.

'*Au revoir, messieurs, la victoire pour les tricheurs* [Goodbye, men, the victory for the cheaters],' I thought at the time. Through the years from Armstrong's seventh in 2005 – featuring Landis, Rasmussen, Vinokorouv, Contador, *et al* – to Wiggins in 2012, I hadn't covered the Tour, and I hadn't missed it. Armstrong's banishment changed things; exiting the building, he left the door half-open and finally I had a way back in.

'It's your comeback Tour, how do you feel?' says a photographer colleague bumping into me in a corridor.

'Excited and holding on to scepticism,' I say.

I'm not just entitled to my scepticism, it is my job to have it with me at all times. We've all been fooled, duped and suckered by this race. 'For years they fucked us,' Jean Michel

Rouet, a colleague at *L'Equipe* once said. I never forgot that. Lamentably there are ties cycling is unwilling to cut. On page 46 of the Tour de France bible, the official road book, there is a full-page photograph of Richard Virenque advertising a Festina watch. In the photo Virenque looks handsome, almost distinguished. If you didn't know his story or understand what he had stood for, you could look in the road book and see cycling's George Clooney, the same tinges of grey.

But beyond the image, there is reality.

Virenque doped throughout his career, his team got caught and they came out with their hands up. All except their leader Virenque, who lied for more than two years and might never have told the truth if he hadn't come up before Judge Daniel Delegove in the autumn of 2000.

By then Virenque's dishonesty had plummeted into pathos, so much so that you weren't sure whether he deserved stoning or pitying. Presiding at the 'Festina Trial' in the autumn of 2000 Delegove, weary no doubt from having heard so much about cycling's sordid business, looked at Virenque in the witness box and said, 'Do you accept this reality, that you used doping products?'

'It was a like a train going away from me,' replied the still self-pitying Virenque, 'and if I didn't get on it, I would be left behind. It was not cheating. I wanted to remain in the family.'

Virenque cheated to win, and his team celebrated with a lethal recreational drug concoction called *Pot Belge*. And still they fete him at the Tour. Officially. Festina is a name synonymous with that shameful 1998 Tour which began in Ireland but exploded when their *soigneur* and principal drug runner Willy Voet was arrested. And still they remain a Tour sponsor.

For Rod Ellingworth, Team Sky's master planner, the road book is the bible. So on the day he gets it, he riffles through the pages, checking the details that underpin his planning. He gets to page 46 with its photo of Virenque and it disgusts and confuses him. Ellingworth can be diplomatic, understated and restrained when talking about most things. Doping is different and in his eyes Virenque has stood for everything he despises about the sport. He stops at page 46, turns the page over to check there's nothing too important on the other side, and tears Richard from the book and bins him.

Returning to the Tour was straightforward for me once the sport had accepted the truth about Armstrong. There would be a new grammar, I hoped. Every new rider, every new effort, every iconic stage wouldn't be compared with how things were when people believed in Lance.

Every living winner of the Tour has been invited back to this centenary race. Every champion welcomed except the evil one. It makes me laugh a little. Yes, Armstrong is no longer a past winner but plenty of known dopers are (Riis, Ullrich, Contador, to name just three of the more recent) and this parade of champions is best enjoyed by those with the ability to suspend their disbelief.

Still, I'm glad that he who once controlled everything can no longer get on the list of invites. His fall has given the sport a new chance but this monster's head has been severed many times before and always it has reappeared.

Sure enough, on the day the race begins, Lance gives an

interview to the French quality daily *Le Monde*. He is determined not to go away.

The interview is the usual greatest hits collection from the cave of his disgrace. The writer Geoffrey Wheatcroft summed up its content perfectly in the *New Republic*.

Yet again he snivelled that, 'I didn't invent doping. I simply participated in a system. I am a human being.' I suggest that readers could try a logical experiment, adapting that defence for persons accused of any other offence, from rape to racketeering to war crimes. He also said that the devastating report last fall from the U.S. Anti-Doping Agency 'did not draw a true picture of cycling from the end of the 1980s to the present day. It succeeded perfectly in destroying one man's life, but didn't benefit cycling at all' – his life, that is, rather than those ravaged by the scourge of doping.

Still, I dream, we will make new memories and finally their weight will crush the past.

Stage One brought the predicted carnage, but with a side order of comedy. First though, Chris Froome, one of the most accident-prone men ever to reach the higher echelons of this sport, had his first mishap. The Tour has two starts. It begins with a 3km ceremonial ride through the town. The riders stretch and preen, the populace cheers, the sun shines. The mood is set. These few kilometres aren't for racing, they are a neutral zone.

Alone of the peloton, Froome punctured in the neutral zone. A more superstitious man might have gone home but he, while the mechanic put on the new wheel, would have thought, 'My good luck that it happened here.'

The carnage came later. Chaos among the athletes and their bikes and parts of each were left on the scorching roads of Corsica in pile-ups and spills.

These scenes of fallen riders and running medics went on as those gathered at the finish line were treated to a pantomime so bizarre and comical that it would have embarrassed a vicar running a village fete. As the peloton steamed towards the finish in Bastia, the Australian Orica-GreenEDGE team bus was going through the finish line when its roof got caught on the timing bridge above the line.

There, under a big sign for Vittel mineral water, the bus got jammed, seemingly unable to move forward or back. When something unforeseen happens on the Tour, the space between the incident and a proper understanding of how it came about is filled with hearsay. These can be juicy and the excitement lasts until the truth comes out.

So this is what came off the production line at the rumour mill: driver is cruising along the road to Bastia when he decides what he'd really like to do is watch the second test of the rugby union series between Australia and the British and Irish Lions. So he stops, orders a sandwich, watches the game, arrives late at the finish line after the gantry has been lowered and his bus gets stuck.

The president of the race jury, Vicente Tortajada Villarroya from Spain, sees the pictures of the bus wedged into the timing bridge and decides to switch the finish to the 3km-to-go mark and communicates this to the team managers. This causes panic among the riders because they're guessing the new finish is now located in the midst of narrow roads, sharp corners and short straights.

What dissuaded Señor Tortajada Villarroya from stopping the race until the bus was freed and then re-starting it, no one knows. But, just in time, the bus extricates itself from the timing bridge and it's decided to revert back to the original finish line. Problem being that some of the riders now knew about the change and others didn't.

Chaos.

Pandemonium.

And the crashes that might have taken place before the hastily chosen new finish line happen just before the original finish line. The stage is won by Marcel Kittel, the German sprinter with the Argos team. People presume this is typical of what happens in the first mass sprint when everyone is fresh and the result is not to be trusted. Kittel, it is assumed, shouldn't beat Cavendish. The following three weeks would dismantle that assumption.

Similarly, the assumption about the rugby-loving Aussie bus driver proved to be false. Garikoitz Atxa who drove the Orica team bus into Bastia that afternoon is in fact Spanish, and is not a rugby union fan.

Things improved for the race from there on. A second stage streaked over the jagged mountains from Bastia towards Ajaccio and Team Sky, depleted and sapped by the first day's crashes, had the pleasure of seeing Froome attack alone on one of the climbs.

Nothing too serious, just a boyish checking out of his own powers and a desire to poach a little lead so that, when they began the descent, he would be able to pick his own lines and decide how fast he wanted to go. While not the worst descender in the peloton, neither is Froome the best. Instead, he uses his class going uphill to pick and choose in whose company he negotiates the descents.

And if the stretching of legs sent a little flare over the heads of his rivals, that would have pleased him. No one with half a brain mistakes Froome's politeness and softly spoken sentences for expressions of timidity. He has come to the Tour to win it and, such is his desire, the challenge for him is not the courage to attack but the discretion to know when not to.

Jan Bakelants of RadioShack took the stage on a day when Geraint Thomas was Sky's big concern. His horrific crash at the end of the previous day's stage left him sore around the hip and pelvis but an initial X-ray didn't show up any break. But soon after leaving Bastia, Thomas was in trouble and immediately after the finish in Ajaccio, he was sent for another X-ray. Not many around the team expect him to last more than another day or two.

Thomas is someone that the team's brains trust – Brailsford, Kerrison and Ellingworth – believe could develop into a Tour de France contender. Without the injured Wiggins, the Welshman's role in this race is greater because his intelligence and outgoing personality make him the obvious man to captain the team on the road.

Brailsford fools around with Thomas in a way he doesn't do with any other rider in the team, but only because Thomas understands that the mickey-taking is an expression of affection. To lose him in the first few days would be a blow.

On Sunday, for television reasons, the Tour raced towards Calvi and then sidestepped the city to finish along a stunning coastal road a couple of miles away. The pictures justified the inconvenience for everybody else but the race was taken from the people of Calvi and the finish played out before a relatively small crowd.

In Calvi one of the sport's newest stars, the Slovakian Peter Sagan, was surprisingly beaten by Aussie, Simon Gerrans, and so two days after the marriage of their bus to the timing bridge, Orica-GreenEDGE were back in the news. Good news. Brailsford and Ellingworth seek out the Orica bosses and offer their congratulations. For all the guff about the English–Aussie rivalry, Team Sky feel an affinity with their Australian counterparts.

The Tour had to move on quickly, all the riders had to board a fleet of coaches waiting to take them to Calvi Airport from where they would fly to Nice. Time was important because planes can only fly in and out of Calvi in daylight hours and pilots need special training before being allowed to do their job there.

If the riders were rushing to get to the airport, staff members had more time to get to the harbour in Calvi for the six-hour ferry crossing to Nice. In the clamour of this migration from island to mainland not a lot was said about the final climb of the day, the second category Col de Marsolino, which came just before the drop down to the finish outside Calvi.

Of Sky's nine riders just two got over the top with the leaders, Froome and Richie Porte. Edvald Boasson Hagen almost made it but was dropped before the top, and then rejoined on the descent. So three finished in the main group of ninety riders and the other six didn't make it. Their time losses ranged two to ten minutes.

Something was wrong.

Sky's team is loaded with riders who can climb and support a leader where he will most need support: in the mountains. So here on the straightforward second category Col de Marsolino, which rises just 425m over 12km at an average gradient of 3.5 per cent, two thirds of Sky's riders are scattered like pieces of paper on the mountain.

A week before the Tour, I had been part of a two-man panel with Team GB's Shane Sutton at a *Sunday Times* event in London. Pretty much everyone in the audience believed Froome was the likely winner of the race and I felt they needed to be reminded that it was the Tour de France they were talking about and there were reasons for wondering if Froome would do it.

Primarily there were legitimate questions about the quality of the team, because it was obvious the team wasn't as strong as the previous year. For different reasons, they wouldn't have three of the strongest men from the 2012 team: Wiggins, Christian Knees and Michael Rogers. Wiggins was injured, Knees had ridden the Giro and wasn't at his best, Rogers had joined the Saxo-Tinkoff team.

It wasn't just their absences that would be felt. To properly support Wiggins at the Giro earlier in the summer, Sky sent the Colombians Rigoberto Urán and Sergio Henao to the Italian race. After illness ended Wiggins's race, Urán became the de facto team leader, won a mountain stage and went on to finish second. It was impressive.

Both he and Henao would have made the Tour de France team stronger but, wearied by their efforts in Italy, they had to be left at home. At the *Sunday Times* evening I argued that the team would not be able to control the race because it just wasn't strong enough. I'd expected Sutton to argue the opposite, but he didn't. Without saying anything against the riders selected, he clearly thought it wasn't a particularly strong team.

I am sitting in a team car at the finish. Rushes and sand dunes outside. Soon we'll be heading for the airport and the flight Brailsford has chartered for those members of staff not needed to take team vehicles on the ferry. I am in the backseat alone as the staff tend to the million-and-one duties they have at the end of a stage. Dave Brailsford arrives, slumps into the front seat and with a sigh he says, 'You know what? We don't have a team.'

'What do you mean?'

'Today we weren't there on that last climb. Just Froomey and Richie and Edvald. Pete Kennaugh was sick, G [Thomas] is in a bad way with his pelvis, and I don't know what's happening with the others. I didn't see this happening on this stage but it's not ideal. On the other hand, Froomey is very strong, Richie's good and we've just got to get on and make the best of what we've got.'

What is impressive is his refusal to be falsely optimistic. I know how Brailsford and his team plan for every contingency. And now this evening in Corsica, just three days into the Tour, Dave Brailsford, master of the cycling universe, is conceding that he has come to the Tour de France 'without a team'.

There should be histrionics. A note of despair. Instead the concession brings an insight into what makes Team Sky what it is. What has just happened is a fact. It is a problem. The problem will have to be solved. It is something to deal with.

At the airport the mood among the staff is subdued. Men hand in and then pick up their bags without much talking. Psychologically these are a group of upbeat people. They feel a responsibility to give off a good vibe and, most of the time, it doesn't involve an effort. Today is a jolting collision with reality that they can't pretend not to have seen. Suppose the team is as weak as it seemed on that 145km spin from Ajaccio. Suppose there is no figuring a way out.

That evening Kerrison, the head of performance, felt bad migraines coming. They can wait in the shadows for weeks and then come to life at the Tour. He deals with them in his way, unable to engage in small or big talk, just concentrating on bearing and banishing the pain. It is noticeable that Brailsford, who is closest to him, leaves him be.

At a table in the airport, the Sky boss starts speaking with Carsten Jeppesen and Dario Cioni. The debrief was under-way but they wear faces which hint at the gravity of the situation. What can we do with the guys who aren't going well? Which of them just had a bad day and will get better? Let's look at this rationally. We still have the best rider in the race.

And on they go, calmly and analytically, knowing they have the team time trial the next day, Pyrenees later in the week and many miles to go before they sleep.

CHAPTER FOUR

'All in the game, yo. All in the game.'

Omar Little, *The Wire*

Team Sky is a road movie with two leading men. Chris Froome and Bradley Wiggins don't have the easy affability of Hope and Crosby. There is no straight man and no fall guy. Froome and Wiggins are ambitious, prickly and acutely aware that even though there are three Grand Tours every year, there is only one that young boys (not brought up in Italy or Spain) dream of.

The chief cycling narrative of the spring of 2013 will be which man gets to contest the yellow jersey of the Tour de France. And whether or not his rival will defer to him and accept the role of *superdomestique*. Their breakthrough as cycling's strangest double act came away from the Tour. They began forging their dynamic of odd couple chafing in the kiln of the 2011 Vuelta.

Those were the strangest of days. Wiggins was already a

star. Three Olympic golds and a fourth place in the Tour de France before being lured to Team Sky for more money than seemed sensible. Froome was half man, half rumour. An infuriating mix of mad potential, comical clumsiness, and undulating form lines. He was Kenyan. He was South African. He was British. He was either the next big thing or heading towards a quiet expiration of his Team Sky contract.

They had worked together before, but the relationship was defined in Spain. This was the proving ground for both men. Through the first nine stages of the race Froome had been the best Sherpa a man could wish for, toting the load for Wiggins in a team which had come to Spain without men like Edvald Boasson Hagen, Rigoberto Urán and Geraint Thomas. They looked miscast if they were expecting to finish on the podium but the defiance of Froome and Wiggins was heroic.

Froome seemed to leave a huge part of his essence on the Spanish roads and mountains every day. On Stage Nine he hauled Wiggins to the Covatilla ski station in the mountains of Sistema Central while Vincenzo Nibali and Dan Martin set the pace.

The 183km stage was designed to have the action loaded right here at the end day. The day would climax with a 10km 7.2 per cent gradient climb up Sierra de Béjar to La Covatilla. The road undulates as if created by a wave machine. Before the Covatilla scramble officially starts there are 8km of lesser gradient as a warm-up. Traditionally the heat here is merciless. Riders are made or broken on this hill.

As the road turned for home and the crosswinds hit the riders, suddenly Froome accelerated, towing Wiggins in his slipstream. Having delivered Wiggins into the lead, Froome dropped back to the tail end of a group of six riders separated now from the field. Wiggins did the donkey work now through the last kilometre leading, leading, leading, until the final frenetic sprint which went to Dan Martin. Wiggins came in fourth though. Froome fifth. Just seconds off the lead.

Going into the long time trial the following day Wiggins had proven he could do more than just time trial. Froome had proven that he had arrived. At last.

That was Sunday. Froome should have been spent. On Monday, in the old university town of Salamanca, he would have been excused for cruising. Instead he sought and was granted permission to put his foot on the gas. And so Chris Froome ad-libbed his way through a gruelling 47km time trial which ran in a loop out from and back to the city.

Time-trial days involve a burst of intense effort but lots of waiting around. Most of the heavy hitters in the discipline were out early. Taylor Phinney (BMC Racing Team) set the early mark. Fabian Cancellara (Leopard-Trek) eclipsed him. Then the German time-trialling star Tony Martin of HTC-Highroad took a couple of minutes out of Cancellara's time. A couple of hours and many riders passed without anybody coming near.

Wiggins came down the ramp like a demon though. His first intermediate split after 13.3km was a second faster than Martin's. Wiggins was in business.

Froome passed the same marker a little later, turning in a respectable time some 24 seconds slower than Wiggins.

When Wiggins pressed the turbo button, however, nothing happened. At the 30km mark he found himself 19 seconds behind Martin. Understandable. Tony Martin is Tony

Martin. But when Froome passed the same mark he had gained 23 seconds on Wiggins.

So to the final run home, 17km into Salamanca and the Plaza Mayor. By the time Wiggins got there he was 1'03" behind Martin. Forgiveable, until Froome rode home 23 seconds ahead of his team leader.

After the heroics on Stage Nine, Sky had expected that this time trial would give Wiggins a substantial lead on General Classification. Instead the red jersey was handed to the gangly apprentice, Chris Froome. He was pleased, but aware of the difficulties the situation presented.

'I'm in trouble. This situation was never the plan. I got the green light to go for the time trial as hard as I could. I'm over the moon.'

They had a rest day before heading into the Cantabrian Mountains. Team Sky who had never seriously challenged for a Grand Tour had the red jersey on the shoulders of their stronger climber. His leader was in third place. The problem was that Chris Froome had come here for weeks of servitude. If it was time for a rethink there was no suggestion of it on the road that day.

Sky's tactic on the mountains remained the same. Keep the speed high. Turn the climbs as far as possible into the time-trial-like efforts that would suit Bradley Wiggins. The workload for the tactic fell on Wiggins's teammates, mainly Froome.

The hallmark of the Vuelta is its unique climbs, which present themselves not as long steady hauls to the clouds but as a series of short punchy gradients coming one after the other. It was on this corrugated landscape that Froome sacrificed himself, hauling Wiggins up the 19km ascent towards the summit finish at Manzaneda. With 3km to go after a day of shepherding his leader, Froome's legs finally went. Wiggins found his way home alone.

That evening in Galicia, Froome realised he had left everything on the roads in order to hand the red jersey to Wiggins. Froome was now 7 seconds down in second place. Still, when he crossed the line he went straight to Wiggins to congratulate him.

The next day, on Stage Eleven, Froome delivered again, responding to a series of attacks before ceding to Wiggins on the long climb home. Wiggins ended the day in red. Froome was second in the General Classification.

His sacrifice had been huge but it was what he got paid so handsomely to do. And with contract negotiations pending, more reward would come later.

Wiggins retained the jersey through four stages before losing it to Juan José Cobo, a local favourite and the eventual winner of La Vuelta. Froome finished just 13 seconds behind Cobo in second place on the podium knowing, in his bones, that first place could have been his. Wiggins was third, 1'39" behind.

30 January 2013: Vanity Hotel Golf, Mallorca. It is Wednesday evening, the fifth day of my first week inside Team Sky, and the moment to speak for the first time with Chris Froome. We have passed each other in the hotel, once he'd sat in the bar reading a serious newspaper. Another morning I'd gone to the small hotel gym to see him work out with Richie Porte, his best friend in the team.

His friendship with Porte is interesting because they are so different. With Porte, what you see is what he is. And what he thinks is what you hear.

Froome has always been guarded – considering, sifting, then speaking. When his rise began, those who managed Sky's media affairs would say: 'We need to get Froomey to give a little more of himself.' And that morning in the gym with Porte, he gave plenty. Ben MacDonald, the Team Sky physiotherapist, supervised a session in which the riders did a tough circuit of strength and stretching exercises.

Porte is small but neatly proportioned. He looked every inch the athlete.

Froome is different, his tallness accentuated by his thinness. More than 6ft tall, he will start the Tour de France weighing 10st 6lb. But when the exercises get tough, Froome's strength leaves an impression that would overwhelm every other memory from that workout. In the gym Porte seemed like a boy to Froome's man.

I am reminded of the story often told within the team to illustrate Froome's physical freakiness. The former American rider Bobby Julich had been assigned to sand the rough edges off Froome in the 2011 season. He began by running some lab tests, the results of which startled him. Rod Ellingworth had to check the calibrations on the machinery but the numbers were right. They knew then that Julich was polishing a Tour de France podium finisher.

That evening, Froome was already there when I arrived. We speak for half an hour or so. He is polite, comes across as intelligent but he is reserved, as if he's learnt that the less you say, the less you get into trouble. Two memories survive from the conversation.

The first was his time at St Andrew's School in Bloemfontein.

How could a 13-year-old from Kenya without a word of Afrikaans have survived at this predominantly Afrikaans school? He said it was not easy at the time but when you looked at the bigger picture you saw the benefits. It toughened him.

Everything Froome says is delivered in well-formed and politely expressed sentences but you soon learn not to confuse politeness with softness. The other memory came from the corner of Froome's soul where you find granite.

The conversation had turned to the coming season and how he felt about riding the Tour de France in the same team as the defending champion, Bradley Wiggins. 'What I want,' he said, 'is to arrive at the start in Corsica with my chance to win the race. Nothing more, nothing less.' What he didn't say but wanted you to know is that he would have his chance to win this year, no matter what. His intensity recalled what Apollo Creed said to Rocky Balboa: 'Now, when we fought, you had that eye of the tiger, man, the edge!'

Two weeks later, Froome rode his first race of the year, the Tour of Oman. On the fourth day he rode well to finish second to Spaniard Joaquim Rodríguez on Green Mountain, took the leader's jersey and attended to the usual podium, media and anti-doping duties. A car waited to take him the twenty kilometres to the team hotel.

'The car's over there,' someone said.

'It's okay, I'll ride back, a little extra training.'

Eye of the tiger, man.

He is the man.

*

When I speak to Bradley Wiggins he appears to acknowledge this.

'When we go to the Tour and the form guide says Chris is the man, I will be supporting Chris, we're in a team and that's why we're successful.'

First though, a brief reminder of some things which happened on the 2012 Tour de France – the race which turned Bradley Wiggins from sideburned mod into knight of the realm and national institution. Froome was there for another stint of stoical servitude.

Stage Seven. The climb into La Planche des Belles Filles. Tough. Tough. Tough. The gradient goes from 14 per cent to 22 per cent. And you've had a long day. Richie Porte did his dog work and when he handed over to Froome only Wiggins, Cadel Evans, Vincenzo Nibali and Rein Taaramäe remained in contention. And Froome.

Froome injected some pace into the business. Evans went with a kilometre to go but he had miscalculated. Froome, Wiggins and Nibali trailed after him like the tail on a kite. With 100m to go the stage was anybody's, so Chris Froome decided to make it his. He nipped around Nibali for his first ever stage win. Wiggins finished a couple of seconds behind Evans. All were happy.

'Now he has got his stage and he is going to be an integral part of me winning this race,' said Wiggins, his presumption barely masking the fear that Froome wouldn't be satisfied with one stage win.

So to Stage Eleven. 148km to La Toussuire. All was looking well heading into the first real mountaintop finish. Wiggins in yellow.

It is said that at a team meeting that morning, Froome had inquired if he had permission to attack from 3km out. That, he was told, would depend on Bradley. Froome's eagerness was fed, not just by his natural competitiveness, but by a puncture on the first day of racing which had cost him 1'25". He felt he could do his work for Wiggins and get a podium finish for himself, but only if he was allowed to retrieve the time lost by puncturing.

Circumstances were different from La Vuelta, as by now Wiggins had two minutes on Froome, but letting Froome jump early could mean that Nibali and Evans would tag along with him eating into Wiggins's lead as he went. Whatever, nothing would be allowed to damage the team's pursuit of the Tour's yellow jersey.

An attack from that far out? It's unlikely, Froome was told, but maybe in the last 500m. As it happened, Evans launched a madcap attack with 56km to go but got burned on the Croix de Fer, the second savage *hors catégorie* climb of the day.

The last climb of the day is La Toussuire, 18km of torture. Richie Porte takes his turn at the front. The peloton stretches out in survival mode now. Team Sky has the same tactic as ever: high steady pace, burn off as many as you can.

Today, though, Vincenzo Nibali is feeling defiant. He shoots ahead of Wiggins's group and makes a break for glory with 12km left. He is asking Team Sky what they have. He goes and he goes fast. Team Sky leave him be and pedal on. This is the Kerrison Way: react by not reacting, continue riding at an even tempo because that way you get to the top in the quickest time. So Plan A is still operational. Richie Porte drops away leaving just Froome and Wiggins to implement it.

Froome pushes on. Wiggins follows, Frank Schleck and Cadel Evans trailing him. Froome, as usual, rides his bike in that almost boyish way, knees and elbows attached but separate from the torso, head down, eyes constantly pointed at the road directly below. It works though. He hauls Nibali back in.

So it goes. Nip and tuck at the front. With just 6km left only Wiggins, Froome and Schleck have any chance of catching Nibali who has broken away again. Five kilometres to go and Froome is working like a faithful sheepdog, dragging Wiggins back to the ambitious Nibali. This time Nibali appears genuinely spent.

Wiggins sits in behind Froome. Sliding uphill. Thus it shall be.

But suddenly Froome breaks. Leaning forward into the incline, accelerating. It is surprising and it is confusing. A sliver of madness in Team Sky's bloodstream. Nibali gives chase. Wiggins is left in yellow, forlornly climbing alone. In the team car, Sean Yates asks Froome had he Brad's permission for this? What is going on, Froomey?

Finally Froome relents. He straightens in the saddle, slows and waits for Wiggins.

In the aftermath Brailsford and his team did what they do best. They controlled the controllables. What were beyond their reach were the storm clouds gathering on social media. Bradley Wiggins's wife Cath tweeted, pointedly thanking Michael Rogers and Richie Porte for 'genuine selfless effort and true professionalism'.

Froome's partner Michelle Cound tweeted that she found this 'Typical'. That she was 'beyond disappointed'. She added later, 'If you want loyalty get a Froome dog – a quality I value although being taken advantage of by others.'

There it lay. For their part, Wiggins and Froome did their best to varnish over the cracks in their relationship. Behind the scenes Wiggins, who at the best of times needs to be handled sensitively, was saying that it might be best if he himself went home. In front of the microphones and cameras, Froome and Wiggins threw each other little bouquets of nice words.

There was one more hint of insurrection. On Stage Seventeen Froome appeared to go rogue again on the finish to the summit at Col de Peyresourde. This would be the last ascent of the entire Tour. Wiggins just needed not to get left behind and, barring unprecedented catastrophe, the Tour de France was his.

But ...

With 4km to go on a mini descent of the Col, Froome conferred with Wiggins. What was said is unclear, but with just over 3km to go Wiggins kicked on and Froome tucked in behind. To the onlooker it looked as if Wiggins was drafting Froome to give him the chance to break after the stage leader Valverde. Froome left Wiggins behind and the lead group of eight riders shattered. Froome kept going.

He took a glance back at Wiggins, however, and Wiggins didn't look right. Valverde was catchable now. Froome seemed to urge Wiggins on but Wiggins's head was in a different place. He was about to seal the Tour. Froome kept urging him on. Wiggins kept declining.

To keep the pot boiling, Froome's partner Michelle Cound tweeted three words: 'DAMN IT GOOOOOOO.' Froome decided not to abandon Wiggins, however, and sacrificed the stage by 19 seconds.

Nobody was impressed. Sean Yates told the media that Froome had a lot to learn. Froome noted that he thought that it had been an ideal stage for Team Sky to win. Wiggins promised that soon Froome's day would come.

They got to Paris as number one and number two in the General Classification, but by then it was becoming clear that Froome expected to be riding with a Wiggo dog working for him in the 2013 Tour. He felt he could have won the 2011 Vuelta, might have won the 2012 Tour and his days of 'could have' and 'might have' were over.

Their relationship will be a key narrative of Team Sky's 2013 season. The backgrounds of the two men each make for compelling stories but they could hardly be more different. Both have clear difficulties in their family upbringing but they grew up in environments so disparate that it is a miracle that their paths ever intersected in pro cycling.

Wiggins was born and reared in Kilburn. He grew up in Dibdin House, a large block of flats owned by the Church Commissioners, but has been swaddled by British Cycling from the time his talent first emerged. From the age of twelve onwards he was riding the eight miles to Herne Hill velodrome for track racing. He follows the programme, understands the system.

He has never clung to a tree for two hours while a belligerent hippo waited to kill him. Froome has. He grew up outside Nairobi, collecting snakes and scorpions, the only white kid in a gang who would spend days and weeks cycling in the Ngong Hills. He came to Europe alone, represented

Kenya alone, did virtually everything alone until he entered the realm of the controlled controllables.

In retrospect, too much perhaps has been made of the breakaway. Froome pulled back. No physical damage was done, Froome did rein himself in, Wiggins lost no time. But the relationship between two leaders in a cycling team can be like an exotic fruit – once mishandled, bruised forever. Wiggins felt betrayed and humiliated by Froome's brief show of strength. The rift between the two men remains.

When I meet with Wiggins it is a logical jumping-off point. Had he really wanted to come home from the Tour de France? Was Froome's jump that serious?

'Because you perceive something to be something, what happens within the race, whether you are right as to how you perceived it is another thing but at the time, it's like what happened there, in hindsight and obviously racing since, a winter has gone by, and you realised that wasn't the intention of someone, but at the time you take it as you see it. Because we had a plan, we were in yellow, everything was going great, we'd dropped Cadel, four of us left, we're nearly at the summit, it's nearly over and then Chris goes and it's like "what's just happened?"

'But in his mind, he was thinking, I want to get rid of Nibali so he is not chasing me for second, you could see now looking back, having spoken to him and that, what he was thinking at the time, in the heat of the moment, in the Tour and everything, on those stages, he has a lot going on.'

What becomes clear as Wiggins speaks is that the relationship with Froome is dysfunctional. I put it to him that he perceives Froome as having betrayed him and that as such there is no way back. He doesn't demur or correct me.

'I don't think I've ever really forgotten it, especially the one in the Pyrenees, right at the end, there was two of us left, it was over, the time trial is tomorrow, the Tour is won, to jeopardise that, I still felt whether we were going for the stage or whatever, Valverde was there, I still don't one hundred per cent understand that, but enough time has passed. I just accept it, that was whatever, but we have a professional working relationship.

'I said in January, we sat in a hotel down there, and they asked what are you two like off the bike. I said we don't room together, we don't mingle off the bike, but we are two very competitive leaders of this team and we both want to win, and that's it really.'

At the end of the day it all worked out. Wiggins won the final time trial. He won his Tour de France. Ultimately Froome obeyed team orders. He stopped and waited. On Toussuire and in the Pyrenees.

'Did he do anything wrong?' says Wiggins. 'Perhaps he didn't. He played ball, Chris.'

But Wiggins and Froome don't have enough of a relationship left upon which to build something new. Here in early 2013 they are still speaking in riddles about their intentions for the season. At the best of times it would be difficult to ask a four-time Olympic gold medallist and reigning Tour de France champion to step down and play *superdomestique* to the man who had butlered for him the year before. With the distance between Froome and Wiggins seeming irreducible, it seems impossible.

Wiggins can almost taste the salt of his rival's ambition and determination. He can see it in the way the season started in Oman with Froome devouring the desert sands. And he knows that this year's Tour will be more mountain than time trial.

'He is a better climber than me. Chris is one of the best climbers in the world, we talk about weight and numbers, he's got that frame of that time-triallist, powerful rider and he's five kilos lighter than me, he's a freak in terms of his frame. That power, and yet he's got this incredibly light climber's weight. I envy him in some respects, I wish I could be five kilos lighter and have the same power. '

I had gone to Mallorca to see Wiggins, to shoot the breeze at a time when he had only his bike and family for company. We spoke at a restaurant where one of his Tour de France jerseys hangs on the wall and the staff invite his two young kids to come in behind the bar and help with the washing and drying. When Cath, their mum, tells the children it's time to give the staff a little space, they come back to the table immediately.

To better understand Wiggins, the contradictions must be embraced. Sometimes he likes to analyse his performance in training and talk numbers with Tim Kerrison. Other times he likes to roll along without a thought about power output and aerodynamic drag. As much as he enjoys Kerrison's intellect, he has learned even more from another Aussie, the no-frills, straight-talking and emotional ex-pro Shane Sutton.

Wiggins's intelligence is as obvious as his fragility. He could rationalise Froome's flexing of muscle on those two mountain stages in the 2012 Tour but not get shot of the feeling he had been humiliated.

*

For his part, Froome is less animated but more open about 2012 when we meet in Nice two weeks before the start of the Tour. He says that he found last year's Tour to be 'quite stressful', and that he would stop short of calling Team Sky a 'happy team environment'.

'There were a lot of questions from the outside about the leadership and the way that Bradley is. He's not very approachable, not very open and communicative about how he is feeling or about the situation we had on the road. It certainly did add to the feeling that, "Wow, we're first and second in this bike race."'

Once again he explains the anatomy of his so-called treachery. From the very first stage when he lost 1'25" having punctured, he fretted about getting the time back. Somehow, he felt entitled to have that time back. He needed to be among the contenders and, in the event of anything happening to Wiggins, he needed to be able to take over.

He attacked on the stage which he won and he attacked on La Toussuire when he felt that Wiggins was safe. He'd gone 200m up the road when he got the message in his ear that Wiggins was 'falling off the wheels' and he sat up completely and paced him home.

'A lot of public and media would have jumped onto that, and said I was trying to attack Brad and I wasn't, I knew the yellow jersey was not an option for me unless something happened to Bradley.'

As for the Pyrenees, it was a miscommunication. Nothing more.

And what was the relationship between the two men

heading into this season when Team Sky were hoping to expand their dominion?

'I think that probably comes back to the way Bradley is, he's not the most open guy, he keeps to himself a lot and a lot of people wonder where they stand with him and especially if it looked like you had just attacked him while he was in the yellow jersey, he's probably got a good reason for not talking to me.'

On the surface it seems so little separates the two men and so much should unite. The rift is counter to everything which Sky stand for. Quietly, as I spend more time with the team, I wonder who is a Wiggo man and who is a Froomey man, for within the squad there are two camps.

Some riders like both men and are comfortable riding in a team led by either, others are more aligned with one or the other, but these are professional athletes. They have their own ambitions. If it's good for them to ride for Wiggins, they'll do that. And they will happily do the same for Froome.

One dividing point becomes evident, however.

Team Sky's house rules are printed on a poster inside the team bus. In no particular order of importance they are as follows:

TEAM SKY'S RULES

We will respect one another and watch each other's backs
We will be honest with one another
We will respect team equipment
We will be on time
We will communicate openly and regularly
If we want our helmets cleaned we will leave them on the bus

We will pool all prize money from races and distribute at the
end of the year

Any team bonuses from the team will be split between riders
on that race

We will give 15% of all race bonuses and prize money to staff

We will speak English if we are in a group

We will debrief after every race

We will always wear team kit and apparel as instructed in the
team dress code

We will not use our phones at dinner – if absolutely required
we will leave the table to have the conversation

We will respect the bus

We will respect personnel and management

We will ask for any changes to be made to the bikes (gearing,
wheel selection etc.) the night before the race and not on
race day

We will follow the RULES

Nestled in the middle, seventh and eighth from the top: 'We
will pool all prize money from races and distribute at the end
of the year', and 'Any team bonuses from the team will be
split between riders on that race'.

Bradley Wiggins has paid his teammates all he owes them
from the prize money and bonuses accrued on the Tour de
France. Paid everybody, that is, except Chris Froome. In
terms of the rules, it is perhaps a tad more important than
leaving a helmet on the bus if you want it cleaned. Inside the
team it is whispered about, nothing more. Even riders who
like Wiggins say he should have paid Froome his cut.

As for the man who recruited Froome and Wiggins, the

problem of their relationship is one which has consumed a lot of Dave Brailsford's thinking time. People close to the team tell him he should have got the two riders in the same room, knocked their heads together and told them to behave like proper professionals.

Brailsford's approach is different, more conciliatory. He starts by recognising that the team exists to win bike races, especially the Tour de France. Having Froome and Wiggins on the same side gives the team the best chance of achieving that, so he feels it is his responsibility to do what he can to bring them closer.

Froome had earned the right to lead the team in 2013 and in his eyes there was what he saw as an accumulation of debts since he had sacrificed himself on the 2011 Vuelta. He'd also seen little things which Wiggins had said or written about last year's Tour and he wasn't impressed by them.

So from early on, no matter what Bradley Wiggins said about this year's Tour de France and his own intentions, Froome was reluctant to trust his teammate to stick to the team plan. They rode together in the Tour of Oman at the beginning of the season. Froome won and seemed pleased with the help he'd had from Wiggins.

Then they went their separate ways. Froome got the preferred route to the Tour: Tirreno-Adriatico, Critérium International, Tour de Romandie and Critérium du Dauphiné. Meanwhile, Wiggins used the Tour of Catalunya and the Tour of Trentin as his principal prep races for the Giro d'Italia. It was an unusual programme, for neither Catalunya nor Trentin had an individual time trial and his normal route to victory in stage races was blocked.

Wiggins rode well enough in both but didn't win. Without victories there was the sense that he wasn't going as well as he did the previous year. Froome was winning virtually every race he rode and the 2012 Tour winner wouldn't have been enthused by the perception that he'd become the secondary man. When Wiggins went to the secondary Tour, the Giro, he announced that while he would try to win the Italian race his focus was the Tour de France.

'Does this mean you see yourself as the leader [of the Tour team]?'

'That won't be decided until three days before the race or maybe not until we're in the race where a natural hierarchy will become clear.'

Across the cyclo-sphere, the sound that followed was the fluttering of wings as pigeons tried to escape the cat.

This was the Tour de France champion standing up for himself. Lest you have forgotten, I am the guy who won last year's race and as the cycling historians in your midst will know, there is little precedent for last year's champion to be this year's *domestique*.

Twenty-seven years had passed since a defending champion agreed to chaperone his successor to victory.

Remember what happened then.

This was 1985-86. Bernard Hinault won the '85 Tour but victory was tinged with controversy as his young American teammate Greg LeMond felt he had been held back. On a key Pyrenean stage to Luz Ardiden ski-station, LeMond broke away with the Irish rider Stephen Roche and with Hinault toiling, the American had the chance to forge ahead and show the world what he could do.

Team manager Paul Koechli saw only the danger, knowing if Roche stayed with LeMond he would take the yellow jersey and jeopardise the team's chance of winning the race. Deciding to override LeMond, Koechli ordered him to sit in behind Roche and not contribute to the pacemaking.

How can you tell a man he mustn't try his best to win?

LeMond was American and blessed with a freer spirit than is commonly found in bike racers from the old continent. He argued. Koechli tried to explain it wasn't in the team's interests while LeMond talked about his own interests. In the end the La Vie Clair boss insisted and LeMond eventually slipped in behind his breakaway companion. Roche's effort petered out and Hinault stayed in yellow.

His victory was a record-equalling fifth but the story came with a footnote. He owed LeMond. Not to worry, he said, I will pay the debt next year.

It is one thing to offer this pledge, another to honour it. Hinault was defending champion and when the 1986 Tour came round, he felt strong. Yes, he was going to help Greg but he wasn't going to gift him the Tour de France. His view was that champions of every era had to earn the right to the yellow jersey.

That year the race began with a prologue in the suburbs of Paris, and Hinault went quicker than LeMond. That got people thinking, most of all Hinault. Maybe he was still stronger than LeMond. The second X-ray of their form took place at Nantes eight days later, a 62km individual time trial. Again Hinault went faster than his team leader, this time by 49 seconds.

What's an old champion to do? Stand aside and let the kid

have a victory he didn't deserve? Pretend he is not interested in becoming the only man in history to win six Tours?

To have done that would have been to say, 'I am not a champion. Not a winner. Not a proud Breton. And my name is not Bernard Hinault.'

Instead, Hinault played the man he was.

Three days later he got his young ally Jean-François Bernard to help take him clear of LeMond in the Pyrenees and at the end of that eventful day, his lead over the American was more than five minutes.

Climbing from his bike that evening, LeMond conceded he was riding for second place. He sounded like a coroner pronouncing his challenge dead. But that wasn't enough for Hinault, who still wanted to drive a stake through his team-mate's heart. On the second Pyrenean stage he attacked on the Tourmalet, the first of four big climbs. On the early slopes of the Col d'Aspin, he was part of a group already three minutes ahead of LeMond.

That meant he led the race by more than eight minutes. It was daring and exhilarating and ... suicidal. On the third climb, the Peyrescourde, Hinault rediscovered frailty. Drained of energy, he wilted and the chasing pack, including LeMond, caught him before the summit.

They knew then how little he had left for the final climb to Superbagnères and LeMond felt like a new man. Away on that climb, winning the stage and though he still trailed Hinault by 40 seconds, the Tour had turned his way. Four days later he would take the jersey from the old champion, never to relinquish it.

The French never loved Hinault as much as they loved him

through that Tour. They didn't want their champion to be the American's *équipier*. Hinault didn't want it. He chose to die with his boots on.

LeMond was invited onto a French television show, expecting the fact that he was the first American and first English speaker to win the Tour de France to be celebrated.

First thing the host of the show said was, '*Greg, le victoire pour vous, la gloire pour Bernard.*' What do you say in response to that?

With this as a precedent, things didn't bode well for Team Sky's attempt at Tour champion relegation. When he spoke about focusing on the Tour and said he believed he could yet be Team Sky's leader, Wiggins showed that a boy from Kilburn in London could be as proud and as obstinate as a Breton.

But Brailsford has a team to run, a race to win and Wiggins's suggestion that he could yet lead the team in France was close to anarchy. Froome was furious and put out a statement saying the team was fully supportive of him as leader. Brailsford didn't need to hear from Froome to know how angry he was. The following day Team Sky issued a statement insisting Froome would be leader of their team for the Tour de France.

'As always the team selection is a management decision and it will be evidence-based,' said Brailsford. 'However, it is crucial there is clarity of purpose and for that reason we will go to the Tour with one leader. Taking that into consideration' and given Chris's step up in performances this year, our plan, as it has been since January, is to have him lead the Tour de France team.'

Brailsford still knew that a strong and committed Wiggins,

riding for Froome, would be a huge asset to the team. Early on the 2013 Tour, we spoke in the team hotel car park and perching himself again on the shelf that runs across the back of the Camper SKY 18, he talked one day about the difficulty he faced when it seemed both men would be in the team for the Tour.

He spent a long time trying to figure out how best to deal with a situation that had the potential to tear the team apart at the Tour.

'I seriously considered this scenario,' he says.

'I would have the two of them in a room and I would say to Bradley, "Are you prepared to fully commit to a role where you would ride for Chris?"

'He would say "Yes, I am."

'Saying that, he might mean it but I couldn't be sure he would follow through on it and Chris certainly would not believe it.

'Money is important to Chris, he makes that clear which I think is good. The guys that are more difficult to negotiate with are the guys who say that money is not a big issue for them, but two months later are not happy with what is agreed and it festers. So what I'd planned to do was ask Brad again, "Are you certain you will ride for Chris?" and he will say, "Yeah, certain."

'Then I would say, "Okay, if you don't follow team orders we will agree to fine you three or four months' wages." This would be a significant amount of money, maybe as much as a few hundred thousand and I believed it would concentrate Brad's mind. "Now, are you really committed to riding for Chris?"

'I was then going to turn to Chris and say, "Right, Chris, if Brad goes against team orders, I'm going to give you that money." And I believe Chris would have thought, "Okay, that's decent compensation if this guy doesn't do what he says he will do." This could have worked. To win, you have to have "goal harmony" but not necessarily "team harmony".

'I don't believe we ever had harmony inside the GB cycling team but when it came to the Olympics or the World Championships, everyone got on the same plan and would be totally together.'

Brailsford never needed to put his plan into operation because Wiggins would go to the Giro d'Italia, lose his nerve on the descents in the first week, pick up a debilitating bug in the second week, and then struggle with a sore knee before being forced to quit the race.

That compromised his preparation for the Tour de France and Dave Brailsford's decision was made for him. The narrative was suspended for a while.

Even in Team Sky fate sometimes runs the business.

CHAPTER FIVE

'You are right, Watson. It mentions the legend in one of these references. But are we to give serious attention to such things? This agency stands flat-footed upon the ground, and there it must remain. The world is big enough for us. No ghosts need apply.'

Sherlock Holmes, *The Adventure of the Sussex Vampire*

On a Tuesday morning in 2010, 19 October to be precise, an urbane, bespectacled physician flew from his home in Belgium to Manchester and journeyed onwards to the higgledy-piggledy assortment of buildings which comprise the National Cycling Centre in Sport City. He was well dressed and well prepared.

Dr Geert Leinders had come for an interview for a part-time position on Team Sky's medical team. He would get the job he came for. And he would get more. He would get to become a symbol of cycling's struggle with its own past . . .

Haters, as they say blithely on social media, gonna hate. And when it comes to Team Sky there are an uncommon amount of haters. It is something you become aware of as soon as you start mixing with the team. The dislike which so many people have for them, and the team's bafflement at their own unpopularity, creates a microclimate around them.

A lot of people simply detest Team Sky. Why? For what they are and for what they are not.

Let us count the ways. Some of them.

Team Sky are monolithical. Those black team buses with the darkened windows, each coming in at £750,000 a pop and looking like something out of Thunderbirds. And the predominantly black uniforms with the azure stripe down the back, a stripe which is supposed to have some sort of meaning. They look like the secret police of the peloton.

Team Sky are uppity. The Jaguars they use for support cars for instance – what's wrong with a Skoda?

Team Sky are in thrall to the new-fangled. All those PowerPoint presentations and business jargon buzzwords and new ways of measuring everything. Did Coppi use PowerPoint? He did not.

Team Sky are slaves to analysis. Riding at a certain tempo for a certain amount of time instead of flaring briefly and dying? Just not old school. Team Sky would need an architectural blueprint and several environmental impact surveys before tilting at a windmill. Analysis? Schmanalysis!

Team Sky are keepers of bad company. Sky. The Murdochs. Not the Sopranos, but for a lot of people they might as well be.

Team Sky are headhunters. The recruitment of so many good riders in a short space of time. So unfair. All money, isn't it?

Team Sky and their bloody detail. The sheer tyranny of it. Team Sky don't move to the music of chance. Ever. They bring their own mattresses everywhere in case they get allergies. Never trust a man who carries his own mattress around with him.

Team Sky carry echoes. They train in Tenerife where Armstrong and the boys used to train. Bradley Wiggins had a house in Girona where Armstrong and the boys ... Two plus two equals?

Team Sky aren't cycling people.

Team Sky test positive for smug.

Team Sky stand for piety. Team Sky speak of their zero tolerance policy as if they invented the idea of being against doping. So when a chance arises to beat Team Sky with their own crosier, a lot of people like to step in and take a swing.

Which brings us back to Geert Leinders. Dr Geert Leinders.

Team Sky employed Dr Geert Leinders. Therefore, Team Sky are a force for evil.

Whenever a Team Sky person is asked about Leinders, they will draw a sharp intake of breath before responding. They don't resent the question, they are just tired of dealing with it. They never say the words but deep in their soul they must want to ask if you will be questioning all the other teams about their doctors and staff too.

The questions have to be asked but they have a point. Katusha, the Russian team, for instance have a doctor [Andre Mikhailov] who was arrested in France in 1998 with a van full of EPO. He said he was making an emergency run to a hospital in Russia. He got a suspended prison sentence. They have a sprint coach [Erik Zabel] who admitted some years ago that he took EPO for a week in 1996 but it didn't suit him. And they have an interesting boss in Viatcheslav Ekimov, who was a lieutenant of Lance Armstrong's on six of his seven Tour wins. Ekimov claims not only to have done nothing, but to have seen nothing untoward in those years. How did the Russian's seeing eye dog keep up with him?

Earlier this year Katusha got their World Tour licence back through the Court of Arbitration for Sport (CAS) after the Union Cycliste Internationale (UCI) had withdrawn it citing several reasons, the principal of which was financial. The team's travel budget was colossal. When the reasoned decision for restoring the licence was published by CAS, it emerged that on top of the two positives in 2009, another in 2011 and another in 2012, Katusha had employed seven riders with doping convictions and had registered twelve 'whereabouts mistakes' for random dope tests since 2009.

(Incidentally, after the 2013 Tour, Zabel would be named as among the positives in those samples retested from the 1998 Tour, news which required him to issue an updated edition of his original tearful confession. Ekimov, with heavy heart, suspended him from work.)

We journalists want to talk about Geert Leinders, however. Always.

Tweeters, bloggers and haters want to talk about Geert Leinders. Always.

The theory borrows heavily from *The Manchurian Candidate*. Brailsford, having spent a good proportion of his professional lifetime building up British cycling and then establishing Sky Pro Cycling, decides to secretly dismantle it all and to destroy

the reputations and lives of those who work with him by bringing in a master of the dark arts. He hires a doping doctor.

Either that or, as he claims, he screwed up.

Worse. When he is caught he doesn't keep hold of his
doping czar by claiming to have had a Damascene conversion
to the way of truth and reconciliation as practised by, among
others, Jonathan Vaughters at Garmin. Brailsford could have
said that it is important that we understand, forgive and
move on. He could have said that those who have sinned in
the past can be part of the future. Instead he reiterated the
zero tolerance policy and the only moving on that was done
was by several contaminated staff members.

Rewind from the Tour for a moment. It is March. Altitude
training in Tenerife. Here, up at over 2,000m, the Hotel
Parador often sits above the clouds but it is never free of
ghosts. A couple of weeks ago it was announced that Geert
Leinders is to face a criminal investigation in Belgium. That
is enough to ensure that the story will have legs all the way
into the summer.

The Parador is located in the Teide National Park in
Tenerife, where the volcanic landscape takes your breath
away, replacing it with the cleanest mountain air. Here professional cycling teams have been coming to train for almost
two decades. The best and the most notorious all came here.

'US Postal,' the man at reception says, 'for five years they
came. First as Postal, then as Discovery. I have my photograph taken with Lance Armstrong. Would you like to see?'

'Did Dr Ferrari stay here too?'

'Oh yes, he come always with his family.'

There were suspicions about US Postal's training camps in Tenerife. Why did they go there? How often did the testers show up? Armstrong and his key teammates came, trained, and returned to conquer. Their doping guru came too. After they'd gone Teide's pure air had the lingering whiff of toxicity.

On this crisp March morning though, it is eight riders from Team Sky who head off on a five and a half hour ride. The team has come to this training camp in Tenerife without a doctor. They like to strip things down when they're in Teide.

Seven times Sky have returned to this island, their faith in the high-altitude location expressed most keenly by their head of performance, the Australian Tim Kerrison, a key representative of all that Brailsford has got right in bringing in new talent from other sports.

'There's a time for giving the riders all the support and a time for focusing them on the things that matter,' says Kerrison, which is why Sky always come here without a doctor. 'Up here we try to eliminate all the distractions.'

To anyone who has spent more than ten minutes with the team, the importance of Kerrison's contribution is clear. He has been Dave Brailsford's key appointment and what has been achieved has much to do with Kerrison's coaching and mentoring of the riders.

Kerrison arrived in 2010 from a background in Australian swimming and rowing. He watched the Team Sky operation for months on end. He studied cycling and its practices and traditions. He crunched numbers. Finally, he told them the three things which would keep Team Sky from the success they had promised themselves.

Heat. Mountains. Altitude.

These three things may seem a little obvious but the team had morphed from the world of track. What makes a great track team doesn't make a great road team. Kerrison went further. He came back with a training schedule and an overall philosophy which would work.

Team Sky were thinking way outside the box now in cycling terms. Coaches to work with individual riders. No more racing your way into fitness. No more assuming that a cyclist can't do 'efforts' in December, that he should start in January. They started training earlier than anybody else. They incorporated power and speed work into their sessions from the start. They had long training camps and from the first race of the season they gave 100 per cent.

And Kerrison brought them to Tenerife, to this absurd landscape, where above a certain altitude the very concept of flatness ceases to exist. One road with its scorched surface runs like a ribbon over the volcano. You toil uphill or hurtle downhill. Six-hour sessions; 4000m worth of climbing.

Heat? Mountains? Altitude? Bring them on.

So Kerrison is in the business of excellence and sometimes he is in the business of ghostbusting. He knows the furtive practices of the men who cycled these roads in the era of Lance & co. He knows the risk he takes with his own reputation in the sport.

I want to get a picture of the environment which Geert Leinders slipped into. I have some straightforward questions, I say to Kerrison. They just need a yes or a no. He nods.

'Have you ever been involved in doping, either in Australia or in the UK?'

'No.'

'Have you ever witnessed doping either in swimming or cycling?'

'No.'

'Have you ever seen anything in any programme you were part of that made you suspicious?'

'No.'

'If you came across anything suspicious in Team Sky, would you immediately tell Dave Brailsford?'

'Yes.'

'Would you leave Team Sky if you felt any form of doping was tolerated?'

'Yes.'

Ask any Team Sky staffer and they will give the same answers. With conviction. So why the traces of toxicity? Why Leinders?

The recommendation for Leinders to join Team Sky had come from Steven de Jongh*, a *directeur sportif* with the team who had worked with Leinders while both were at the Dutch team Rabobank.

That Leinders had come to Manchester at all was indicative of a change of policy at Sky as, when the team was founded a

---

*By the end of 2012 de Jongh would have moved on from Team Sky in difficult circumstances too. He elaborated on his career in an open letter which included the passages:

> My doping was done by me, and nobody ever forced me. Of course, I always knew it was wrong and was scared of the risks I was taking. And I will always regret what I did.
>
> I took EPO on a few occasions from 1998 to 2000. It was very easy to get hold of and I knew it couldn't be detected. I was a fairly young rider, the opportunity was there right in front of me and it was a pretty big challenge to stay away from the temptation. There was no pressure at all from my team, the Directors or the Doctors to take it. This was my choice.

year before, it had committed to employing doctors who had not previously worked in professional cycling. Brailsford wanted to create a team above suspicion and with a clear code of ethics, but a disappointing first season was followed by a review.

Brailsford and those around him point to the context in which the Leinders appointment was made. The death of one of the team's more beloved carers, Txema González, during the Vuelta doesn't justify the mistake, but when they analyse where their heads were at the time they understand the anatomy of their mistake a little more clearly.

Right from the start of the 2010 Vuelta, the riders were feeling poorly. A virus had spread through their ranks, weakening them and causing upset stomachs. Txema González, the friendly Basque *soigneur* was suffering worse than anybody and had to be hospitalised. The team struggled on, losing Ben Swift, John-Lee Augustyn and Juan Antonio Flecha to abandonments as a result of the virus.

It was a nightmare period. The team which had headed into the season with so many idealistic notions and policies about supplements and nutrition etc., found its riders ailing and crying out for medication. The heat was oppressive, the racing was hard, the bulletins about Txema González's declining condition upset and frightened everybody. Riders are twitchy thoroughbreds and many were used to different regimes. The team felt impending pressure on its policy of no intravenous drips and no needles. The new team found itself making calls and decisions it had never anticipated having to make.

On the Friday of the Tour's first week, on the day of the

seventh stage, Txema died in a hospital in Seville. It transpired that he had contracted a bacterial infection which entered the bloodstream and developed into sepsis. The toxins had damaged his organs and his body went into septic shock. It was a different illness from that which the riders had been suffering but there was a difficult period of confusion which was reflected in the official statement of the Vuelta itself.

'The Spanish masseur Txema González has died in a hospital in Seville, where he was transported from virtually the start of the Tour of Spain, as a result of a viral illness from which he could not recover ... Team Sky have suffered since the beginning of the race from a viral illness that has affected not only its riders, but also one of the members of the backroom staff ... from the beginning it was discovered that Txema was worst affected.'

Brailsford said later that, 'When someone dies on your team, you feel you're putting riders at risk ... for all we knew the riders could have had the same thing... We sat down and realised that as a group of people we did not know enough about looking after people in extreme heat, with extreme fatigue. We were making calls like "No, on you go, mate."'

The outcome of the team's review of the Vuelta raised a question mark over whether the policy, of having new doctors from outside of cycling dealing with the extremes that professional cycling offers, could be sustained. Brailsford found it difficult to locate and recruit medics from the real world who had the experience and knowledge of the demands placed on riders while riding Grand Tours. It was agreed that the team's medical outfit had not been focused enough and that, contrary to the team's charter, they now needed doctors with experience in bike racing. So the policy was changed. There would still be no IVs, no needles and a severe discouragement of supplements but these things would be dealt with by an experienced cycling doctor.

Thus, Geert Leinders came to Manchester with good references and recommendations and at just the right time.

Leinders was interviewed first by the team's medical chief, Dr Steve Peters, and then by team doctor Richard Freeman, before Peters again spoke to Leinders and two other applicants.

Dr Steve Peters is a typical Brailsford appointment. A forensic psychiatrist by profession, his CV includes a stint working at Rampton High Security Hospital (at a time when Soham murderer Ian Huntley was there). He has made the journey from working with mental illness to working with elite athletes and has brought the same degree of success to both arenas. He is a fascinating, deeply thoughtful man and, one suspects, an accomplished judge of character.

'We needed a doctor with experience and the guy I met [Leinders] appeared very ethical, very professional and very compassionate,' says Peters. 'He was also very knowledgeable about cycling, training, the different races. This wasn't an appointment made lightly. Dave [Brailsford] and I had spoken a lot about how we could get tarnished by our involvement in pro road racing and how that would diminish everything we achieved with the track team. It was a massive fear.'

Peters doesn't claim to have an encyclopaedic knowledge of sports. When he moves into a new discipline he asks questions constantly until he understands the nuts and bolts.

As such his experience and expertise at the time of the inter-view were in track racing and its world. On that October day in 2010, Steve Peters knew little about professional road cycling.

He didn't approach the interview as an interrogation. It was one professional interviewing another. He didn't know about Rabobank, the cycling team Leinders had been with from 1996 to 2009, and he didn't ask Leinders what he knew about the team's Michael Rasmussen being withdrawn while leading the Tour de France on suspicion of doping. Neither did he ask what breach of 'internal rules' had led to Thomas Dekker being kicked off the team.

'I could have grilled him and grilled him but when some-one assures you that he has not been involved in doping, that doesn't seem appropriate,' says Peters.

After Peters's interview, Leinders was then interviewed by Richard Freeman, another doctor, who quizzed the Belgian on his medical skills and was impressed. Peters and Freeman recommended Leinders be hired and Brailsford offered a con-tract that meant he could be asked to work for up to eighty days in 2011. He worked sixty-seven days for Team Sky that year, starting with the Tour of Oman and covering some one-day races in Belgium, the Giro d'Italia and the Vuelta.

He was liked by the riders for his ability and admired by the management for his professionalism. If he treated a rider for an injury he would follow up with phone calls and advice after the race. If the truth and reconciliation movement within cycling was looking for a poster boy, Leinders might have been it. Sky found him in tune with their policies and keen to make a contribution.

Peters insists that Leinders was scrupulously ethical in his time with Sky. 'We agreed as a team that if a rider, suffering from asthma, got into trouble with pollen we would pull him out of the race rather than apply for a therapeutic use exemption on his behalf.

'Once, one of our riders was in this situation and the doctor got in touch with me and asked if we could get an exemption because the guy was in a bad way but was very keen to finish the race.

'Using my discretion, I said "Okay."

'It was Geert who rang me afterwards to tell me I was wrong.

'"We've got to have consistency," he said.'

Leinders had worked forty-four of his eighty-day contract in 2012. Leinders was present for a couple of days in Majorca at a team training camp, then spent a week on Paris-Nice, worked six one-day races in Belgium before working the Tour de Romandie and the Critérium du Dauphiné.

Then in April Theo de Rooij, former *directeur sportif* at Rabobank, did an interview with journalist Mark Miserus for the Dutch newspaper *de Volkskrant*. De Rooij said there had been a doping programme at Rabobank and that Leinders had been part of it. Brailsford asked for an explanation and Leinders claimed de Rooij's words had been misinterpreted and insisted that he, Leinders, had not been part of any doping programme.

In his modest and obsessively uncluttered office in Manchester, Brailsford thought deeply about the problem. He judged finally that to keep Leinders on while this allegation was being investigated would damage the reputation of the team. Brailsford has a fondness for coinages which sum up situations. This was a reputational risk.

Leinders's contract was paid up for 2012 and he was told the team would not use him again. Since then, Leinders has given interviews to Miserus and another Dutch journalist, Maarten Scholten, from *Handelsblad*. To both he said his role with Sky was 'minimised', meaning he had worked purely as a doctor. With Rabobank, he was involved in the conditioning and preparation of the riders and, it is alleged by Rasmussen, Dekker and Danny Nelissen, in doping. The fall-out continues for Team Sky.

Just last week when Richie Porte won the Paris–Nice his greatest challenge came in the press conference afterwards. Half the questions concerned doping. The Australian, riding for the English team was even asked to pass judgement on the state of Dutch cycling vis-à-vis Rabobank.

The team have noticed that when they go badly the questions subside. There is a danger therein which they need to address. Failure bringing the reward of a little peace is a dangerous concept.

In Tenerife Mat Hayman, the thirty-four-year-old Australian rider, took a call from a cycling journalist who wanted to know about his memories of working with Leinders at Rabobank. Hayman said he would prefer not to comment, an answer that didn't please Brailsford.

'It was a legitimate question and Mat should have addressed it.'

Sitting on a couch in the lobby of Hotel Parabor, I asked Hayman how he looked upon his ten years at Rabobank.

'From the beginning, I let it be known I wouldn't dope and

no one tried to push me. I didn't want to go to bed worrying about testing positive. I suffered because of that, never got to ride in the Tour de France, and settled for the life of a *domestique*. I felt it was unfair and there were lots of performances I was suspicious about, from riders in other teams and riders in my own team.'

And Geert Leinders?

'I have no proof, I didn't see any doping, but I felt there were riders in the team who used doping and I was sure some members of staff were helping them.'

'I spoke to a lot of guys from Rabobank, both on and off the record,' says Mark Miserus. 'They pointed the finger at each other but no one mentioned Hayman in connection with doping.'

Brailsford accepts that Sky's recruitment processes weren't sufficiently rigorous. 'We asked questions about Geert, no one raised an alarm and we didn't see the need to grill people. As the person responsible for bringing him in, I thought maybe I should resign. I got it wrong and if the board had wanted me to step down, I would have.'

In the post-Armstrong era many saw echoes of Armstrong everywhere. Leinders was depicted as the new Ferrari. Online cynics began referring to Team Sky as UK Postal. Leinders never covered a Tour de France for Team Sky but his ghost haunted the 2012 Tour and even though he had been dismissed in October 2012, he would still be a feature of press conferences at the 2013 Tour.

Brailsford points out anytime he is asked that there is no evidence, no hint that Leinders was ever even slightly unethical in his time with Sky. He was a good doctor, an excellent one. He understood the job and, in an environment where riders are being pushed to their limits day after day, Leinders was an invaluable asset as a medical practitioner.

And yet, he concedes with a sigh, it was a mistake. Not to have asked more. Not to have dealt emphatically with the issue sooner.

After Leinders's departure, Team Sky reverted to its policy of employing doctors who haven't previously worked in cycling and the new head doctor is Alan Farrell, recruited from a practice in Dublin.

On the Tour I will ask Farrell about the Leinders appointment and for such a genial man he will be quite blunt.

'Erm, when all you have to go on is rumour, and not facts, it's difficult that one. I'm glad I wasn't in that position. I think, I think, given the undeniable history surrounding the sport and the influence that doctors with questionable ethics had had on the sport, I think that hiring somebody from that era would surely have come with a couple of question marks . . .'

And if the team could turn the clock back would they ask more searching questions, do you think?

'Or even not involving themselves with anyone from that era. But, in fairness, as soon as it materialised, his association with doping and the Rabobank team, what more could they do other than expel him? Once the decision was made that I was going to the Tour, Geert was no more really after that.'

Geert Leinders was no more. Not in body. But his ghost still haunts them. Back on Tenerife where Michele Ferrari used to calibrate Lance, Geert Leinders is another spook from the past. Team Sky press on, trying to exorcise him, trying to find their space in the brave new world. Sometimes they wonder if cycling is interested in a brave new world at all.

They have been to this island eight times now on training stints. Every time they fill out the forms telling the authorities which riders will be where and for how long. Tenerife is a two-hour flight from Spain and the hotel is a fifty-minute drive through spectacular landscape. Only once in those eight times has a random drug-testing team made the journey to see them and test them.

'Now that,' says Tim Kerrison, 'is truly disappointing.'

CHAPTER SIX

*'Damn everything but the circus! ... damn everything
that is grim, dull, motionless, unrisking, inward turning,
damn everything that won't get into the circle, that won't
enjoy. That won't throw its heart into the tension, surprise,
fear and delight of the circus, the round world, the full
existence ...'*

E. E. Cummings, 'Damn Everything But the Circus!'

Some things send a peloton of shivers racing down a man's
spine. In the team car Alan Farrell could hear the voices of
the Team Sky riders ahead of him, familiar voices crackling
on the radio.

'Awesome, G!' they were shouting. 'Awesome!'

It was Stage Three, the last day in Corsica, and Geraint
Thomas had just hauled himself and his famous cracked
pelvis out of the grave to briefly join his team at the top of
the field and roar them on. They were responding to his
extraordinary courage.

Alan Farrell allowed himself a grin. When you run away

with the circus, when you elope with the love of your life, these are the moments you cherish.

For the first three days of the Tour, Team Sky's race head-quarters and its media centre have been on a boat, the *Mega Smeralda*, a ferry anchored in the dusty old port of Bastia. To get from the finish to the press centre, we journalists jumped on one boat. Then we get to work on another boat. It may have been *Smerelda* but it wasn't mega. The Corsicans never tire of pointing out that Christopher Columbus came from the town of Calvi where the third and final Corsican stage finished and Napoleon came from Ajaccio. Had either man seen the Tour's difficulties in extricating that bus from under the timing bridge at the finish line on Stage One, they might have gone out into the world a little more timorously.

For Team Sky the chaos and carnage of that first day of racing on the island are still being audited. Alan Farrell, the team doctor, is on his second Tour and the sight of Geraint Thomas lying on the hot asphalt beside the kerb unable to get up, having somersaulted over his own handlebars, was novel but worrying. Ian Stannard had been brought down too and Froome had squeaked past, narrowly avoiding the chaos.

Thomas, or G as he is affectionately known, was the principal casualty though. Very little stops G Thomas. Eight years ago his handlebar impacted with his torso so violently that he had to have his spleen removed. After a few weeks of morphine-masked pain he was up and about, gleefully show-ing his scar to innocent bystanders and claiming that he had been bitten by a shark.

A regular X-ray on the day of the crash failed to show the

small fissure in the rider's pelvis. Thomas must have suspected he was suffering from a little more than bruising the next day, however, when having been lifted onto his bike he set off on the second stage, an undulating 156km slog to Ajaccio. The first 10km of the race were punctuated by roundabouts and the process of slowing into them, and accelerating out, produced an exquisite pain the like of which he had never experienced before. He couldn't generate any power in his left leg and was seriously worried that despite his bravery he would finish outside the time limit and everything would have been in vain.

By the time an MRI scan showed the full damage to his pelvis he had ridden the second stage and could see no reason to let the team down by not riding on. He submitted to a regime of pre-race coffees, ibuprofen and paracetamol, as well as three sessions of physio and some acupuncture daily with Dan Guillemette, the team's head physio and a former elite amateur cyclist himself. Other than that he was devouring Jo Nesbo thrillers to keep his head occupied and to stop himself thinking about his mother's encouraging words – that he should get some sense and quit the race.

On Monday morning at Ajaccio the onlookers were wincing empathetically as G tried twice to get his leg over the saddle. In the end he was hoisted into place again.

Stage Three went fine for Team Sky, yet the moment on everybody's lips at dinner that night was the same one that sent shivers down the spines of those in the team car. G, bloody G Thomas, materialised on the shoulder of his colleagues, shouting at them to lift it. What a bloody war!

Nobody was sorry to leave Corsica behind but for G

Thomas the road ahead is as treacherous as the road behind. Today, Tuesday, in Nice brings a 25km team time trial. Geraint Thomas has been told that, as much as his team-mates love him, they won't be waiting for him. They can't be waiting for him. When he gets dropped early as he inevitably will, he is alone with just his pain for company.

C'est la guerre, mon amie, c'est la guerre.

Nice, France. The Promenade des Anglais.

Team Sky is another country. They do things differently here. With the three Corsican stages out of the way the race organisers arranged to fly the riders to Nice for Stage Four. Everybody else was to make the long schlep via ferry. People who have worked the Tour for a long time see nothing unusual here. The Tour is the Tour. As the miles go by, as the days pass and as the stages mount up, everybody gets more fatigued and more jaded until a caravan of wall-eyed zombies rolls into Paris. The Tour is the Tour. There is no need to see it any other way.

David Brailsford can't accept that. He himself often sleeps through portions of race stages in the afternoon so that he will be fresh and at his best when he swings back to work later. Days are long, beginning with a cycle with other staff at 6.30 in the morning. There is little for Brailsford to do when the riders are on the road and he trusts his staff entirely. He recharges daily and stays fit and sharp. As such, the decision to fly riders to Nice but to send those whom the riders depend on by boat made no sense to Brailsford. He investigated the cost of a private plane, found it to be good value, and flew the fourteen staff who didn't have to drive the vans and cars onto the ferry straight to Nice. Little wonder that the view which other teams hold of Team Sky is jaundiced by some jealousy.

For Alan Farrell his days during a race are long and hectic. He doesn't have the luxury of running in the mornings or taking a spin on the bike with his colleagues. Availability he sees as being a key part of his job. He is available in the team hotel first thing in the morning. He goes to the race in the bus so he can continue to be available. He is in the race car during the race, available for any calamity the stage might bring. Coming up to a stage finish there is a deviation for the support cars, so when he gets dropped off he has to get himself to the finish to be at anti-doping with any of his riders chosen for testing. To be there he has to get through the crowds and the security. He doesn't have to be there but he likes to be. Availability.

Today's team trial means a short day on the road. For the riders the effort is short and intense. For the team around them the day allows time to catch up on all the other things which make Team Sky tick.

When life slows down for Alan Farrell he will probably appreciate the strangeness of these days. For now the young doctor is immersed in this world. When Thomas cracked his pelvis and rode on Farrell wasn't much fazed by it, or unduly surprised. The heroics were wonderful and Farrell knows that the more Thomas works on the bike, the more pain he cycles through, the better he will feel. Everybody has their reasons for running away with this circus. The sense that anything can happen during a working day on a Grand Tour is one of the attractions.

Farrell had been working in pro cycling for just six weeks when he found himself acting as Sky's full-time doctor on the 2012 Tour de France. The first major issue he had at the Tour was when Kanstantsin Siutsou [Kosta, to the team] broke his leg on the third stage. One of those moments. You're not in Kansas anymore, Dorothy.

Farrell learned quickly that this job was different from any he was used to before. He was an Irish doctor. Here he had a rider from Belarus who was living in Italy, riding his first Tour de France for a team based in the UK. When Kosta broke his leg Alan Farrell was up all night trying to organise a flight to get the rider to the UK to have an operation. At the last minute he realised that being a Belarusian, Kosta didn't have a visa for the UK. He would be turned away. Alan Farrell switched his attentions to Paris, found what he was looking for and resolved to improve his linguistic capabilities.

Today's team trial isn't an annual feature of the race. Last year for instance it didn't figure at all but when the team trial is included it makes for a fine spectacle. Teams operate what they call a rotating pace line with the members of the team, taking it in turns to lead the group. This is called taking a pull. Thus the cyclists share the responsibility of punching a hole through the wind. That's the theory. The challenge is discipline. You want the group to maintain a steady pace rather than have each rider who goes to the front upping the ante until the team gets strung out and the system breaks down.

In this context G Thomas is expected to be dead wood today. Yesterday in Corsica was wonderful but winning is about pragmatism, and finishing close to the top of the pile in Nice will send Team Sky towards the Pyrenees in pretty good shape.

When he finished his medical studies at Trinity College, Dublin, back in 2001, Farrell taught anatomy for a year in the University. He served an internship in a Dublin hospital and then did a year and a half of anaesthetics before heading off to travel for six months. He returned to Ireland and settled into life as a General Practitioner for four years. His last job in Ireland was working in an urgent care centre, best described as a halfway house between an A&E department and a GP surgery, where he dealt with people with acute injuries. By then he had fallen in love with cycling, but nothing suggested to him that he would someday be watching Geraint Thomas be helped onto his bike to head off with a cracked pelvis.

Farrell had given up his own athletic pursuits when he was in his twenties. Middle age wasn't exactly crowding him when he decided to get back out and do a bit of running, but he felt the need for exercise and for competition.

He joined a triathlon club in Mullingar in the Irish midlands and that got him back into running again. He was a novice swimmer and that was hard work, but the bike? The bike just sang a siren song to him.

As soon as he started cycling properly he was out of the triathlon business and pledging himself to the bike. He bought himself a Trek 1000, the bikes used in the Discovery Team, bought it at Trevor Martins, a bike shop in Longford. Trevor had raced at a decent level and the connection and the 6000 euro Alan paid for the bike fuelled his interest. He still has the bike, preferring it to the Pinarello he got from Sky.

Soon he was addicted. He went from feeling slightly comical wearing a cycling helmet to staying up into the small hours devouring YouTube footage of old races.

By 2009 he could no longer conduct the affair by long distance. He went to the Tour de France, three of them driving from Ireland. They met with some other lunatics – three from the UK and two from Australia – when they were in the Pyrenees and they joined forces cycling around after the Tour like a supporting trip. In Longford where Farrell comes from you could stand on two phone books and see for ever, so the mountain terrain was very new from a cycling point of view. Now he was racing his new friends up mountains and finding that he had the legs for it and that he certainly had the competitiveness for it.

For six weeks they were based in Barèges, a village in the high Pyrenees just to the west of the Col du Tourmalet. It was 2009, Lance Armstrong's comeback but the beginning of the end of cycling's lowest period. Farrell sat on top of the Tourmalet as the race passed over the summit. Thinking. Thinking.

The addiction bit him hard and wouldn't let go.

Still. Nobody predicted what would happen in the spring of 2012. Late one night in Dublin, with his girlfriend Rhona away in Boston on a trip to see her sister, Farrell was enjoying a quiet evening in, watching the television and sipping a glass of wine. Still thinking, thinking, thinking. He would like to work in professional sport, he thought to himself. What sport would that be? Cycling. What team would he like to work for? Well, language was going be an issue. He had just the standard Irish person's linguistic skills – fluent English and Gaelic. And game to try anything else.

So. Cycling. A doctor. English speaking. Sky were the newest team on the block and the obvious choice. So he literally Googled 'Team Sky Cycling Doctor' and the first thing that came up was the *British Medical Journal* and an advertisement for a job with Team Sky with the closing date two weeks later. His jaw fell open as if its hinges had been removed. He had actually Googled his specific dream job. Eureka. The phone rang. Rhona, from Boston. He told her what had just happened. She heard him say it and some voice inside her told her that he was going to get the job.

He wasn't so sanguine.

'I applied, not expecting a reply. I got news of the interview in an email on a Saturday night. I was running a race, a ten k, in Carrick on Shannon the next day. It was a particularly hilly ten k. I smashed forty minutes, I broke it. I was on an absolute high. I was thinking I'm not going to get this.'

Still. It was a high just to be getting interviewed.

Two weeks later on 14 March he went for the interview in Manchester. He wore his good suit and his competitor's face. He was offered the job that day. He was leaving Manchester when his phone rang and they asked him to come back into the velodrome. Tim Kerrison and Dr Steve Peters were there.

'Look, do you fancy this?'

He did.

The interview had been freighted with small reminders of what the world of cycling was going through and clear messages as to what Team Sky saw their response and their responsibility being. One scenario put to candidates was to tell the interview panel (Kerrison, Peters and Dr Richard

Freeman) how they would deal with a young athlete coming in and saying, 'Look, I want to try this ... uhm "method".'

What would the doctor do in that situation? Bring it to management? What would the response be to the athlete?

Farrell was quite direct. First and foremost from a doctor's point of view was concern for the health of the athlete. One reason why the athlete would be told to scrap the idea. And secondly?

'This is cheating, okay. And then the question was would you bring this to senior management's attention? And I said, absolutely. Of course I would. You have to respect ... there's laws governing medical confidentiality, and I'm bound by those, but at the end of the day if somebody is doing something that is potentially endangering their own lives, then you have an obligation to intervene there. So there are times that you need to breach that. If they're a danger to themselves or others.'

Doping didn't crowd his thoughts though. He had his views and was relieved that his new employers genuinely seemed to share them. They did what it said on the tin.

He saw himself though as getting into a medical job, not a policing job. He wanted to work as a healthcare professional in a professional sports environment. The job was described to him as involving covering a lot of races and race days, but not big races.

'It was kind of made, not clear, but, implied that – don't think you're gonna be covering the Tour de France. Don't think you're gonna be on Grand Tours any time soon.'

He was still interested. He still wanted to get in the door.

What was on the other side of the door changed quickly. He did the Tour de Romandie. The Giro, the Tour de Suisse. Then went to Manchester for a catch-up with Rod Ellingworth, Tim Kerrison and Carsten Jeppesen.

At the end of that day of talking and debriefing they asked him if he would be available for the Tour de France, starting just two weekends later. He gulped. He'd done the Giro d'Italia. This would be his second Grand Tour in three months. The Tour de France!

It was sometime around then that they explained to him that Geert Leinders would no longer be working with the team. Farrell had heard the rumours running around but wasn't sure how seriously Team Sky were taking them. He wasn't at the level to make a judgement. He'd spent a week with Leinders in Romandie and found him personable on the human level.

'If you had asked me I would have said I'd be very surprised if they weren't taking this very seriously, but I wasn't privy to exactly what their position was.'

And so Leinders was gone and more painful bloodletting would follow later in the year as Team Sky discovered that their zero tolerance policy was a stick with which their detractors could beat them. They had perhaps been a little naïve in trusting job candidates to answer a simple 'yes' or 'no' when asked at interview if they had ever been involved in doping.

Farrell hadn't been anything more than a spectator during the doping era. Pro cycling represented a new beginning for him. And in his own quiet way he represented part of a new beginning for cycling. What team operating a doping programme would turn over the medical duties on the Tour de France to a bright young idealist who had been just over six weeks in the job?

He sees the extent to which Team Sky have gone, not just in terms of the painful sundering of relationships, but in educating their athletes, in batch testing any nutritional products a rider might express an interest in. Chris Froome for instance expressed an interest in fish oils. Nigel Mitchell, who looks after this area for the team, wrote to the manufacturer concerned looking for details. When no reply was forthcoming, no nutritional information received, it was decided that Froome had best abandon his interest in the supplements altogether.

These stories, these attitudes reassure and enthuse Alan Farrell. In the course of a long conversation he welcomes questions on the issue of doping and repeats his employer's offer of complete transparency so long as the rules of medical confidentiality aren't breached.

As we talk he says things which would surprise the cynics and which surprise me. A frequent source of scepticism in chat rooms and tweets is the issue of TUEs or Therapeutic Use Exemptions. These are exemptions granted to a team to administer a listed drug for a genuine medical reason and not for performance enhancement. There is a perception that TUEs are thrown about like confetti. In his fifteen months with Team Sky, they have applied for two TUEs. One earlier this year, in season but out of competition, to treat a respiratory problem, the other to treat a medical condition before the rider went for a surgical procedure. The rider specifically needed a medication which was on the prohibited list. The operation was at the end of the season and he didn't compete for another three or four months.

Other issues?

'Having Festina as a sponsor of the Tour de France is not good for the image of the sport. I'm sorry I'll probably get in trouble for saying that, but, I don't care . . . I think there are doctors still involved in this sport that would have been involved with teams in the dark days. Sponsors should be more insistent with that not being the case. Now this isn't going to go down well with my medical colleagues on the world tour, but I just don't think it gives the right image. And sponsors need to show more power on that front, should put pressure on people running teams to follow the lead of other teams, like ourselves.'

'People are accusing us of not being transparent, but, we really are trying to be transparent. It's not just the anti-doping, it's everything surrounding that, so it's about the education and changing the culture, it's about things like the first international federation to introduce a no-needle policy into the sport. Massive, massive change. It got that culture of an athlete requiring an injection of anything, out of the sport. So successful was that that a lot of other sports are taking that policy on now as well. The summer Olympic Games 2012 in London was the first no-needle games – so if anyone required a needle or injection of any description, they had to bring that to the attention of the medical authorities in charge of the London games.'

He is aware too of cynicism surrounding the biological passport and isn't naïve enough to believe that any testing system will ever produce a 100 per cent deterrent in a world where cheating can mean survival or riches. But within a changing culture he sees the passport as a useful tool.

'People say that the biological passport hasn't been that

effective; well certainly some of the information we have regarding reticulocyte percentage [immature red blood cells, typically composing about one per cent of the red cells in the human body] and haemoglobin values, has been one hundred per cent effective. I would argue that an effective deterrent shouldn't catch anybody. People say the passport hasn't caught many people; it absolutely has changed the culture of the sport.

'But obviously the collaboration with the police and a more forensic approach to the use of drugs and sport is another part of that . . .. Another tool in the toolbox. So you've got your anti-doping, you've got the education, you've got no-needle policy, you've got collaboration with the pharmaceutical industry, collaboration with the policing organisations, more interaction between the national anti-doping organisations – the international federations, the athletes' entourage including coaches, doctors – more of an appetite to get drugs out of sport. And cycling is doing a good job of that. It's got a bit to go, but it's doing a good job. I definitely think there are a few other sports that really, really are in the Stone Age when it comes to this.'

Still, he knows that his own sport has yet to fully deal with its past and cannot bury that past. A lot of talk on this Tour concerns the recent publication of *Blood Brothers*, a book written by two Dutch journalists. The book throws a little more light on what was going on through the first decade of the new millennium. It is the story of the Rabobank team and it is extraordinary. It is also a little chilling that one recalls Rabobank so often cited as an example of a team with good ethics.

Head of the US anti-doping agency, Travis Tygart,

described US Postal's doping as the most sophisticated in the history of sport, but Rabobank's wasn't far behind, though manager Theo de Rooij denied that the team either suggested doping or paid for it. They had a recognised world authority in haematology, Paul Hocker, supervising their transfusions at a clinic in Vienna. They washed the water from the red cells, added glycerol, froze the blood and re-infused it when it was needed. US Postal by comparison could only chill their bloods in a fridge. Being able to freeze the blood gave Rabobank total flexibility as to when they used it.

As the UCI's testing improved, Rabobank's team bosses bought a Sysmex XE-2100, the same $100,000 machine the authorities were using to test riders' blood. With that, Rabobank ensured that their riders didn't test positive.

The single most remarkable story in *Blood Brothers* concerns the Rabobank leader Michael Boogerd, who the authors say got a blood transfusion directly from his brother Rini the day before winning the Alpine race to La Plagne in the 2002 Tour de France. Boogerd denies this took place but the journalists claim to have two sources for the story.

Blood Brothers makes difficult reading for anybody involved in Team Sky, as Geert Leinders is depicted in the book as a central figure in Rabobank's doping programme. According to Michael Rasmussen, a rider who has now admitted his doping, it was Leinders who advised the riders to persuade a family member to donate their blood for transfusions.

It was when these homologous transfusions became detectable that Rabobank's riders turned to the clinic in Vienna and started transfusing their own blood.

Leinders is no longer working in the sport and the Rabobank

team has changed, evolving into the more credible Belkin team. Sky have no option but to learn from their own mistake.

'This team,' says Farrell, 'it made very difficult decisions at our London meeting about its no-tolerance policy [parting ways with Steven de Jongh and Sean Yates. The American Bobby Julich had gone earlier] and even though I was sad to see some of the people that I'd worked with leave the team, I believe that they made the right decision. But that's not to say that the staff on this team, we're not machines, we're not robots, you've seen us, we're pretty normal people, you build up relationships with people that you're working with, especially when you're working on the road like this. So when I saw people like Bobby having to leave the team, and Steven de Jongh, that wasn't something for us to celebrate, it was a sad day. But at the end of the day that's the team's policy, and I fully support that.'

Alan Farrell represents some of the hard-earned wisdom which has come to Brailsford and Sky. He is the sort of clean break from the past which cycling needs. A man who doesn't want his personal adventure contaminated.

Out on the streets of Nice there is a story unfolding which explains why an Alan Farrell would choose to run away with the circus.

Geraint Thomas, whom Alan Farrell says has more physical courage than anybody he has ever met, hasn't been dropped by Team Sky right at the beginning of the time trial.

Dave Brailsford had spelled it out the night before. It would be unreasonable in view of his injury, to expect that G Thomas would be part of that team time trial in terms of really being able to contribute. The team could live with that. G would be a dead man riding.

G Thomas hasn't been dropped though. And he hasn't just stayed in touch. He has pushed the team on, taking his pulls at the front. He was there for 24 of the 25km, making his last contribution just at the return to the Promenade des Anglais at the end of the stage. He submitted another significant turn at the front, shouting at the boys and telling them to give every last ounce of gas they had. How could anybody not?

Then, job done, he dropped back.

The team finished third. Three seconds off first.

It was an ideal result but those gathered at the end including Alan Farrell would have noticed a cloud of disappointment cross the face of one rider. A Team Sky win would have put Edvald Boasson Hagen, the team's highest ranked rider, into the yellow jersey.

The race though is about the team and its needs. Chris Froome, the team's leader, had made up 6 seconds on Alberto Contador and 23 seconds on Cadel Evans, perceived in these early stages to be major rivals. Froome is seventh overall, now just 3 seconds behind Simon Gerrans, the Australian race leader who is commonly perceived to have a very short-term lease on the yellow jersey.

At this stage of the Tour the team emphatically do not want to be defending the yellow jersey and wasting energy for a marginal advantage. Geraint Thomas has established the mood of the day. Poor Edvald Boasson Hagen's personal ambitions or disappointments are of no interest for now.

There are warm-downs and doping tests to be looked after. Today has been one of the days that Alan Farrell dreamed of when he ran away with the Tour.

CHAPTER SEVEN

*'Not everything that can be counted counts, and not every-
thing that counts can be counted.'*

Albert Einstein

When the Tour leaves Nice, and after the drama of the team
time trial, we have a few days of shadow boxing and photo
opportunities as we meander to Marseille and on to Montpellier
and then to Albi. Three days of drum roll before we get to the
Pyrenees.

Froome narrowly escapes a crash in the last kilometre to
Marseille but otherwise there is a dearth of drama. He arrives
in Albi lying seventh in the General Classification, 8 seconds
behind. It's been an eventful first week for Sky. Bad luck with
Thomas's crash, worrying performance into Calvi on the last
day in Corsica, but that was then countered by the boost of
the team time trial.

By and large, judgement on the team is being reserved.
Those who expect a re-enactment of their performance of

2012, gathering around their leader in a protective cluster, haven't been paying attention.

Fans and journalists collect around the bus in the morning, crowding around like Freddie Mercury has reanimated for one last reunion tour. And how do people try to comprehend this celebrity treatment? To explain it they talk about what they imagine lies beneath. And mustn't what lies beneath be all lies? No? That's the residual taste in our mouths from the Armstrong era. Shan't get fooled again.

They have to be micro dosing. They have to be taking something which isn't even banned yet. They have to be. Doesn't that drug AICAR make you thin? Aren't they really thin? How else? Faulty syllogisms that wouldn't pass in a philosophy undergraduate's logic class. X was a doper. Yesterday Y was faster than X ever was. Therefore Y is a doper.

My worry is this: from 1999 onwards it was easy to add up the questions that Lance Armstrong should have been answering but wouldn't answer. A lot of people who got fooled and refuse to get fooled again didn't want to know back then. A lot of those same people don't want to know now when there are rational arguments for not pointing the finger at every exceptional performance.

If we allow ourselves a culture of not believing anybody whose performance rises above the mediocre, we're not avoiding getting fooled again. We are asking to be fooled again. If we believe nothing, if we take away the stigma of cheating by denouncing the entire peloton as cheats without asking the right questions, we leave nothing of value left to defend. The right of an honest athlete not to be accused just because he is an excellent athlete is worth defending.

I go back to Bradley Wiggins speaking to me in a bar in Mallorca earlier this year. He is talking about his dad, a man who once smuggled amphetamines in Bradley's nappy.

'He left me when I was two years of age. That always stuck with me since I've had children, I can never allow what happened to me to happen to them. My kids must stay true to their mother and respect their parents and I want them to look up to me when they're adults and go, "He was a great father," and I never want them ever to say, "I don't like me dad," like I grew up saying.

'It would crucify me if they did that.

'How I conduct myself in my sport is the same. They can come into this bar [in Mallorca] in twenty years' time and my yellow is hanging over there. They can walk in and say, "That's my dad's, he won the Tour de France," and be proud of that. Not coming in and going, "He did win the Tour but he tested positive later," and that means more to me than anything. I would rather not have won the Tour de France, not been knighted, and not got all the other stuff, just been a professional bike rider and not have any issues and go back to work in Tesco's but still have my children be proud of who I was as a father.'

When a man says something like that to you he shows you what is in his heart. Men can't always live by what is in their heart but when you know it's there; when you hear Wiggins articulate all this in his soulful way, it moves you. You have a responsibility to tread softly when you decide that he is very good and therefore very guilty. You have a responsibility to go and gather all the evidence before you frame a question. Even with Lance we had that responsibility. We need to remind ourselves of that more than anything now.

Let me offer up a confession here.

On the last Sunday of the 1999 Tour de France, I advised readers of the *Sunday Times* not to applaud Lance Armstrong as he rolled down the Champs-Elysées in the yellow jersey. Mistrust was based on his radical improvement, his bullying of the anti-doper Christophe Bassons, the US Postal cover-up of a positive test for cortisone and Armstrong's refusal to engage in intelligent conversation on cycling's doping culture.

We called the story 'Flawed Fairytale'.

I didn't actually feel great about that story. I was certain Armstrong had cheated but a gut conviction wasn't evidence. But from the moment the 1999 Tour ended and there was time to delve I wanted to find the evidence that would convince others of what I knew. And I can't recall this without a nod of appreciation to Sandro Donati, Stephen Swart, Betsy Andreu, Emma O'Reilly, Greg LeMond and many others.

I've been with Team Sky for some time now on and off. Living with them and talking with them. I do my best. I keep my eyes peeled for a 'Motoman' character ferrying drugs through traffic. I check the car park for a camper van in which the health freak and bean sprout addict Chris Froome might perform blood transfusions on himself.

I check the trash for syringes. I look at the riders' arms and legs for puncture marks. I narrow my eyes when I see Søren Kristiansen, the chef, just to let him know I am on to him if he tries anything. I am on the alert for East German doctors. I would know a testosterone patch if I saw one. I ask Claudio Lucchini, the driver, if I can help him hoover the bus in the evening, so I can check for things hidden under the seats. I drift over and block the exit if a doping control chaperone comes into the room.

Nothing so far.

It might be better and more logical journalistically to sift through the available evidence first. Take what we can see and hold it up to the light. The things which Team Sky reckon make them go faster? Let's see if they all add up. Many of those things come straight out of the head of Tim Kerrison, the team's head of performance, who comes up with those marginal gains which so many denounced as madness at first. Let the investigation of Kerrison and his so-called 'science' commence.

Mr Kerrison, you stand accused of masterminding the most complex doping programme of the modern sporting world.

'Come, Watson, come! The game is afoot!'

In the Sky hierarchy there are maybe five supreme beings whose roles I would crudely sum up as follows.

Brailsford is unimpeachable as spiritual leader, Dalai Lama, guru, oracle, sage, swami, keeper of the fire, with a weakness to lapse into presumption on the question of others' honesty.

Fran Miller, head of business operations, is the conduit to the outside world, marketing, persuading, charming, correcting, chiding, far from a pushover.

Carsten Jeppesen, head of technical operations, deals with the team's partners like Pinarello or Rapha in getting the best equipment into the arena. Made for the world he moves in.

Rod Ellingworth, performance manager, co-ordinates the sports directors and race coaches. Plans for tomorrow, next week, next season. As close to the soul of the team as one man can be.

And Tim Kerrison, a quietly spoken, understated character

who moves in the background but affects everything in the foreground. His influence is everywhere.

The model under which Team Sky operates doesn't mean that these five enjoy any more privilege or leeway than anybody else on the team. When there is work to be done, you do it. It is common during the Tour to see Kerrison and Jeppesen standing on the roadside, being accosted by cycling fanatics of all stripes, for a couple of hours waiting for the Sky riders to come past so they can hand them their *musettes* of gels and drinks.

I like to watch Kerrison from a distance as he deals with the riders. Reconnaissance. He is that rarest of coaches, the man who can make you a better performer in half an hour. Riders would like him regardless of personality, because liking him and listening to him are the best thing they can do for their performance. Still, when he talks to riders in his quiet and reserved way he gives off liking and respect for them too, but never in such a way that a Chris Froome would imagine he was more special to Tim Kerrison than a David López or Pete Kennaugh.

Glowing character references. Still, they won't save you from the weight of cold hard evidence, you mark my words, Kerrison.

Every rider is a person as well as a scientific project. A challenge of data, science and coaching, but also a human being needing to be understood. On my first training camp with the team, which was in Mallorca, I spent a lot of time shooting the breeze with Kerrison. We ran together, talked about sport and life and the team and the riders. Let's see how he deals with good cop first.

At different times he spoke to me of the importance of his chats with riders after training when they would explain how they felt while doing it. That feedback, he argued, can be as important as the numbers produced.

It frustrated him that because he didn't speak all the languages necessary to be conversant with every rider in the team, and because many of them had limited English, he couldn't access the information he needed to set against the numbers.

Kerrison despaired when he came into professional cycling and Google searches started linking him with doping. He talked with Dave Brailsford about it and though his boss told him not to let it worry him, it hurt Kerrison and caused him to wonder if he should be involved in the sport.

His upset at his ethics being questioned was understandable. For a man who sees each of his charges as a separate project and different challenge, the notion of pumping a hatful of drugs into a rider and watching him go faster was profoundly insulting.

There were things I would remember from that week in Mallorca. How Joe Dombrowski and Jonathan Tiernan-Locke hated being blood tested because of a fear of needles. Tiernan-Locke, the others were saying, used to turn green. Another memory is of the other young American Ian Boswell sidling up to me and introducing himself with an assurance that seemed very un-European.

But the strongest memory was of the time spent with Kerrison and the absolute conviction I felt that whatever doping might still be happening in the sport, he would have no part in it. When Brailsford brought him into the team, it wasn't because he was looking for the next Ferrari.

So far so good, Tim, but we're just getting started.

*

Kerrison is an Aussie. He worked down under in both swimming and rowing before being lured to British Swimming in 2005. Kerrison is from Toowong in Brisbane and in 2002 Steve Kuzma and Michael McBryde from his home rowing club won the World Under-23 championships under Kerrison's tutelage. How long since that had previously happened? Toowong, much Toowong.

That isn't the sort of joke one makes to Tim Kerrison. Well, actually, you could but you might have to pick your moment.

Kerrison's move into swimming performance at the Queensland Academy of Sport coincided with a time when the Australians were starting to worry about their inability to produce top-class female sprinters. In Athens in 2004, Queensland provided the answer when Jodie Henry of Brisbane took three golds. By the 2005 world championships there were sixteen Queenslanders on the Aussie swim team.

Kerrison was underpaid and in demand. Another famed Aussie swim coach, Bill Sweetenham, was already in Britain and he lured Kerrison over – the latest transfer under the historical convicts for modern sports coaches exchange scheme, which saw a lot of Australia's best coaching talent head to the UK.

In Australia, Kerrison had constructed success on the back of his Interactive Race Analysis and Video System, which allowed coaches to analyse particular aspects of races as performed either by their own swimmer or by rivals. They could isolate increases or decreases in speed at certain intervals, instantly access the number of strokes taken, the distance travelled with each stroke, and so on. The system was launched with a library file of 2000 swims already loaded.

When Kerrison came to Britain he developed a further advanced version of the system. The results were noticeable. His influence on performance and training gained a large part of the credit for Britain's success in the pool in Beijing.

During his years with the swimmers, Kerrison would meet regularly with a small group of coaches and sports scientists from a range of sports. Cycling was one of those sports. Dave Brailsford heard the word and was seduced by the message. He had his high performance director. Brailsford signed Kerrison just before he was snapped up by cricket and lost forever.

Background checks look pretty solid.

Kerrison is an earnest and likeable man. Not a lot of the loud Aussie stereotype survives in him. Put him back to back with Bradley Wiggins's personal coach for 2012, Shane Sutton, and the two Aussies seem drawn from different species. Kerrison is guarded and doesn't do *bonhomie* as a rule, but he would cheerily admit that when he came to Team Sky he knew little about cycling. He didn't feel he needed to. He knew the human body. Everything else is just applications thereof. So Sky sent him out in a camper van. Usual Sky style. Even a camper can look ominous. They nicknamed it Black Betty. They told him to come back whenever he felt that he knew enough to make a difference. And by the way, no need to rush.

The result of his famous recce of the cycling world in 2010 was Brailsford's announcement that Team Sky had, to that point, been worrying about the peas more than the steaks.

Kerrison had watched and learned. Cyclists thought they were training hard. They weren't.

Famously, late in 2010, Brailsford and Wiggins had an

altercation. Brailsford had travelled to Australia to the World Championships and had watched David Millar grind out a silver medal through gritted teeth and bloody-mindedness. It didn't matter so much that Brailsford had gone to the edge by not inviting Millar into Team Sky when it seemed like he was an obvious signing. It mattered that Bradley Wiggins, highly paid and temperamental, was at home resting while Millar was medalling down under.

Brailsford started the conversation with a phone call and continued it in person when he got home days later. Wiggins came to see the point. That is the easy bit. Leading the horse to water. Brailsford, though, was coming to realise that he had the man who could change all that, a man who was convinced that even elite athletes are only in the foothills of exploring the potential of the human body. A man who could get the horses to drink. Tim Kerrison.

The culture of cycling bemused Tim Kerrison as he learned about it from within the bespoke confines of Black Betty. Riders clocked off at certain periods of the year then came back to train, riding hours on end in unsupervised bunches, gradually getting strength into their legs and stopping periodically for espressos. The same riders would use the early season races for more conditioning. The hope was that by the time the Grand Tours came about the races had worked as a whetstone for their bodies. The blade would be sharp. Hopefully.

A lot of the time they peaked too early or too late. And a lot of the time they didn't know what was keeping them from peak performance. Bradley Wiggins, for instance, couldn't time his talent to be on tap when he wanted it. And he couldn't ride above 1700m without experiencing difficulties.

Training was often long but unfocused. When the season really got going the intervals between races were just a couple of recovery days, enough time only for getting ready for the next race. Riders might go through a whole season and scarcely ever train properly. Not doing any training meant not getting any coaching, which meant not improving technique.

'So with quite a few of our riders we stripped the race programme down, so they were getting enough race days, but also enough blocks between race days to get some good training in. We tried to dispel this myth that you have to race to be ready to race.'

Things changed. Riders' schedules were carefully designed. They took warm-downs after stages. They took their long morning cycles – hours on end depending on bodily resources – before they had breakfast. Don't worry, all this was monitored and a protein shake helps you go a long way. Coaches went out with riders and actually coached them. Guys who had been riding bikes from the time they could walk relearned how to ride their bikes.

As well as trying to recreate the uneven rhythms of real races, the training sessions became harder. 'There were days during our pre-season when I wanted to punch him in the face. But they're the days that got me Paris–Nice,' Richie Porte told me one evening before dinner.

While at team training camps in Mallorca and later in Tenerife I noticed Kerrison insisting upon a reduced training day for any rider showing signs of fatigue or any hint that he might. And when they go well, he is pleased because he has grown to like them. What they seem to like is his even-handedness: he's there for every rider, as interested in one as the next.

After every ride a Team Sky rider performs he comes home, takes his SRM power gauge off his bike, downloads the day's data and sends it straight to Tim Kerrison. The coaches who supervise the riders' long rides know where the weaknesses are. They know where the improvements are to be found.

So Bradley Wiggins found that he would go to Tenerife for two weeks and ride 32,000m of climb. He found that getting ready for the Tour de France involved him riding 100,000m of ascending asphalt. As well as everything else he did. Surviving in the mountains meant not handing back the advantages gained in the time trials.

A few weeks before the Tour started, Chris Froome went to the wind tunnel at the University of Southampton on his new Pinarello Bolide time-trial bike to learn how to shave some more seconds off his time-trialling ability. Different rider, different challenges, different tactics.

Most cyclists have experienced wind tunnels before. In Team Sky they want to go back often. The wind tunnel has become an instrument of such usefulness that they can see the point of building one just for themselves.

In time-trialling, it is a natural law that if you get super low on your bike you are going to go faster. You're going to get a more aerodynamic ride. Speed is largely about punching as small a hole as possible through the air. For a long time cyclists thought these things are set in stone. If you are a bad time-trialler, you are a bad time-trialler. It will say so on your grave.

So, in Southampton, at first the riders would demur. The

usual moans. I feel uncomfortable. I can't get the power out with my hips angled like that, etc. So Sky educates to persuade. They let the rider take off in whatever way he feels comfortable and give them the figures and calculations in real time. Now they can see precisely what a repositioning of the hands, a tilt of the hips, a tucking-in of the elbows or a duck of the head can cost or gain over, say, 4km. Just lost a second. Another one. And another. So they adjust and they can see. Just gained a second. And the scales fall from their eyes.

And suddenly it's all coming from the rider. Two seconds could take years of training to shave off. But now with this new tilt of the hips and tucked-in elbows ... they take ownership of it and off they go. Now instead of the physios dictating, 'You have to learn to ride in this position,' it comes from the riders: 'Help me get the same power out riding like this.'

The team embraced the wisdom of Kerrison's theory of reverse periodisation. So instead of spending a large chunk of the early year building endurance and aerobic base, the rider focuses on introducing all the power and speed from the start. Gradually the duration of the sessions would increase, leaving Team Sky with their defining ability to ride long periods at high tempo.

Anywhere that he could see a better way of doing things, Kerrison would do it. He is the embodiment of Robert Kennedy's ideal of the man who asks not 'why?', but 'why not?'

Hate to say it, sarge, but he looks clean as a whistle.

There is a story from the 2011 Tour which describes part of his genius. Having lost Bradley Wiggins to injury, the team were finishing out the Tour as best they could, learning their lessons. The seventeenth stage began in France and ended in Italy, running from Gap to Pinerolo. At 179km, mid-stage, the challenges began, with a series of climbs culminating in the category one Sestriere, then a long 45km descent before sweeping up the Côte de Pramartino, a category two climb.

And then the finale, designed by race organisers keen to inject a little more thrill and spill into the race. The descent into the finish at Pinerolo was twisting, technical and steep, and described memorably by Andy Schleck as 'fatally dangerous'. Collectively the peloton was nerved by the prospect. Sticking in the group meant danger. Going fast enough to get away meant danger.

Kerrison had brought the Sky boys here before, though. They had done this three times in one day. Back to back. Kerrison hadn't left it at that. He had filmed the descent. He showed it to them before they went to bed in Embrun the night before. He showed it to them on the team bus on the way to the stage. Every twist and turn was implanted in their brains.

On the descent Edvald Boasson Hagen rode with glorious abandon and won the stage. Two riders, Thomas Voeckler and Jonathan Hivert, on the other hand, rode straight into a private driveway. Nobody died but everybody was forced to tread carefully. Everybody except those who knew what they were doing.

Kerrison moved to Nice this spring. It's just a thought, but France has the toughest anti-doping laws in the world. If Kerrison were the new dark overlord of doping, well, Nice wouldn't be the place to fetch up. That stretch of Med from

Nice to Monaco has become a home-from-home for the Team Sky lads, though.

What the Manchester velodrome was for the track boys and girls, the Riviera is for the road warriors. Richie Porte is in Nice. Froome is up the road in Monaco. G Thomas, Ben Swift, Joe Dombrowski, Ian Boswell, Luke Rowe, Ian Stannard – they are all around. And Team Sky bought a house on the Promenade du Soleil for other riders to drop down to. So between training camps they don't float un-supervised. They get daily face-to-face guidance and contact.

Kerrison has come to appreciate the history and lore of cycling both for better and for worse. The climb in the Med from which Team Sky are building their own database is the Col de la Madone – the ride out from Menton to the Col and then down to Peille. It has been used for a long time, but most famously in recent times by Armstrong and Ferrari in the weeks leading up to a Tour.

Aha! Gotcha. Cuff him, lads.

The taint is inescapable and regrettable, but every working day of his life Kerrison feels Armstrong's bony claws reaching out from the past and contaminating his present. Kerrison is a scientist though. Armstrong and Ferrari having been on the mountain does nothing to diminish the mountain or its fit-ness for purpose.

Oh . . .

'Everyone knows it was a test climb of Armstrong's and Ferrari's back in . . . the bad old days . . . So we have some ref-erence data, but then that sort of reference data you never quite know in what condition they did it, and you hear lots of stories about times and time trials up there. [. . .] It is the most conveniently located climb for us to use as a test climb, so we've started using that and we've started to build up a database of our own times up that climb.'

The idea of coaches being present on a daily basis – watching, learning and cajoling – seems too obvious for it to ever have been new, but having Shane Sutton tag along with Bradley Wiggins, or Bobby Julich with Chris Froome, brought considerable benefit. Julich was initially old school in his view of Kerrison's gospel.

'At first when I saw the way Tim was working I was pretty sceptical. Then as soon as I'd figured it out I was like wow! Why doesn't everybody do it like this?'

Kerrison hoovers up cycling data with an addict's voracity. Numbers are his bricks and from the bricks he can build models. The models tell him how to determine what it takes to be the best in the world.

He casts a cold eye on this year's craze, the hula-hoop which is home-brewed power stats.

He sees people happily making big assumptions while watching a rider perform and then throwing the assumptions into the mix as a power-to-weight quantity is determined. The result is a set of rules which supposedly determine the physiological limits of an athlete. Any athlete going past those limits is red flagged. These home-brewed stats are much like their liquor counterparts: rough, inconsistent, and coming with a distinct risk of blindness.

Contaminated evidence.

If you live on a diet of numbers it is interesting to watch but not definitive. His own range of data occupies that no-man's land between Team Sky's desire for transparency and

Chris Froome leaves teammate Bradley Wiggins and 2011 Tour winner Cadel Evans trailing in his wake during Stage Seven of the 2012 Tour de France, which he would go on to win.

But it was when Froome took the lead on Stage Eleven on La Toussuire and had to slow down to allow team leader Wiggins to catch him up that their relationship really took a turn for the worse.

Wiggins finished the Tour in the yellow jersey with Froome the runner-up at 3'21". It was clear that Froome was ambitious to go one better.

In the aftermath of Lance Armstrong, doping is always a topic for debate, but when Wiggins was questioned during the 2012 Tour as to whether his performance had in any way been enhanced, his response was explosive. 'Bone-idleness' was one of the few repeatable terms used to describe his anonymous critics.

Former Team Sky doctor Geert Leinders is quizzed by the media in January 2013 after he had been implicated in doping while working for Rabobank earlier in his career. It was an embarrassing moment for the zero-tolerance British team.

Tim Kerrison, head of performance support, discusses a point with Chris Froome during Team Sky's training camp in Mallorca in January 2013.

Chris Froome (right) leads the group in high-altitude training on Tenerife during April 2013, but their venue raised unfortunate echoes with Lance's US Postal team, who also came here to train.

Ian Stannard leads the way for Team Sky on Stage One of the 2013 Tour de France – perfect teamwork on the route to Bastia.

But a crash soon left the strategy in ruins, not least because Geraint Thomas suffered a broken pelvis in the accident.

At least things didn't go as badly for Sky as they did for the organisers and for Orica-GreenEDGE, whose coach got wedged under the finish line at Bastia on the first day.

The ultra-calm Edvald Boasson Hagen talks to the fans before the start of Stage Three in Calvi, but by the end of the day Dave Brailsford would be lamenting, 'We don't have a team.'

But the spirit and courage of Geraint Thomas, broken pelvis and all, coupled with the planning and strategic thinking Rod Ellingworth soon helped them to regain their customary authority.

The peloton winds its way through the Corsican countryside en route to Calvi.

Peter Kennaugh leads the way, with Richie Porte and Chris Froome in close attendance, setting a furious pace.

His work enabled Froome to blow away his rivals as he climbed Ax 3 Domaines and take a grip on the race that was never relinquished.

Afterwards, Froome was debriefed by mechanics Gary Blem (left) and David Fernandez.

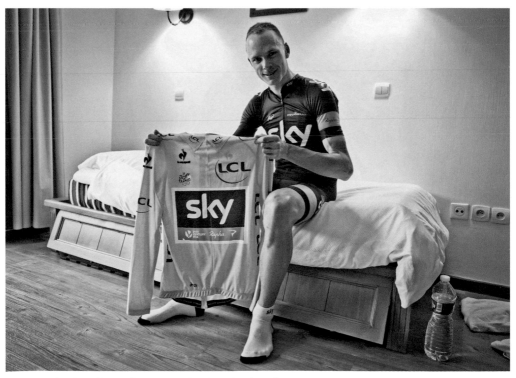

Froome displays his yellow jersey back in his hotel room, sitting on the mattress that Team Sky transported everywhere during the Tour.

Vasil Kiryienka on the last day of his Tour, 7 July, when he exceeded the time limit for Stage Nine by just a minute. He was devastated to miss the rest of the race.

The Team Sky cyclists head to the press conference during the rest day at Le Baule, just as the police were jam-busting performance assistant Oli Cookson.

Team Sky's need for a competitive edge. As a scientist he doesn't discourage the use of data to make for more informed viewing of the sport but he is saddened by the notion of guilt by association. Saddened but somewhat used to it.

Let him go boys, there ain't no flies on this one. Case dismissed.

CHAPTER EIGHT

'You cannot teach a man anything; you can only help him discover it in himself.'

Galileo

Saturday, 6 July

Kaboom!

Chris Froome blew up the Tour de France today and almost got lynched for it. On the short final climb of Ax 3 Domaines he ascended in what we were told was the third fastest time ever. He might as well have had a cannula in his wrist attached to a giant IV drip marked 'EPO'.

Suddenly, this Saturday evening, it is raining conclusions. People are shaking their heads in sadness. Some are wagging their fingers in anger. To me it is all meaningless. Now, I've never worn the leader's jersey in the race for a Field Medal in mathematics, but I do know this: today is only the fifth time that the Tour has used Ax 3 as a climb. It is also the earliest ever appearance which the climb has had in the race.

Today's stage was the eighth and the riders are fresh (in 2001 Ax 3 was on the twelfth stage, on the thirteenth stage in 2003 and was fourteenth stage fodder in both 2005 and 2012). The length of the stage was different each time. Straight off the bat this is a flimsy and unreliable shred of evidence for anybody to be drawing any conclusions from.

Inevitably times set in the doping era will someday be surpassed by clean riders. A well-supported and talented rider doing that on a climb that lasts a little less than 24 minutes is not going to convince anybody that the Tour has gone needle crazy again.

So you would think.

It took until just the third question of the press conference before somebody confessed to having had a US Postal flashback. Froome was asked to assure everybody that what they had seen was bona fide.

Herein lies part of the disconnect between the riders and the media. When I spoke to Froome about the questions, he was of the view that most media believed in his team because there was no concrete reason not to. In reality it is more likely that journalists *won't* believe in a team because there is little concrete reason *to*. These competing starting points inevitably cause problems. Froome thought that the questions came from a need, especially post-Lance, for journalists to be seen to be asking questions about doping. But without real suspicion based upon real evidence, the inevitable doping questions lack rigour and mainly serve to just irk those within Team Sky more than anything else. It's not exactly Pulitzer material.

I remember during the Armstrong years doing an interview in the course of which I said that no one part of the evidence I had amassed amounted to a smoking gun. The evidence was substantial: a suppressed positive, eyewitness testimony of Lance listing what drugs he had done, the tales of Emma O'Reilly, the confession Betsy Andreu heard, Stephen Swart's inside story about Lance pre-cancer, the Ferrari/Conconi chain etc. etc. What I meant in that interview was that, taken together, this evidence amounted to a serious case to answer for, but I didn't consider any one piece of evidence alone to be proof of Lance's guilt.

That seemed reasonable to me and still does. Tonight it seems that the damage done by the Lance era has led us to an environment where one short performance can be taken as conclusive evidence of guilt.

I am uncomfortable with that.

Just as alarming as the outbreak of statistics is the death by anecdote routine gaining popularity. To pull this off, you just need to quote one Ax 3 figure and then drop in a line about how this performance has come from a guy who was disqualified for taking a tow on a mountain in Italy not so long ago.

This is the obligatory reference to the 2010 Giro, which Froome raced in following a bout of sickness (it was a habit of his in his early times as a pro to keep his mouth shut about feeling unwell). Anyway, on Stage Eight his knee gave him trouble and by Stage Nineteen, trailing the stage leader by 35 minutes going up Mortirolo, he was in agony.

There was a feed zone at the top of Mortirolo, and Froome decided to abandon the race and jump in the team car when he reached it. He grabbed the back of a police motorbike, got a pull to the top, stepped off his bike and duly quit.

A commissar saw him hanging off the bike and, thinking that Froome was stealing an advantage and was still in the race, the commissar reported him. He was fined and disqualified, somehow, having already quit.

Ergo? Froome could never climb. And as an aside, if you were going to take an illegal tow would you really choose a police motorbike?

I like to tell another motorbike story which Froome told me. It goes back to the 2007 Giro delle Reggioni in Italy, an Under-23 race. This was where Rod Ellingworth first spotted Froome. Ellingworth is no mug. Froome wasn't long out of Africa (two weeks at the UCI World Cycling Centre in Aigle) and admits sheepishly that he didn't know back then that downhill riding is done 90 per cent on the front brake. He crashed four times on the first stage. Next day was a mountain finish.

'I'd trained really hard to get ready for it. I actually trained at altitude in Lesotho, which is an "island" entirely inside SA with very high mountains, and in J'burg where I was staying at the time. I got over to the Reggioni and this second stage was the mountain-top finish. I was surprised how I rode away from the bunch; going up the last climb, I was with a Russian and a Slovenian, Grega Bole, who is still on the circuit. We dropped the Russian, I think in the last kilometre.

'Grega was on my wheel and he begged me to slow down. He said he would give me the stage, "Just don't drop me, don't drop me."

'I said: "Okay, okay, not a problem."'

'We got to the last hairpin and they pulled the front vehicles away, the front motorbikes veered off. I was following the vehicles and blindly I followed them into the deviation when they veered off! That was one hundred metres before the finish line and the Slovenian went the right way and won the stage. I had to do a bit of a U-turn there and got second on that day.'

He got second place despite his chain going metres from the line.

A few days later they had another mountain-top finish in Montepulciano in southern Tuscany. This time Froome waited for nobody. He went early and then put in a sudden burst of acceleration on the final 1.5km to the finish line. Something familiar about that.

'I just went on my own, went from the last five kilometres, up through cobbled streets, it was beautiful, my first win in Europe. I was blown away.'

Guys like Rui Costa, Bauke Mollema, Ben Swift and Ian Stannard were behind him, gasping.

Ergo? Ergo, nothing actually. They are mere shards drawn from a career of thousands of races. A Reggioni yarn doesn't trump a police motorbike tale or vice versa. It just doesn't work that way. Meanwhile, just because we want to urge people not to leap to conclusions by isolating performances, we shouldn't fail to acknowledge when those performances are exceptional. Froome has been trained and paid to be exceptional and today he was.

The stage was the moment on the Tour for Team Sky to lay its cards on the table. This is what we've got and we believe it's good enough. Froome was the ace they were holding back and the question, endlessly debated, was 'when to play it?' Twelve months before, Sky controlled the Tour by playing safe, covering every attack in the mountains and gaining enough in the time trials to win.

But Froome is not Wiggins. He's good against the clock but not as good as the Londoner. In the mountains he's different and better. Can't just sit there when the road rises, he wants to attack. See what the others have got. He'd spoken so positively, not to say aggressively, about the stage to Ax 3 that Brailsford and Kerrison became pacifiers.

'Chris, we know you're going to attack on that climb but, mate, better not go too soon.'

Froome told them he'd waited the whole year for this stage and he knew if he felt good he'd just want to rip the race apart. And, dutifully, they reminded him that this was only the first of six mountain stages.

When it came to the nitty-gritty of where and how the race would pan out, they saw Vasil Kiryienka making the tempo on the Col de Pailhères, then Kennaugh would take over, lead over the top, make the descent and keep going for as long as he could. On the climb to Ax 3, Porte would take control and burn off many of those in the leading group. Then on a really steep section 4km from the summit, 5km from the finish, Froome would launch his attack. They expected him to take the yellow jersey on this day because they knew he'd set his heart on it.

And he's a pretty stubborn guy.

This was going to be a big hit. Some guys wouldn't be getting up off the canvas.

The first 120km of flatness was unremarkable. A four-man break was indulged with a lead that stretched to 9 minutes at one point. The action on this stage comes at the end though. By the time the race hit the *hors categorie* Col de Pailhères (bigger than its neighbour Ax 3), the breakaway boys could feel breath on their necks. The lead had been eroded away and was down to around 60 seconds by the time the leaders had reached the Col de Pailhères. From Sky's point of view, perfect.

There were some solo bids from here on, but it was young Nairo Quintana who made the attack that counted. He broke away on the Pailhères, so far from the finish it was clear his Movistar team were sacrificing his chances for team leader Alejandro Valverde.

Sky had to chase Quintana, spend a lot of energy in the process and they would then be vulnerable on the final climb. It was a shocking miscalculation by Movistar because Quintana was much stronger than Valverde and, before the Tour would end, he would show he was easily the second best rider in the race. Not bad for a man being used by his own team as cannon fodder.

In Team Sky they fret a little that this long stage race is too much too young for Kennaugh. I don't think anybody dares say that to the face of the Isle of Man rider. He's saucy and tough and does a brilliant ride to the top of Pailhères. On the descent he gives life to the expression 'poetry in motion' and Froome is comfortable taking his teammate's lines into every corner.

Quintana had a minute at the top of Pailhères. Thirty seconds after the descent.

As a postscript, Kennaugh rode at lunatic pace into the final 7.8km climb to Ax 3 Domaines. He was astonishing, almost comical to watch in his fury. He paid the price, dropping away with 6km left, but his work was done.

As planned, that left Richie Porte to pace his friend and roommate Froome. Porte grew up riding the Sideling, a famous climb in Tasmania, and he looked comfortable here at the other end of the world as the two Sky boys reeled Quintana in.

Just the finish left to execute. Froome, relatively fresh, took a look around and surveyed the state of his competitors before striking off on his own for a win which hurt all his rivals. Quintana and Contador lost 1'40", and he put more than four minutes of hopelessness into Cadel Evans. He reached the top 50 seconds before teammate Porte and, when the jerseys were re-allocated, he had yellow.

Froome was the story of the day, but Kennaugh's toughness on the descent of Pailhères is highlighted by another tale to which little attention is being paid.

The Pyrenees should have been the making of one Thibaut Pinot, France's great climbing hope. He finished tenth on his Tour de France debut last year. Unfortunately, for a great climber, Pinot finds there is one thing he can't do. Come down again.

'Some people are afraid of spiders or snakes. I'm afraid of speed. It's a phobia.'

On Pailhères today when Pinot was separated from the yellow jersey group on the way down he lost six minutes.

Poor boy. Imagine the horrors to come.

Sunday, 7 July

The horrors came.

Mainly for Dave Brailsford.

On the other hand, if Team Sky wanted to send out a message about the ethical nature of their work they could hardly have done better than today. Chris Froome had breakfast with his team and then scarcely saw them again until they reconvened for dinner twelve hours later. 'Hey, guys, what've you been doing today?'

Guys like Porte, Kennaugh and Vasil Kiryienka, who all did shifts at the coalface yesterday, might have been forgiven more moderate performances today, but no one at Team Sky could have been persuaded it was possible for their team to collapse quite as it did.

Consider the basis on which the team was picked: Porte, Kennaugh, Kiryienka, G Thomas, David López and Kosta Siutsou were selected because they should all be able to help Froome in the mountains. But, today, they didn't have it. Just not there. There could be good reasons why two or three struggled, but all six?

If Team Sky are cheating, it seems like they are doing it with just one rider. Everybody else in the team should ask for a little of whatever Chris Froome's having.

It was a gripping and engrossing stage in the Pyrenees that saw Kennaugh go down in an early crash, falling off his bike on the descent of the first climb, the Col de Portet-d'Aspet. 'When he was down, we drove past him and didn't even know he'd crashed. Luckily, Servais Knaven came in the second car and helped him,' Brailsford said later. Kennaugh never really recovered.

Porte, who looked so strong on Saturday as he helped Froome claim yellow, slipped badly off the pace and eventually finished long after the stage winner. Starting the day in second place in the General Classification, the Tasmanian lost time on the first climb and continued to lose more time until business closed with him 18 minutes behind, the team having finally told him to cool it and save his energy for what lay ahead. Kiryienka would have settled for that. Unfortunately he had tracked down a lot of early breaks and then run out of steam.

Kiryienka is a tough Belarusian. You suspect that Belarusians aren't available in any other model than tough. I haven't got to know him. Nor will I. This is Kiryienka's first year with the team and one glance at his lantern jaw suggests why he is here. He was hired to shovel coal into the furnace on hard days, and yet no rider in the team pedals with anything like Kiryienka's classily elegant body position.

He comes across as a serious and proud man. When he joined Team Sky they gave him a light-hearted questionnaire to fill out so that fans could get a flavour of him. Under 'Interesting Facts' he recorded, 'I have no special talents.' Asked about his interests away from cycling he says earnestly 'I'd like to have a role in the development of my country. I am worried for the future of my children and my nation.'

He'll get to see those children a little sooner now, but it won't be a happy flight home. The Belarusian exceeded the time limit by one minute and was forced to abandon the race. Kiryienka's pride means that his loss is a serious blow. This evening at the Majestic hotel in La Baule, most of the talk is about him.

'Kiry okay?'

'Devastated. Feels he's let people down.'

No one sees him depart and those who got to speak with him say that his eyes looked towards the ground. How could it happen? Why wasn't the second team car behind Kiry? Encouraging him, coaxing him? In the end, he only missed the cut by a minute. Shame.

While Team Sky struggled they had to watch Movistar doing a passable impression of themselves, pushing the tempo on the front of the bunch. They achieved the first leg of their master plan which was to get rid of Porte and isolate Froome, but things got tougher after that.

Froome was part of a thirty-two-strong group which included most of the race favourites and, instead of belly-aching about his loneliness and isolation, the radio conversation with Nico Portal revolved around improvisational tactics. (It was a characteristically classy touch of Froome's when questioned afterwards about how he felt being alone in the group to point out that in fact he wasn't alone, he'd had Nico with him the whole way.)

You deal with the problem by reducing it in size. So Froome doesn't have thirty-one rivals in that lead group, he has just three. He needed to keep the cuffs on the Movistar pair Valverde and Nairo Quintana, and Alberto Contador of Saxo-Tinkoff.

The Movistar boys maintained a strong presence at the front of Froome's group but couldn't shake off Froome in the valleys. Valverde tried to break clear on the flatter valley roads but Froome was on to him every time. Because he reacted decisively, Valverde got discouraged after the third or fourth attempt.

One final throw of the dice. They would try to bust him on the day's final mountain climb.

Three times Quintana attacked. Three times Froome reeled him in.

Contador should then have been able to profit from the energy the race leader spent on the Movistars, but the Spaniard in the Saxo colours just didn't have it. The favourites reached the top of La Hourquette d'Ancizan together and though Garmin's Dan Martin would escape with Jakob Fuglsang and beat him in a two-up sprint, that didn't hurt Froome.

Afterwards Brailsford was thrilled with Froome's tactical nous. A lot of time and energy at Team Sky has gone into teaching Chris Froome to be patient and discerning about his use of energy.

'When he was attacked on the flat, he had the wherewithal to go with Valverde; when Quintana went on the climb, he had the wherewithal to go with him; he knew he couldn't let those guys go. Then when Dan Martin and Fuglsang went, he knew to sit there with the other guys.'

In the end Dan Martin won the stage, clear from Fuglsang. The final 30km had been largely downhill and the leading pair got home 20 seconds in front of the bunch. That Froome was in the bunch was enough to keep him in yellow.

Not a great day for Team Sky though; Brailsford had a lot to think about.

'It was one of those days that was challenging, and the hammer blow if you like, the thing that made the day a lot worse was Kiryienka missing that cut-off time. The Pyrenees were a game of two halves, you've come out in the first half, absolutely screaming and you've taken a two-nil lead. Then in the second half you're a different team and you've taken a mauling, you go down to nine men and you've still won the match two-nil. It felt like we just scraped through three-two, but the reality is it's still two-nil. It felt like we had lost, but we came out of the match having won. With Richie, it was the element of surprise. I don't think any of us saw that [time loss] coming.'

Post-race? The match might have been won but there were many casualties, and Brailsford had a job on his hands.

'We tend to leave them on their own, emotions are running high, you want to take information in calmly, react rationally, but that's a very difficult thing to do just after you've competed. I think that's something we've taken off the track in British cycling, we let them do their warm-down, we leave them to it. Our urge as a management team is to want to talk about it, most people cope with stressful situations by talking about it. But in reality it's not the greatest thing to do from a rider's perspective, we tend to leave it.'

And what about Kiryienka? To have seen Geraint Thomas suffer an early injury in the Tour was unfortunate. To lose a second engine through being one minute outside of the cut might seem a little careless. One of those casualties which can occur in the fog of war.

'If you are the last car, and you have to go forward, what you say to one of the other teams is, "Just keep on the lads for me." Back towards the end of the race on a mountain day, you are not racing. You're all just trying to survive. So if your guy gets a puncture, he will be given a wheel by one of the other teams. From what I gather, Kiryienka was dropped when he was really struggling, and he came back again, and then I think Matt Goss might have been dropped and the Orica-GreenEDGE car was looking after him. And Kiryienka dropped out behind, then he was gone, and nobody knew. There was no malice.'

Brailsford recognises that Kiryienka, being such a proud man, would never have said, 'Look, I'm really struggling here.'

'I think with hindsight, he should have said something because our guys would have dropped back and got him home within the time limit. On the other hand if somebody is literally walking the bike up a hill, there's no point in losing other riders.'

What did he find when he spoke with Kiryienka that evening?

'You have to recognise how devastated he is, because he's a proud guy. You could tell that he felt he let people down and in that situation you've got to reassure someone. He didn't do anything wrong, and he certainly didn't do it deliberately. Get yourself home and get yourself right, there are moments where you can push people and moments where what the person needs is one hundred per cent support. No matter what, you've got to put your arm around someone and say "Look, it's going to be okay."'

That was one of those moments.

The Tour is going into a rest day. Brailsford can leave his team to eat and think tonight but there are too many signs that Team Sky aren't functioning as they did last summer. Tomorrow will be about calming things down and putting together a rational review of the situation.

Team Sky do still have the yellow jersey. Things could be worse. They certainly are for Thibaut Pinot, the speed-fearing

French racer. Today he lost another 25 minutes when he came in with the *gruppetto* and was in tears soon after the finish.

Speaking candidly to *L'Equipe* afterwards, the tachophobe said: 'When I saw that I was not able to stay on the wheel of a rider like Mark Cavendish on the descent off a mountain pass, I asked myself, "What am I doing on the Tour?" I received the clear response that I have nothing to do here.

'This is a very sad situation for me, I'm the person who is most disappointed about it . . . I don't know if I will be able to get over this trauma. During yesterday's stage my only objective was to survive. I don't know if I will recover, but that's life and that's cycling.'

Pinot's difficulties go back to a crash he suffered when he was younger, which has resulted in him being extremely tentative on descents. Imagine if he gets his head right. The time improvements. The things which will be written. Death by the firing squad of social media. Commentators armed with anecdotes each expressed in 140 characters or fewer.

Monday, 8 July

Often on a Grand Tour Dave Brailsford arrives home fitter than when he left. He likes to get up early and hit the roads on his bike for about two hours.

This Monday morning though he has a management task. Not something that would get studied in an MBA class. Not a case-study from a text book. Eight riders whose heads are all over the place. One leads the Tour, the other seven aren't sure where they are. The ninth is going home. This

Monday morning Dave Brailsford doesn't go for his usual ride. He waits. Morning rides are Brailsford's little slice of sanity during the race. Today he's brought the whole cake to share out.

When the team go out on their bikes to loosen the limbs and clear the minds, he slips into Lycra and goes with them. Wordless. He has seen his team virtually in disarray but this morning that same team are comfortable with his presence. He just hangs there.

One by one the riders drop back to him and speak. These are men who spend their working lives in the saddle and talking frankly while riding comes easier to them than while sitting down across a desk. So one by one they drop back and open up, and by the time the ride has ended Brailsford has gathered together the pieces of the jigsaw.

What do you think about the other guys, he asks them, is everybody contributing do you think? Are you contributing as much as you can? What should change?

He asks his questions, receives his answers, and one by one the riders seem glad to have spoken. Brailsford has managed to get a feel for where they are at, any personal angst. He has isolated those few issues which he thinks need to be addressed.

They get back to the hotel. Dave Brailsford begins putting the jigsaw together.

Tuesday, 9 July

Morning. Eight riders and Dave Brailsford on the Death Star bus. He speaks. They listen.

Brailsford leads the team into an open discussion. A classic Stop, Start, Continue.

What are we going to stop doing?

What are we going to start doing?

What are we going to continue to do?

A typical Brailsford solution. He is not the boss man here. He is the solutions guy. He outlines the state they are in. It's all okay.

'If you bring any group of individuals together these things happen. We have been together for two weeks. We went into Corsica under pressure.'

He knows the boys can't get away from each other and after two weeks' imprisonment little things become big things. Splinters under the skin. He said this. He did that. The way one guy picks up his fork starts pissing another guy off. It's irrational but human. He will try to reset the bar.

They know they had a bad day to Calvi. They know they had a worse day on Sunday. They know where everybody is at.

Now, here on the bus, this is the time to have the discussion. Not in private, guys saying what's on their minds in front of everybody. This is Brailsford on his *terrain de prédilection*.

He looks to Edvald, his talented young Norwegian. Edvald has the feeling that the team hadn't cared if he got the yellow jersey or not at the time trial in Nice back at Stage Four. Yellow was so close that Edvald was already picking out his matching cleats but he gave it up for the team. He wasn't resentful because that's not Edvald, but he had carried that disappointment with him like a lead weight.

'Edvald is disappointed he didn't get the jersey. He feels that you guys felt no disappointment for him. He isn't sure if you guys even want him sprinting. How do you feel about Edvald sprinting? Let's have some honest opinion.'

Honest opinion. Of course it comes from Pete Kennaugh, the oldest tyro in town.

Always when Kennaugh speaks they are reminded that the young rider from the Isle of Man carries the same chippiness that his fellow islander Mark Cavendish once brought to this team.

'We are a racing team,' says Kennaugh, 'of course we are going to sprint. If Chris is safe and he says, "Okay, go for it," then of course Edvald must go for it.'

This is okay by Brailsford, who believes if Boasson Hagen gets the chance to win stages he will then have the morale to go and empty himself in the mountains for Froome. The same for Richie Porte. Richie bombed in the second day in the Pyrenees on Sunday. Brilliant the first day. Crushed the second day.

There is an individual time trial coming up. Richie's shot at a top ten finish is gone. Should he take it easy in the time trial or go out and give it everything?

The old school would have said, 'No. Richie, you are here to conserve your energy.' Porte would have said, 'But the TT is my thing. I need that for me.' The old school wouldn't have been interested, but Brailsford is not old school.

So he asks and Porte says that he would like to do the time trial flat out. That would give him the morale to give it everything in the mountains. He rooms with Chris Froome and they are close. He won't be letting anybody down.

Brailsford knows Rod Ellingworth feels that Porte should conserve his energy and Rod knows when to keep his counsel to himself.

Brailsford says, 'You should go for it, Richie.'

Porte's teammates want him to prove to the world that the guy who suffered this body blow could go out and show the world that he is one of the top time-triallists.

He adds that the team needs Richie and Froomey and Pete in top shape when they arrive at the bottom of Mont Ventoux. The team has targeted Ventoux from a long way out, they have always held it as crucial in their march to Tour de France victory.

Ian Stannard is assigned a new job. From today he will chaperone Froome from 30km out to the finish. 'Ian, you will be our guy for taking him there.'

This simplifies Stannard's job. Gives him a new status in the team. He perks up.

Through this first week of the Tour, David López and Kosta Siutsou, who were expected to be two of the team's strong climbers, have not been riding well enough to contribute significantly. There were whispers from other riders that indicated dissatisfaction and, after Froome was left on his own for most of the ride to Bagnères-de-Bigorre, things worsened.

So Brailsford addresses the issue right here before the start of Stage Ten in Saint-Gildas-des-Bois:

'David,' says Brailsford, looking straight at López, 'you are at eighty per cent, right?'

López quietly nods his agreement.

'Nobody can blame you for that. It happens to everyone, but David what we need is one hundred per cent of your eighty per cent. You do that and everyone on this bus will be happy.'

Brailsford is taking reality and reshaping it for his riders. What López had been doing through the first week was to measure out his effort each day to ensure that he got to the finish without blowing up. Respectable on a personal level but not much good for the team.

Brailsford looks to the other riders and reiterated.

'David and every other rider in this team needs a little success in the race, and we've got to make sure they have that.'

It wasn't just López, but Siutsou as well. Brailsford outlines his new plan for the two under-performing riders.

Instead of expecting them to work for Froome at the end of the more difficult stages, they will now try to control the first 150km of the flatter stages. After the customary breaks of riders low on General Classification clear, López and Siutsou will make sure it gets no more serious than a five-minute gap. For two thirds of the race they will give it everything and then pass the baton.

Brailsford turns to the rest of the team. He tells them that he understands their disappointment that certain riders are not at their best, but that those riders are going to need to feel a little bit of love and appreciation in the days to follow. When they do their job, and when they do it well, they will need the others to notice their contribution.

This is a reversal of the usual roles for López and Siutsou but in the coming days it will work. This morning both are pleased to be given jobs they know they can do. They feel drawn back into the fold. As their morale improves, so too will their performance level.

Brailsford will meet his riders before each morning's stage on the Tour, but in the three weeks of racing no other meeting will be like this. No other meeting will impact the team as this one is going to.

In the space of a few minutes he has relaunched them psychologically and he has scrapped and redrawn the best-laid plans that he brought to France.

CHAPTER NINE

*"'The rule is, jam to-morrow and jam yesterday – but
never jam to-day."*

"It must come sometimes to 'jam to-day'," Alice objected.

"No, it can't," said the Queen. *"It's jam every other day:
to-day isn't any other day, you know."'*

Lewis Carroll, *Through the Looking Glass
and What Alice Found There*

Sometimes the Tour de France is as much a planes, trains and
automobiles experience as it is a bike race. Compared to the
old days when different imperatives informed the selection of
the route the Tour took, this year's route was three stages in
Corsica, a ferry back to the mainland, a few days in the
Pyrenees and then a jump up to Brittany. In 2014 the Tour will
linger amid the Francophiles of Yorkshire for two days before
heading south and then evacuating to mainland Europe.

The hopping, skipping and jumping between stages is a
logistical difficulty but it often brings sharp reminders of the

new ways in which the Tour interfaces with the real world outside. When you spend hours on end baking in a press tent, the talk of doping becomes so constant that the subject almost becomes abstract. People know because they know. Only rubes, dupes and suckers don't know or deny knowing. You forget that outside it is France, and these days in France doping is no longer a game.

Lest we forget when the French got serious on doping, introducing biological passports for sportspeople resident in their country before any other sports associations did the same, they also handed the bulk of the responsibility for enforcing their policies to the police. Lance Armstrong moved from the south of France to Girona in Spain like Jumpin' Jack Flash. Doping was no longer an administrative issue, it was a big legal problem. A gas, gas, gas it ain't.

On the first rest day of the Tour, the candidates for the UCI presidency circulate their messages. One such is Pat McQuaid, the controversial incumbent. The other is Brian Cookson of Great Britain. Cookson has the rare distinction of being a sliver of common ground between the fallen Lance and me.

At the time he announced his candidacy for UCI presidency, I tweeted that all cycling fans should unite and support Brian Cookson in his attempt to end McQuaid's reign. Armstrong was impressed and retweeted my advice to his 3.9 million followers. Three point nine mill . . . all comes to he who waits!

Brian Cookson's son Oli works for Team Sky as a performance assistant. You will never hear anybody tell you that he got the job because of his surname. It doesn't work that way at Sky and, by the way, Cookson junior is an impressive young man.

On the day in question, Oli picked up Rod Ellingworth from the airport at Nantes, after Rod had been home to help his wife Jane look after their little girl Robyn who was unwell. They drove towards La Baule and the Hotel Majestic not far from the centre of town where the team were billeted.

Oli was driving the Jaguar XJR, the long wheel-base VIP car. Tremendously flash. It's the top of the range and Team Sky use the car for ferrying VIPs.

Eight of the Tour teams are in La Baule on this main strip facing the sea and as Oli drives along he comes to a round-about with a police check. He presumes the police are diverting the traffic. Nothing out of the ordinary. He continues with this presumption until the police pull the Jag over onto the verge just by the roundabout.

So, a check of some sort. There are three or four of them. Bit heavy, but here goes.

He winds down the window. Naturally the policeman speaks in French. Oli can understand him but isn't confident enough to converse. Rod can speak French but, when asked if they can, the pair of them shake their heads, no. It's easier that way. Nothing lost in translation.

The local constabulary aren't planning on beating around the bush or admiring Oli's wheels.

Are you carrying medicine?

Are you carrying blood?

The question is not asked in a neutral tone. More like a policeman asking a guy with long hair and a ratty kaftan not to waste any more time and to just hand over the hash. So straight off it was 'show us the medicine'.

'Oh, we don't have any,' said Oli.

He could tell he was disappointing the police.

'I've found a lot with French police that, maybe it's just their way of being, but it seems like sort of aggressive to start and then once they talk to you then it's fine and relaxed, but, it was just, you know, not the best way to start these things.'

They spoke for a couple of minutes through the open window. One policeman spoke English and repeatedly he asked where the drugs were, the medicine.

Then he asked Oli what his role was, his job in the team?

'Okay, performance coordinator.'

'Ah, so you carry medicine?'

'No, no medicine.'

It went on like that for a while. Then to Rod.

'Performance manager.'

'Oh, so you carry the medicine, no?'

'No. No medicine.'

'Okay, out of the car.'

They get out. No hustle and bustle. Things still cool.

'Okay, empty your pockets.'

Oli had nothing in his pockets, he had placed it all in the central compartment of the car. Rod got his phone and his wallet out, but as he did so, laying them on the bonnet, Oli noticed one of the other policemen had opened the back door and was going through his bag.

Oli couldn't see what was going on: 'Sorry, you can't do that. You can't go in my bag without me watching you going in my bag.'

'Yes, we can.'

'So what happens if you put something in there or, you

know? I go to jail for two years and the whole team folds, it's ridiculous.'

'No, no, we can go where we want.'

'Okay, well, let me see.'

So Oli started to walk round the car and told the policeman that now he could look where he liked.

'Okay!'

At this point, another policeman went around to the other side of the car and they found the cooler, the mini little cool box of sandwiches. The policemen got excited at this, and Oli and Rod could hear them going '*Oi oi oi oi.*' Surely the perfect equipment for storing blood used in mobile transfusions?

The mini cool box was tucked in behind one of the front seats.

'It was a Vittel bag, and then inside it there was a small hard cool box which the team use for VIP sandwiches because we don't have much space, so it's kind of a mini cool box, about 25cm by 25cm by 30cm or something.' The cool box turned out to be empty, because there were no VIPs that day. And it all would have been a bit comical if it hadn't been so serious. The police weren't seeing any funny side.

'Okay, well where are the drugs?'

'Sorry, we don't have any drugs. Well, not "sorry", but we don't have any drugs. Why would we have drugs?'

'You are cycling, cycling you carry blood, you know?'

'No, we don't. Maybe that was the old cycling.'

'No, it's still today cycling.'

The conversation was going nowhere. Oli looked to wrap it up.

'Okay, well, maybe you've come with a preconceived

agenda unfortunately, so please, let's search. You can search us every day, you'll never find anything that's, you know . . .'

One of the policemen opens the boot and Oli has his main bag in there, his big travel bag. Oli had just seen his girlfriend for a day, because he'd had three days of the race with no VIPs, and driven up north, a 900km drive, to Paris and then to Tours. And he'd stayed a night in Tours with his Spanish girlfriend Lucila and, anyway . . . long story.

The policeman started to go through Oli's bag.

This was taking too long and Oli was watching Rod, to see if he was getting itchy. And there's a funny side to it but there are people passing now, blowing their car horns and taking photographs. The BMC team drove past and waved triumphantly.

It's comical . . . but . . . it's just not funny . . . this doesn't look great. Team Sky have an image . . . people always jump to conclusions.

Rod is sitting on the fence – literally, not figuratively – and one of the policemen is going through Oli's bag and, ta da! He pulls out a jar of French jam!

He holds the jam up in the air and looks at it.

Clouseau has triumphed.

'What is this?'

'It's jam, mate.'

Oli laughs.

The policeman doesn't.

Then the policeman pulls out another jar. Major bust.

'What is this?'

'Jam. Toast. You know toast, mate?'

So then he pulls out another. Huge. Again he asks, 'What is this?'

'It's jam, mate. For toast.'

And Rod had sort of had enough by now . . .

'Oli, what the fuck are you doing with loads of jam?'

'Rod, just don't ask. It's a long story.'

And then the policeman starts to pull out bottles of shampoo.

Rod's jaw is hanging a little loose now.

'Oli? What the fuck are you doing with a bag full of jam and shampoo?'

By now the police had figured out that the body language of Oli and Rod wasn't that of major drug traffickers. They lost heart with the searching. Instead they left Oli by the side of the road, blushingly trying to explain to Rod about the nice French deli which sold certain flavours of jam that you can only get in continental Europe. Oli tells me later that Lucila's embarrassment about the story is still all-encompassing: 'If there's any kind of dinner or something with the team then she'll say, "Oh, I can't come, I can never show my face in the team again when the team was stopped because of all my jams!"'

The shampoo remains a mystery . . .

You wonder if it might have struck Oli that he could have been carrying blood and drugs unknowingly.

'That's the beauty of the team we work in, I'm pretty sure, and I'd hope, pretty sure all the teams, all the guys working in cycling, don't ever have to worry about that, you know. From what I've read in Willy Voet's book and other books, and obviously . . . that's a different era. The only disappointing thing was the way that the police started off so aggressive and they already had the idea that we were carrying it, unless that was what their tactic was.'

But, the story was funny and the vigilance was reassuring to Cookson and Ellingworth.

'Well, that's what we like, we're glad we were stopped, you know, it's not like ... well for me, and you can stop me, er, every day, and the whole team, that's what we want, really. Although we also want them to do it to other teams, and, just because we're winning doesn't mean you shouldn't stop other teams, you know?'

If that sounds a little too good to be true, sometimes it is okay. It reflects Team Sky's understanding of the world they live in and the challenges their sport faces. In a lifetime of covering drugs-in-sport stories there are few things more discouraging than encountering athletes and teams who have a hostility to the entire business of being tested, nothing uglier than competitors who respond in ugly fashion to good people's attempts to keep sport clean and trustworthy. It isn't easy to stand with a stranger and pee into a bottle but everybody's life is easier if athletes understand why it has to be done.

In La Baule the police came at Team Sky car with a little too much aggression for sure, but that is the world that these men live in and it is, to use another buzzword of the post-Lance era, the legacy which has to be dealt with.

For a long time to come, cycling will be working hard to make a telling breakaway from its legacy. The Faustian deal with the dark side was a rolling contract in every way. Many cyclists are gone but their pee is not forgotten. Their urine and their blood remain sitting refrigerated in labs waiting for technology to catch up. Cycling's cold cases.

In the Mercure Majestic in La Baule I am sitting with

Brailsford and Ellingworth and I drop a little reminder that cycling's murky past just keeps giving and giving. New technology has given the French the chance to alter history. The results of the retrospective testing on the 1998 Tour de France by the French anti-doping laboratory AFLD are due out three days after the Tour ends. According to reports, there will be forty-four positives from that race. Given that the protocols were such that stage winner, race leader and two riders at random were selected for doping control, that means that half of the 1998 samples were found to be positive.

We wonder what might come out in this latest wash of 1998 linen. Thinking aloud, I ask if Chris Boardman won the prologue in '98, meaning he would have been tested. Ellingworth and Brailsford say no, they don't think he did, and anyway, he wouldn't be in any danger of testing positive. I say that more than one French rider has claimed that Boardman used EPO at a certain point in his career and, specifically, that Philippe Gaumont, who has since died, wrote in his book that Boardman had doped.

Nobody at the table believes that Chris Boardman's reputation is in danger. Rod Ellingworth immediately starts flicking and swiping on his iPhone screen and brings up the 1998 Tour de France; from there he goes to the prologue and there it was, Boardman the winner by four seconds. The result he brings up gave the top ten in the prologue, the riders Boardman had beaten by four or more seconds. Unlike him, most of them were later implicated in doping.

Brailsford and Ellingworth both shrug. It doesn't change their instinct or their opinion. They don't expect to see

Chris Boardman's name connected to any of the forty-four positive samples. They will be proved right of course, but it must have crossed everybody's mind what damage even a British positive from the dim and distant past could do to Team Sky in 2013.

Later that evening I am sitting in the bar talking about doping stuff with Alan Farrell. The subject of the past and the battle for the future is never far away. Team Sky fights on two fronts all the time. The battle to be cycling's top team through constant reassessment of the targets and potential benefits of training. And to be demonstrably clean, insofar as that is even possible in a world where we say, 'Well, let's see in ten, fifteen years' time just how clean you were in 2013.'

Farrell's nightmare though is not a positive test. He doesn't toss and turn worrying if a guy will decide that he wants to cheat intentionally.

'Because if a guy does that he'll be caught and he'll suffer the consequences. And if that is, for example, blood doping and it can be proved that he did this intentionally, then as far as I'm concerned, out of the sport.'

Alan Farrell's nightmare is not that guy.

'It's the guy who's living with his friend from another team who gets some supplement over the internet, takes that and it contains a contaminant, and then us trying to explain that this was an accident. Because people will say, same old story, same as what people are saying about the Jamaican sprinters at the moment. Well, they're entitled to their defence, and it may well turn out that it was the result of contamination. But it looks bad. And people have been using it as an excuse for years and years.'

So Sky provide their own supplements.

'We'd be pretty severe on guys that we thought were taking anything that didn't come from us, and we have . . . I mean Nigel [Mitchell] our nutritionist deals mainly with that side of things, but at least we know where our products are coming from and they're subject to proper quality control.'

That sounds small but on a team of twenty-seven riders with different needs it is quite an undertaking in order to avoid the cynicism which would greet a claim of accidental contamination.

The waves of the past beat relentlessly against the present. All the cheats who have gone before play their part in erod-ing this great sport today, even if they are just central figures in the ongoing argument between a future for cycling which involves truth and reconciliation, and a future which involves zero tolerance. By opting to set the bar higher, Team Sky have left themselves open for a surprising amount of vitriol.

Yet here in La Baule, Brailsford persists with the blue-sky thinking which is the hallmark of the operation.

'The doping stuff is a lot less intense than last year,' he says, 'Twitter is still relatively new. Loud voices and you couldn't put a name to the voice and they were saying very hurtful things. You think people will think less of you and that is very difficult to take. Last year it was like, "We're bust-ing a butt to run a clean team and we're getting slaughtered for it." Last year it seemed full on, and I had never been exposed to that level of aggression. I couldn't get my head around how unjust it was, and this time last year I felt just rotten.

'I could take Leinders on the chin because I fucked up

there. I watched the performance on the bus on Saturday, as Froomey broke away, and I loved that performance, and the second it ends and I'm getting out of the bus, I'm thinking, "I'm going to get some shit now." And that's what I got. The elation lasts for a second, then you get off the bus and someone says, "You've killed the Tour. You must be doping, you guys are definitely doping now."'

If Brailsford composed a list of the most asked questions, they would be:

Number One. 'What do you say to people who say your team is the modern version of US Postal?'

Number Two. 'The similarities between Lance Armstrong and Christopher Froome are there for everyone to see, what have you got to say about that?'

Number Three. 'How do you explain Christopher Froome's performance? It doesn't seem normal to us.'

Number Four. 'Can you look us in the eye and tell us you are not cheating?'

Number Five. 'Is it true you go to Tenerife because you can dope there and mask it?'

They're not really the sort of questions that Woodward and Bernstein would have put to Nixon, Liddy or Hunt.

'Can you look me in the eye, Mr President, and say you didn't know anything about the break-in at the Democratic HQ at Watergate?'

'Damn you and your journalistic brilliance. You have me bang to rights.'

On Saturday in the Pyrenees, the Team Sky boys had the

perfect day. On Sunday they collapsed and Froome was on his own, without support, and the team lost one of its strong men, Vasil Kiryienka. The question that followed this turbulent day of racing was not one of Brailsford's most common, and it was the most insulting yet.

Brailsford was asked if he had instructed his riders to perform badly on the Sunday in an effort to convince the public the team was not doping, if he'd told one of his riders to get eliminated. This question was posed by Nicolas Jay, an otherwise sane journalist working for the official television broadcaster, France 2.

Sky's boss needed to speak sternly to his chimp before answering.

'He starts it this way, "Dave, it is not me asking, but there's a lot of people saying you asked your riders to drop back to make it look less suspicious."

'Then I was asked, "When you realised that Froomey was going to smash Tony Martin's time in the time trial, did you ask him to back off?" And I'm like "I wish I was that clever," I was sitting at the back of the bus having a kip at the time!'

Police and cheats. Testers and cheats. Media and cheats. I'm here so I don't have to ask the same questions as my colleagues. An intelligent, original question at a press conference gives an intelligent, articulate answer to all your colleagues and competitors. The real work of looking at this sport and where it is at, is done elsewhere.

These weeks behind the scenes are a revelation.

And they have their funny moments too.

On the Saturday stage to Ax 3 Domaines, I watched the final 8km climb to the finish from the team bus parked at

Ax-les-Thermes down in the valley. Brailsford was also there, the driver Claudio Lucchini, the physio Dan Guillemette and perhaps one or two others. We watched as Pete Kennaugh and Richie Porte prepared the way for Froome to attack.

Everyone on the bus knew how much this stage meant to Froome and that he would definitely go for it. He was supposed to wait for the murderous 10.5 per cent gradient that began 5km from the finish and stayed that steep for a kilometre. But Froome couldn't wait and once he attacked, Brailsford's reaction was the loudest. 'Go on, Chris, go!' and when the gap began to open, 'Holy moly, look at that.' He cheered him all the way to the summit and he seemed like a boy supporting his football team. At one point the TV coverage showed Porte riding strongly in second place. 'And who said we didn't have a team?' he asked triumphantly.

Then, after a two or three seconds' reflection, he remembered.

'Actually, I fucking said it.'

CHAPTER TEN

'Great, just great. You're on an exciting adventure with Mario. Talk about unfair.'

Luigi, Paper Mario

Meet Mario Pafundi. The man who felt life offered him a choice. One year as a lion or twenty as a rabbit?

Before you meet Mario you know that you will like him. All the charm of an Italian matinée idol but none of the arrogance. And even his name has a lyricism to it that makes you want to repeat it again and again. Mario Pafundi. MARIO PAFUNDI! Eeeeeeeeeeet's MARIO PA-FUNDI!

Mario is the oil on the wheel, the pacemaker in the heart, the guy Dave Brailsford met in 2006 and told, 'If I start a professional cycling team, you will come and work for me.' He is head *soigneur* or lead carer depending on whether or not you speak fluent Sky. As with all jobs in Team Sky though, demarcation is a dirty word. Mario does something of everything, says no to nothing.

Chances are it is hot outside, temperature in the high

twenties, and when you meet him, inevitably it will be in a hotel lobby. You're loitering. He's hustling through. He spends more time in hotel lobbies than most concierges. Mario will be setting up the hotel for the arrival of the riders hours later. He may be hauling three physio tables along the corridor but he knows the score.

Everyone knows Team Sky likes to work on the outer boundaries of what's physiologically possible and they will wax lyrical about the accumulation of marginal gains, but morale of the team is built on simpler values.

'If you see somebody struggling with a heavy bag,' says Brailsford, 'if you're not willing to go, "Hey, come on, I'll give you a hand with that," and you walk past them because you're the doc or the physio, you're in the wrong team. The physios have been more challenging in this regard.

'"I'm a trained physio, I'm a professional, I'm not here to wash bottles." Those guys should never have been part of a sports team. I mean someone saying, "I'm not here to do this." Right, come on, mate. I wouldn't work with them. They'd be gone. In a nanosecond. I used to tolerate it, but I now know it causes aggravation, it causes friction. You can't build a team with people who want to be precious and individual about themselves.'

Mario fits into this team because he gets it. The Pafundis are from a small town, Pietragalla, near Potenza, in the south of Italy. To give their son a better chance, his parents sent Mario to Turin to continue his education when he was fifteen. Mario missed home but learned to live with loneliness and after a time, he didn't feel it anymore.

Mario was especially close to his dad, Canio. They could

talk about anything. Canio treated his son as if he were a man and so Mario tried to act like one. Once the boy spoke with his father about the loneliness he'd felt through the early months in Turin. Canio asked his boy to see this in another way. 'You were sad,' he said, 'but can you imagine what it was like for parents to be separated from a son they loved?'

Early in life Mario understood the world did not revolve around him.

Gracie, Papa, gracie.

It was almost as if Canio knew Mario would one day work for Team Sky.

There are people who envy you, Mario, who think you have an exciting job?

'I am glad you are seeing this,' he says as he hauls massage tables along tight corridors, 'that this is what it is like when you get to the hotel.'

Rooms, beds, bottles, *musettes* aren't prepared by accident and when you joke with Mario that actually his life is pretty unglamorous, he agrees.

'Yes! Yes!'

Mario brings people with him. No request from him seems excessive and when Sky's army turns up at the hotel later in the day, they find enemy defences have been dismantled. Team Sky, staff at the hotels say, are a nice team but that's mostly because their first impression has been created by Mario.

He has been around riders long enough to know it's different for them. Physical exhaustion can make '*bonjour*' feel like an effort.

Like thoroughbred athletes in every sport, they adhere to a

non-negotiable schedule and move with such languid grace when not at work that you would hardly know they're in the hotel. Each man serves as wingman to another, lest their thoughts be interrupted by a fan or, worse, a journalist. Some of them insulate themselves with headphones.

For all but the dullest and most meaningless of stages, their heads will have been programmed full of information about terrain, distance, corners, inclines, ascents and descents. They are walking sat navs. They then race for four or five or six hours, are forced to hang around for thirty or forty minutes at the finish and by the time they get to the hotel, they're ready for a lie-down.

For them the hotel is a place to rest and eat and sleep and rest.

Mario gives them their room numbers, so they bypass reception. Inside their rooms, their suitcase and water awaits them. Bedding is in place, sheets washed, pillow cases pristine and they're at the back of the hotel, away from the noise. They know all this doesn't happen by accident.

One thing, Mario.

Could you have been a contender? He was riding bikes in the south of Italy from the time he was eight years old. In Turin he got better. A pro contract was the dream. He got it, lived it for six months and then turned his back on it. He had six months as a pro and decided to do something else.

So, could he have been a contender?

'Yeah, yeah,' he says with a grin that precedes humility. 'Maybe not strong enough for do this job. The rider, you need to be a superman.'

On the Tour he is beloved. Welcomed everywhere. You know Mario Pafundi? Most people know Mario. The young woman at reception who pretends not to have noticed him. Daryl Impey, the South African who now rides for the Orica-GreenEDGE team, says he can never forget him. They crossed paths at Barloworld four years ago.

Seeing Daryl become the first African to wear *le maillot jaune* in this Tour brings Mario back to that time. Daryl was in the leader's jersey for Stage Eight of the Presidential Tour of Turkey. Close to the finish line Theo Bos, the Dutch rider, appeared to grab Impey and fling him into the railing. Impey smashed three vertebrae and his mandible, and lost a tooth in the bargain.

As the race moved on, Impey was left in a hospital at Antalya, a long way from home. Feeling for him, his team asked if he would like anybody to stay behind with him. Daryl asked if Mario could. The team booked a hotel for Mario and it was agreed he would stay for a week and see Daryl through the worst of it.

At the hospital, they suggested Mario slept at the hotel during the day and spent the night in the hospital with his friend. Just call a taxi around midnight and it'll take you to the hospital. He rang for the cab and when none came he walked the couple of kilometres to the hospital. He asked why taxis were so scarce.

'It's very dangerous at night,' they said and asked how he'd got to the hospital.

Mario said he'd walked.

'Crazy man,' they said, 'you are a crazy man.' Maybe.

Still, he got the message. After that he spent twenty-four

hours a day in Daryl's room. He would sleep on the sofa. The doctors weren't sure of the extent of Impey's internal injuries and worried that he would suffer internal haemorrhaging.

Mario waited night after night with Impey. Don't give him food, the doctors said, don't give him water. Nil by mouth. Impey was stuck on his back, immobile, unable to move a muscle. He would beg his friend.

'Mario please, water! Mario please, some water.'

It killed Mario to say no. He was allowed only to wet Daryl's lips with a sponge. Mario saw how Daryl suffered, how he dealt with it and the experience brought them close. Tough though it was for Daryl, it was still a special time in their lives. 'Always,' says Mario, 'when he always see me he says, "I never forget what you have done for me."'

Impey's day in yellow pleased Mario. The best victories are wrung from adversity.

But don't misunderstand him. Mario's sympathy is not for one rider, nor for one team but for all those who take on the challenge of racing a bike for a living. Anytime he sees a crash in the peloton it feels like one of his children has gone down.

Everyone in Team Sky has their special tasks. When the team are on the move, which is most waking hours, they operate like worker ants, with fierce efficiency and the ability to move more than their body weight when needed.

Everybody is a leader although, as Mario says, some are 'leaders without the wallet', referring to himself.

And by the way, just because you ran away with the circus doesn't mean that you get to see the circus. When the big top goes up, Mario goes to work.

Every day starts the same. Movement. Out of a hotel and

onto the road. Mario is always the first to leave. A one-man recce crew. He hits the road and stays in radio contact with everybody behind. How is the road? Any diversions? Any change of route for the truck or the bus?

New hotel. First job is to charm the manager. Things to impress upon the manager. Good parking. Space for the mechanics to work. Quiet rooms away from the road. Bags of ice. Oh, and fill him in about the special mattress and beds with gels that will be arriving soon. And remind him that the team chef Søren Kristiansen will need access to the hotel kitchen for a while later. Mario calls this process 'introducing our priority'.

The beds arrive in the second movement of vehicles. Once a rider shows for breakfast back in last night's hotel, his cleaning, his bedding and his suitcases are swept away. The stuff goes into the truck. Anything which will need to be replenished Mario keeps stocks of.

Having arrived first and spread the charm, he begins setting up everything he can till the bedding arrives. It doesn't dawn on him to have a quiet espresso and swan about in his Team Sky polo shirt for a while. No time for that.

The truck arrives and bang. The bedding goes to the allotted rooms. Five rooms for the riders, four being shared and in the odd one, David López the Spaniard on his own. Froome and Porte are together, Stannard and Kennaugh, Thomas and Boasson Hagen, the two Belarusians until they lost one.

Five or six massage tables get set up. If there is bed linen to be washed it gets done. The routine is a two-hour 90-degree wash every couple of days if you are thinking of beginning your own team. The riders have high metabolisms and sweat a lot at night, Mario says, so every second day the sheets get done. Sometimes if a rider has had a crash he'll come in and lie down and take the pristine look off things.

On his journeys through the lobby Mario will wonder what's happening with the race. Maybe the boys are at the start area now. Dave Brailsford at the back of the black bus talking to a few journalists. The riders stretching their limbs, warming up feeling where the strength is, if it is there at all.

Rest days mean 'rest' for the riders, not their valets. On the evening before the first, the riders fly from the south of France to Brittany, the support team make the 700-kilometre journey by road. It doesn't matter if the next hotel is in Timbuktu or in the adjoining building, everything has to be right for the riders to sleep well and be out on their bikes doing their rest-day ride at ten in the morning. The long drive from the south leaves the carers and mechanics needing to do a lot of catching up.

If it's a time trial, the day has a different texture to it. The riders will be waiting around for longer than they like. A few will race on full gas, others will take it easier, almost as an unofficial rest day. For Mario, it's just another day. Sure, if Froome does a good time trial and gains on his rivals, that will lift the mood of the team. Mario says the true professional acknowledges neither victory nor defeat.

'I don't feel a difference between a big day and a little day, because I always do my work one hundred per cent. I try to put the rider in the best condition possible for them to think just about the race. If it's a flat stage or a mountain stage, I don't care. I don't want to say I don't care because I am really happy when the rider wins. But I am not disappointed when he loses, because I'm pretty sure I have done one hundred per cent.'

Generally on the Tour, each day unfolds like a decent-sized novel. Lots of scenery and sub-plots early on. The narrative takes the characters to a place of jeopardy. On good days that place is a mountaintop and the story breaks men on the mountain. On bad days there are just breakaways which nobody heeds because the breakaways are just shoals of small fish. It takes more than that to bring out the sharks.

By the sides of the roads the personality of the crowds change as the miles are left behind. Early in the day people are just out to see the race go by. The Tour is woven into the fabric of France and they like to come and wave, to see the gaily coloured jerseys and to talk about old times. It's a good day when the Tour passes through your village or valley.

But as the stage matures, the hard core take their places on the kerbs and grassy knolls. These are the students of cadence and chain rings, they know their history and get the tactics. Appreciation of the near emaciated band of men is heightened by fans' understanding of how much pain it takes to keep churning the power out at this rate. For cycling is democratic. These roads and mountains will be empty tomorrow, just like they were yesterday, and anyone with the heart and the helmet can take up the gauntlet.

The *soigneur* has a unique bond with the rider. Not always but mostly. It was with Emma O'Reilly that Lance Armstrong let his guard down and his mouth loose. How that came back to haunt him. Sometimes the *soigneur* can be just like a priest. Giver of counsel, taker of confession. Sometimes the massage takes place in silence.

The *soigneur* can be the connection between the rider and the team. Sometimes, says Mario, he is left knowing things which just need to be kept private. Sometimes he hears stuff that he cannot keep private. He'll need to talk to the boss. Sometimes the rider talks about family, about a wife or girl-friend, they talk about the kids they miss, the things they want to do when the race ends.

This year Mario is working on two old friends. Kostas Siutsou who he has known since their Barloworld days, where he also met the other guy now in his care.

'*Allez le Pelvis!*' he says. '*Allez le Pelvis.* You know? Geraint Thomas.'

Old friends. Lots of old stories. Characters. He looks for-ward to that part of the day, listening, getting the inside stuff. That's why he ran away with the circus. But he never forgets that however close he feels to those who come to lie on his massage table, he doesn't work for one member of the team. Not for Team Le Pelvis. Not for Team Wiggins. Not for any rider. It is Team Sky who employ him.

This lies at the heart of what is bothering Mario as the Tour snakes its way from Brittany towards Mont Ventoux and the Alps. Suddenly his mood isn't as cheerful as it has been and on different evenings, he is seen having heart-to-heart conversations with Dave Brailsford in the hotel. He is concerned that David Rozman, the carer who has been look-ing after Chris Froome, is spending so much time with Froome that he struggles with his other chores.

One of the Slovenians in the team, Rozman is good at his job and has worked closely with Froome for some time. Much earlier in the year, when Rozman's partner delivered their child, Christian was going to be the name if it was a boy. But that changed in the moments after the birth when David understood he wanted to name the boy Chris after a guy he considered a great athlete and an even better person.

Mario, though, feels Rozman has temporarily lost sight of who he works for. 'When you are a father, there is one favourite child. You will not say this, but you cannot hide it. But you don't need this to take away the stuff for the rest of the children. You need to give one hundred per cent for everybody and one hundred and one per cent for your favourite. Until now, we understand this.

'But if you give one hundred and eighty-one per cent to one person and just nineteen to the rest of your children, that's not right. If that happens, the rest of the carers need to cover for the eighty-one per cent you forgot, while you were giving so much to just one rider.

'At the Giro d'Italia, you never see me come to dinner one and a half hours late because I was spending one and a half hours more with Wiggins. You never see me not carrying all the other suitcases because I'm taking just his suitcase from the room. You never see me walk straight to him when everybody else is around. You see, at the Giro I was in the same position as David Rozman.

'When everybody else is around, I treat Brad same as everyone else. When we were just me and him, I give him five per cent more. I think if David Rozman speak with the rest of the carers and say, "Guys, I need your help because Chris is the strongest one and we need to support him more and how can we do this without damaging the other eight guys?" that would have been the right way.

'But he spoke with the management and tried to cut out the other four guys [carers] and that wasn't the right way. The carer must remember that his mistake might help the rider to lose the race but he cannot do anything to make him win it. When they win, it is by their performance, not ours.'

Brailsford listens when Mario says something isn't quite right. They've been together since the start and there is mutual trust. When Sky sent Mario his first contract, he called Brailsford and said, 'The salary is wrong. What we agreed was in euros, but in the contract you're paying me this amount in sterling. It's too much.'

'Mario,' said his boss, 'you deserve what we're giving you.'

When a stage finishes, the hierarchy of the peloton is never felt more keenly. There are media and podiums and doping control for some. For others a wait on the bus until it is time to move. With Froome leading the race and needing to do podium, press conference and anti-doping, he gets caught up in so much protocol that the bus cannot wait for him. A car will take him to the hotel half an hour or so after the bus.

Team Sky handle all this stuff pretty much as they deal with all detail. They see what can be got out of it. It bothered head of performance Tim Kerrison that Froome had to do so much after the stage ended. So they timed him from the moment the race ended to the moment he got in the car waiting to take him to the team hotel. It came in at forty minutes.

That showed Kerrison it was pointless for Froome to warm down when he got back. But Sky's way is to find a solution and so a warm-down bike was positioned right at the finish for Froome. And so the warm-down came before the podium, press conference and anti-doping. Sky was first to initiate warm-downs, a development so obvious that you wonder about the collective wisdom that went into a century of cycling before that.

Mario likes the attention to detail. Water? Well, Mario would like it fresh and cold if he was riding these white hot roads, but too much ice on the drink is dangerous. There has to be sugar for energy and of course it shouldn't be too warm either because some riders just like to pour it over their heads.

The *soigneurs* make up two bottles. One is filled with a special drink made by British Cycling nutrition management. It is full of electrolytes and some carbohydrate, and given a neutral taste. This bottle is denoted by an 'x'. Not too much isotonic reaction, says Mario, because that can be hard to digest and there is a risk of diarrhoea and, well, there are those sheets to maintain …

The other is a bottle of water. But some riders have their own favourite drink as a mid-race treat. Some want protein shakes, and Mario lets them choose between strawberry, vanilla or banana. A key thing for Sky is their own drink, a special hydration tipple, which riders get as soon as they step onto the bus.

The *musettes* handed out to riders at feed stations during the race have as much thought in them as food. Tart with jam or some baguette, and rice cakes which the team prepares in the hotel the day before they get used so that they can have a twelve-hour setting in the fridge.

When a stage is climaxing you will always be able to find a man somewhere nearby making rice cakes for the next day. Detail, detail, detail. Give them a little flavour. Some soft cheese, agave, special nectar or honey. Maybe a little chocolate or chestnut jam. The feedback is good. The rice cakes get wrapped in special paper, not aluminium foil (the horror!), a softer wrapping so that riders don't cut their lips trying to open them as they ride.

That's the life. With the team, parallel to the team. For the team.

Mario has a son. Christian is three years old.

How does he feel about the possibility of Christian going into cycling?

'Yes. I can suggest him into this sport,' he says. 'But, he likes the food a lot, the only problem! A grandmother always say, they say the boy looks really skinny but he's, already . . .'

As big as Richie Porte?

'No, I don't want to say, I don't want to say this, Richie's really professional guy. No, I mean he's a really good Italian, he likes eating well, you know?'

He also has a wife, Tiziana. He travelled the world meeting women and ended up marrying the girl he went to primary school with and he couldn't be happier. Sometimes she nudges him and asks if they might move. Somewhere more exciting, somewhere a little nearer the team's new base in Nice.

The Côte d'Azur has much to recommend it but it's not for Mario. 'If you found a place where you drink amazing coffee espresso in the morning, sixty cent [as it is Pietragalla], then we move there.'

He is satisfied with what he's made of his life.

'Because when I go to sleep, I sleep on seven pillows. Like in Italy, they say when you have nothing wrong in your life, they say that you sleep on the seven pillows. Like, "Aahhh no problem." I haven't done anything wrong, nothing can talk bad about me.'

I've come to know Mario. I understand why Dave Brailsford wanted him in the team three years before he got the team on the road. Mario's important, a keeper of high standards and good morale. He can be like this because he was nurtured by a good man. Canio Pafundi.

Seven days into the Tour, I ask Mario to take me with him on the 200km journey to the next hotel, that I want him to tell me about Canio. And to tell me what happened when he came to that fork in the road that offered him a choice: this way one year as a lion; that way twenty years as a rabbit?

We are alone, the road disappearing beneath our wheels, the distance that separates us diminishing with each mile.

'Mario,' I say, 'you speak well of your father?'

'The car was the best place for us to speak. In the car together we would speak about important things.'

He recalls telling Canio about Tiziana when he knew she was the girl for him. He'd known her from their days in the village primary school at Pietragalla. Then he'd left for Turin at fifteen, travelled round the world with cycling teams, met the most beautiful women, there was a Swedish woman, an Australian, good times, but not what he wanted.

'You know you go all the world looking for something, you feel you have it but you don't know where you put it. Then you see you've left it in the most obvious place. The women I met, they helped me, but it's only when I arrive back where I start that I find it. Tiziana is a fantastic, amazing girl.'

He told all this to Canio, who spoke solemnly to him.

'Mario, you can play your game with whoever you want

but if you play the games with this girl, from our village, where we all know our story, it is different. The distance between you and Sweden or Australia is great, the difference between you and the other side of the street is nothing. Whatever happens between you and Tiziana will affect your parents and your brothers and her parents, and all our families.'

Mario never listened to anyone else as he did to Canio because his advice was never wrong and his support was unwavering. 'When I was a little boy, he told me I had two parents, I would never have any more. I had two brothers, never any more. If you don't like each other, you will still be brothers.

'He grew us up. He never touch any of us with his hand, he always try to teach us. All three of us, no one ever smoked, no one drank, no one got in trouble with the police, no one ever did anything very wrong.'

Mario became a professional bike rider in 1999, the year of Lance Armstrong's first Tour de France victory and a time when most riders wouldn't go to the start without EPO coursing through their veins. But Mario decided against eating that mushroom and turning into Super Mario.

'Ah, yeah, yeah, yeah. But, you know that I think, my private opinion, it's not private, it's just a legal one. Maybe at the height of it the UCI, they chose a haematocrit limit of fifty. It was like you can steal, but you can steal just five thousand euro. But your mum and dad they say since you was young, you are not allowed to steal anything. Anything! A lollipop . . . you are not allowed to steal. If I say I have stolen the lollipop, my dad say, "Yes, but it doesn't matter, you have stolen." Yeah but it was just a Haribo. "Doesn't matter, you have stolen."

'That was the principle they put on me. They say you have a surname and you have family, our little village are so proud about you. They tell me I can live one year like lion? Or twenty years like rabbit? It's just a choice. I have lived twenty years like a rabbit but I have stolen nothing.

'In 2010, Team Sky want everyone in the team to sign this paper, saying you have nothing to do with banned substance, that you never helped anybody to do something. I say, "Why not, this is no problem for me." And then last year, in October, they say you must sign this paper again. Nothing to do with doping. Easy for me, I sign.

'And I realise, three years after he passed over, my father has given me the best thing.'

And so Mario continues to realise that the values Canio and his mother imbued in him were the right ones. The decision to quit racing rather than dope has meant that, over a decade later and three years after Canio's death, Mario can sign up to Sky's zero-tolerance policy with a clean conscience. If he had lived one year like a lion, Mario would not be lead carer for Team Sky right now. The decision to live twenty years like a rabbit proves itself once again.

Canio Pafundi was a carpenter, ' . . . like Giuseppe,' says Mario. Towards the end he developed an allergy to wood dust and then got sick. It almost broke his son's heart. When it seemed sure that Canio wouldn't pull through, Mario told him he would be lost.

'When I see he is going to pass over, I said to him, "How can I do this, you need to still teach me. Without you, I don't know anything. Every time you've given me a nice advice. Every time I did the wrong thing, you tell me, "Okay, you did this mistake, but you now try to sort it out. We can find the solution.""'

'And you know what he tell me? He said, "I always thinking it's much better for a child to lose a parent than for the parents to lose their children." He passed over two days later and this was the last advice he gave me, to help me through this difficult moment. Some of my friends and family have lost a child, and I say, "Fuck, I am lucky."

'After he passed over, everybody talks about him and I learn it was not because he was my dad but because he was the right person.'

After Christian was born, Tiziana said something Mario has never forgotten. 'If this little boy loves you half as much as you loved your father, you will be a very lucky man.'

And Mario knows, he would be.

CHAPTER ELEVEN

*'Now the general who wins a battle makes many calcula-
tions in his temple ere the battle is fought. The general who
loses a battle makes but few calculations beforehand. Thus
do many calculations lead to victory, and few calculations
to defeat.'*

Sun Tzu, *The Art of War*

I'm taking the back stairs in the team hotel one night and I
meet the leader of the Tour de France hiking the same route.
I suspect he does this sort of thing a lot. David Brailsford
sometimes describes himself as a loner but he is an outgoing,
gregarious loner. Chris Froome is more in the traditional
mould. The dizziness and giddiness which come with the
Tour circus don't appeal to him.

He is a serious man with a good sense of humour. A card-
carrying Brit with an African heart. A leader who always says
please and thank you. Even when he texts his friend Gary Blem
for an alteration to his bike, he makes it sound as though Gary
will be donating a kidney which might save Chris's life.

Cycling, though, awakens the general public once a year when the Tour starts and people are torn between the sunflowers of rural France and the strawberries and cream of Wimbledon. It takes a long time for a quiet man to impress himself on the minds of the greater public. Even longer when the acrid smoke of the drug wars still distorts our way of seeing everything to do with the sport.

If you are wised up and street savvy and reckon that you won't get fooled again then there are certain givens about Chris Froome. Be honest, you hold them dear.

You know, for instance, that he once had to be towed over the top of a mountain in Italy. And not when driving his car. Enough said. And last week he was riding kiddies' bikes around Kenya and singing the 'Up With People' theme song as he went. Now he has the *maillot jaune*. What's that all about?

While we are talking, let's just point out that Froome's cadence is an abomination to all right-thinking people and will hasten the apocalypse. And his bilharzia (so we're told but you're not buying it) is his sooo convenient response to Lance's missing testicle.

His partner Michelle Cound takes no prisoners on Twitter. She wears the lycra shorts in that house. And anyway, Chris Froome rides for a team whose motorised transportation choices alone announce them as the axis of evil. Everybody knows that the team Chris Froome rides for has a golden syringe which they unsheathe every sunset, like Excalibur. The golden syringe is for Froome's use only. Not nice.

It's a movie script, this story they are selling. Tarzan does the Tour. You're not having any of it.

It may transpire in years to come that some of these things which you believe to be true are actually true. I don't think they will, but it would be derelict today for any journalist not to ask questions. Yet to close the mind off to the possibility that this is an interesting man, a man with a great story and an outlier in his sport – that would be to let Lance Armstrong win twice. That would be to let Lance's toxic cynicism enter your skin and your system like the waterborne parasite that you say Chris so conveniently suffers from. You once loved this sport and when Lance turned out to be a phoney it hurt. So now you feel safer believing in nothing than believing anything. So Lance wins again.

In the house of Team Sky they expect you to look around. They want you to believe. Well, so did Lance, you say. He wanted us to believe. Team Sky expect you to ask questions. Smart, intelligent questions. Well, actually, Lance didn't want that. Team Sky simmer with frustration that all the good things they do weigh as nothing on the scales of perception compared to the mistakes they make. Lance didn't own a set of scales. Not for that purpose anyway.

So here he is, Chris Froome on Stage Thirteen of the Tour de France today wearing the yellow jersey. He is 3 minutes and 25 seconds ahead of Alejandro Valverde in the General Classification as the riders mill about the start in Tours. Behind Valverde lie Bauke Mollema, Alberto Contador and Roman Kreuziger. All in pounce position.

Today's stage isn't billed as a game changer, but when we look back on it we can see that perhaps it has been. For the old Chris Froome this might have been the day to give it all away. When he hit Europe first he had a talent which he didn't know how to handle and a love of racing which wasn't matched by any deep understanding of how to race.

In the end Mark Cavendish will win today's stage, a 173km pull to Saint-Amand-Montrond, and it will be the twenty-fifth stage win of his career. The Manx sprinter will use the tactics of a cuckoo riding off in a break with Alberto Contador's Saxo-Tinkoff team before sprinting home. Cavendish, for all that his heart is forever beating luminously on his sleeve, has that street savvy, especially when there's a timing bridge at the end of the street.

Team Sky will have their own problems today. Down to seven riders now and one with a crack in his pelvis. Of the others, one is Froome and five are here to support Froome, but their willingness to do so isn't always matched by their ability or their energy. Still, the crisis has prompted Dave Brailsford to issue another of his business maxims. The fewer resources you have, he says, the more resourceful you get. Dave should work in the newspaper business.

What is left in the Team Sky gang might well be wrung out of them by the time they reach the end of the neutral zone in Tours today – 14.5km to be ridden before racing proper begins.

That's a long preamble. Time to think.

How did Chris Froome get here? Sift through his life story and calculate the odds on each passage leading to the next passage, ending up in Tours this morning wrapped in yellow. Impossible.

In the shorter term though, he started training to be in this place last winter when he was at home in Africa. Six-hour stints every day. He'd head out, sometimes to the Lowveld, and ride hard for six hours at altitude. Over those lush mountain passes and peaks he'd picture the road he would be taking this summer. And he would push on. It's the constant theme of the journey that has got him to this place this morning. Chris Froome keeps on, keeping on.

On those African rides he was tended to by Stefan Legavre, a masseur who has worked with the Springboks but who has a love of cycling and turned his hands easily to the art of the *soigneur*. Otherwise they were lone ventures, this matchstick man on his sleek Italian Pinarello, sailing past the odd worker toiling over the handlebars of the ubiquitous black mamba bikes of Africa.

Those sessions were typical of Froome and of Team Sky. When few in professional cycling are working, Team Sky are clocked in and the SRM details gathered on riders' every training run are being downloaded and whizzing down the wires to Tim Kerrison.

Froome jokes that his two brothers are both accountants and it was his fear of falling into that sort of life which sent him into pro cycling. In fact what he discovered is that there is something inside him which refuses to quit or die.

'I think a big part of it is a, it's almost a ruthless . . . determination, desire.'

Stubbornness?

'Stubborn. Yeah, I mean, I've found with my training, I've been very, very particular with my training, and I know it's something that all my coaches sort of remind me of is that, when I set a workout or I set a ride I'll, say, ninety-nine per cent of the time, do exactly what's been set out. It would be very rare that I get halfway through an effort and I say, "Ah I don't feel like doing it any more," or anything. Even if I felt rubbish I'd turn myself inside out to do whatever I'd set out to do.'

So he goes out every day during that time of the year that many in the peloton consider to be holiday time and he leaves the soul of himself on the dark roads of South Africa. He never lets up on himself. And the day he chooses for a quieter, shorter training he makes sure to eat less that day.

Froome spent a lot of time in the career neutral zone. Or so it seems at a cursory glance. We have never seen anybody arrive in the peloton with quite his back story so we aren't too sure what to measure it against. Perhaps he should have been an accountant like his brothers. The guy who turns out to be rather entertaining when you get talking to him at the office party, but who says nothing for the rest of the year. Just another guy who keeps his dreams locked in a dusty box in the corner of his head.

There is an early escape today, once racing starts. There always is on these types of stage. Five or six guys making off like desperados. Or so they imagine. From outside the race they look like plankton getting on with their day before the whale is roused. Still, one of the breakaways is Luis Angel Maté. A different kind of dreamer. It is fair to say that Maté has never seen a break he didn't like the look of. So he tucks in his hair braid and rides off with such optimism every day, like one of those persistent escapees in World War II films who always end up back in the cooler but still dreaming. You would have to like him. And why shouldn't Maté dream big? He's twenty-nine and never going to win the Tour but one day the peloton won't quite catch the break and he'll get a stage win.

Maté has five companions today. I wonder what exactly they talk about as they ride – great breakaways that nearly paid off, maybe this will be the day when the big bosses say, 'Let those guys have it,' or are their hearts heavy with fatalism? Maybe one breakaway in twenty will pay out big. *Directeurs sportifs* of smaller teams say if you're not in then you can't win. Pragmatists say if you're not in, you can't lose. The dreamers go with each escape. And when they look at the man in yellow today, why not?

Still, whatever they talk about they must suspect that this is another day for the sprinters. Yesterday, Mark Cavendish had urine thrown at him by a spectator. His old friend Chris Froome tweeted that such behaviour left a bad taste in the mouth. Especially Mark's mouth. Cavendish has just a single stage win to his name so far on this Tour, which has seen him involved in far more drama than he would have planned for. Marcel Kittel is the new sprinter on the block; even Cavendish has called him 'the next big thing'.

But not so fast. Cav may not be at his best in this Tour, but he will get himself right and reclaim everything. He's Mark Cavendish, serial winner, and not ready to leave the stage.

Wow. The peloton itself is riding with a Cavendish-like attitude today. The breakaway group gets caught with over 90km to ride and the serious pace is a rebuke for their temerity. The main tyrants when it comes to punishing through pace today are Cav's Omega Pharma-Quick Step who are really whipping things along, hoping their man will deliver at Saint-Amand-Montrond. At this speed everybody is happy to follow the wheel in front.

*

Froome's stubbornness and the sense of self-sufficiency he carries make him different. He recalls that from the time he was a young kid his upbringing was unique. 'I was allowed to make my own decisions, I wasn't sort of kept in a house and told, "Okay, these are the rules, don't go outside, don't speak to strangers," or anything like that. That sort of typical English upbringing, or a European upbringing would entail.

'Even when I'd, sort of, leave home in the afternoons after school, on a bike, and then be back at night, that would have been when I was quite young. I think under ten, sort of eight, nine, ten.'

Off to the townships or the Ngong Hills following David Kinjah and his dreadlocks. It was a perfect education in the old sense of the word. He absorbed a whole world. And as regards his apprenticeship as a cyclist he grew up deficient in technique but pushing himself after older riders at an altitude of 1800m or so.

When he finished with boarding school in Johannesburg he went to university and, though he churned out good results, he regrets having spent yet more time dawdling in the neutral zone.

'Yeah. I mean I was trying to get the degree behind me before going off and doing anything, but, I just got offered the opportunity I think a little bit earlier and I thought, "Right, I'm going to go for it now and see where I get to, and if it does fail then I'll come back to the studies." But, it certainly would have made my life a lot easier if I'd switched, just focused on the cycling straight after finishing school, instead of going on and doing another year.'

So people say he can't be as good and as clean as he seems

because his progress wasn't signposted a long way back along the road. It wasn't. Not even to himself. When he and a pal started an Under-23 team in Johannesburg, not even a decade ago, he is remembered for his lank hair and bangles, his clothes, often *kikoys*, made of hemp and dyed in the colours of the Swahili race and his white Golf car with tinted silver windows. Everybody saw him coming. And nobody saw him coming.

The one thing he had then and which people commented on from the time he arrived in pro cycling with Barloworld, was his attitude. Chris Froome was a 'training fundamentalist'.

His early years in Europe read like amusing misadventures, a comic strip of crashes and illnesses and training rides where he would get thoroughly lost. But those experiences were punctuated with races. He learned from every one and when a team came along that believed there was more to be had from a £900,000 rider with a coach than a £1 million rider without one, Froome was in the right place at the right time.

Timing. The ultimate good luck when it comes to beating the odds.

Interestingly, but not to Team Sky, the Lotto-Belisol sprinter Marcel Kittel has allowed himself to get dropped off the peloton as they come through the feeding zone. At roughly the halfway mark, Kittel's group is over a minute behind. The peloton are hammering it today. It doesn't look good for a sprinter to be dropping out the back.

Now. Alejandro Valverde suffers a puncture. It costs him 37 seconds and what gets people talking immediately is the fact that Chris Froome doesn't slow the entire peloton down to allow Valverde to catch up those 37 seconds. The immediate reaction is less condemnation and more sympathy. Froome doesn't look like he could take off his cape and place it over a puddle at the moment. His chivalry levels aren't the ones depleted.

There's too much at stake here. Alberto Contador and his Saxo-Tinkoff teammates see an opportunity, so too the Belkin team of Bauke Mollema and Laurens ten Dam. Valverde is second overall and if he's not allowed to regain contact, there's more space on the podium for everyone else. So Saxo and Belkin aren't slowing.

Besides, given that Kittel is still in the chasing group, Cavendish's Omega Pharma team and Peter Sagan's Cannondale squad have good reason to keep the hammer down. Kittel's been winning and when a sprinter does that he ceases to be a rival. He becomes an enemy.

At first Valverde's Movistar teammates swarm around him clucking with concern and vowing to reclaim those 37 seconds. If they were that concerned, one of them should have switched bikes with Valverde the moment he noticed the puncture, but Movistar haven't been working like clockwork on this Tour. Subsequent glimpses show poor Valverde at the front of the Movistar group doing most of the grunt work for himself. It won't be a happy evening meal for these boys.

As the afternoon sun keeps rising, this stage gets more interesting. Valverde is riding with the desperation of a man knowing his Tour is on the line. Kittel's foot soldiers try for a time to help but in this cat-and-mouse game, momentum is everything. And it is with the leaders.

They smell blood and the chance to kill Valverde off. The sprinters' teams are also pleased to have Kittel back there, out of their sight. Encouraged, this coalition of General Classification and sprint teams increases the pace. The gap stretches.

We should freeze the frame here for a second. For all the talk of how Team Sky have made the Tour a procession and how boring they have become, we have a stage here today, a flat stage with just one bump in the road and the plot is almost Shakespearian. The race is all strung out. Knives are being flashed at Valverde by the GC boys and at Kittel by the sprint set. Froome is gritting his teeth and settling in for another hard shift. If it all goes wrong he could be handing over the jersey. It's that unstable right now.

A few minutes later, Kittel and his team accept that in a race that will run for another nine days, there are no prizes for flogging a dead horse. They accept today will not be their day. Valverde keeps pushing, in second overall he's got to. This turns into one of the most thrilling days on the Tour and the Spaniard shouldn't feel too depressed, he's just had a puncture on the wrong day.

Some of the guys at the front, who would have been counting their blessings to be on the right side of the split, are now counting the cost. The lead group is coming apart like an ageing boy band right now. Richie Porte is struggling again. Richie was told he could give his all in the time trial two days before. Is he getting the bill for that today?

Bilharzia. It sounds as unattractive as it is. You meet up with your little parasitic friend in the waters of Africa and from then on as it develops into a flatworm it chomps your red blood cells, promotes rashes, lethargy, headaches, fever and lots of other nice surprises. For an endurance athlete the impact is crippling. Having something consuming your red blood cells and depriving you of oxygen is a nightmare. Your bilharzia eats the body, steals the breath and gnaws the confidence.

For Chris Froome it was something to be ridden through. His time in the neutral zone was extended considerably by the fact that he paid no attention to the debilitating bouts of sickness.

When people are being cynical about Team Sky, one of the things they are most cynical about is bilharzia. Which is odd. It is a rampant disease in Africa and the fact of Froome's condition is easily ratified if anybody ever cared to ask. After malaria, bilharzia is the world's second most common parasitic disease. He has been straight up about it since diagnosis. Late in 2010 in Kenya, while seeing his brother Jeremy, the UCI performed a routine blood check on him for his biological passport. Given the patchworked history of his health he asked the doctor to scan his blood for anything irregular (doping mastermind?) and the doctor told him that his insides were crawling with bilharzia.

For those interested, the treatment for bilharzia isn't a dose of EPO or anything else which might provide an excuse for elevated numbers of red blood cells. The treatment is a drug called praziquantel (or more ominously, biltricide) and it just lays waste your flatworm population.

The idea is that having paralysed or killed most of the flatworms, your immune system will do the rest. If you are consistently underweight and riding yourself to the brink of exhaustion, your immune system may not get around to finishing the job.

Froome had his first dose in January 2011. The side effects are brutal. The drug doesn't question and ID everything it finds. It just wipes stuff out. For a week to ten days the patient is wiped out as well. By spring of 2011, Froome was showing signs that the treatment was working and he raced well through March and April. In May, though, at the Tour of California the bilharzia was back in business.

Froome battled on until the Tour de Suisse where his legs turned rubbery on the hills. When the Tour was finished he took another dose of biltricide and with his preparations already behind he said goodbye to the Tour de France for that year.

Meanwhile, 2011 was the year he began working with Bobby Julich, the retired American rider who had set up home in Nice. Froome had moved from Italy to Monaco and was getting specialist coaching every day. The components of a great racer were already there for anyone to see. The right-sized block of good-quality stone.

Julich just needed to keep chipping away. Life skills. Bike skills. Race skills.

According to Team Sky's daily plan for Stage Thirteen to Saint-Amand-Montrond, Rod Ellingworth and Carsten Jeppesen must travel ahead of the race and, among other things, they will check which way the wind is blowing and how it will affect the race. Like scouts in old Westerns, they go ahead of the cavalry and send back messages.

Jeppesen drives while Ellingworth writes notes in his race bible on the page that shows the day's itinerary. At the top of the page, he writes '56km, out of town, straight and open roads, full crosswinds'. Often Ellingworth asks Jeppesen to stop the car so he can get out and feel the wind on his face and better understand how it will be for the riders.

From 50km to the finish, his pencil works a double shift. At the town of Segry, he notes, 'real open after town and heavy surface'. On the right margin little arrows point towards the last 30km: 'small roads and crosswinds,' 'open road and headwind'. Ellingworth then texts his notes to the two *directeurs sportifs*, Nico Portal and Servais Knaven, in the race cars and the information is passed on to the riders.

Riders need to know what's coming up, but knowing is not a guarantee they will act upon it. And there are a few teams sensing possibility for carnage now.

The first beneficiary of the chaos is a big fish. Alberto Contador, who up until now, with about 30km left, has been content to hang in with the lead group and let his teammates contribute to the workload. They have been buffeted for much of the day but they've a plan that will show the truth in an old maxim: it's an ill-wind that blows no good.

Suddenly, Contador and his five teammates are gone as if they have heard a signal outside of everyone else's audible range. The move is initiated and led by Mick Rogers. Later, there will be rueful smiles in Team Sky land. A year ago Rogers was doing this sort of thing for them.

Others in the lead group sense what is happening as the Saxo riders gather at the front. Mark Cavendish, finding himself alongside Geraint Thomas, whispers a warning that something's going to happen. Be ready. Thomas isn't in the best position, trapped a little on the right-hand side.

Then the Saxos have gone, created a gap, and because there are six of them, they team time trial at the front, open a gap and create a no-man's-land between their break-away and the pursuit. The ten seconds after the attack are vital. Cavendish is lucky. 'I nearly missed the final split. Kwiatkowski [teammate Michał] got me halfway across and then I shouted to him to move left. I sprinted and just managed to get in the echelon. When echelons form it's similar to falling through ice . . . you've got five seconds to save yourself or it's all over.'

They latch on like two drifters catching a departing train.

All eyes switch to Froome. The membership lists are closing for this break right now. Mollema is safely there, so too his teammate ten Dam. In fact, every rider who will be in the top seven this evening is there. Except Froome. Fifteen are gone and not coming back.

In their team cars and on the bus, Team Sky's back-up men are surprised. Why isn't he there? What was he thinking? 'I looked at Cav's back wheel and thought, "I'm going to get there," but Cav took a hand sling from one of his teammates and then sprinted to get on. Minute I saw that, I thought, "No way am I going to be able to do that on my own."'

Froome's brothers Jeremy and Jonathan are accountants and Chris, the youngest, received the same calculating gene. If he surges after Cavendish he enters the open space between breakaways and those behind and he will end up fighting the wind on his own.

He's strong, he's determined, even bloody-minded, but he's not a sprinter like Cavendish and he's not stupid. Refusing to plunge into that no-man's-land is probably the single smartest thing he has done on the Tour. Instead he looks around to check on what support he's got.

Richie Porte is gone. Pete Kennaugh has just slipped off the back like a drowning man disappearing beneath the surface. Kosta Siutsou is visibly fading. David López drove himself hard early on as per instructions and his race is already ridden. Geraint Thomas is residing in his private house of pelvic pain for this Tour, yet it will be himself and Ian Stannard who are in position to help. Thomas will be the last to fall away.

The lead stretches. Soon it is clear that Sky's reduced and bedraggled team are riding not to catch the leaders but to limit the damage they will suffer. With 5km to go they are one minute behind but Froome is on his own, leading the chase, refusing to panic. He now shows the rider he has become. When everyone misses the bus, what matters is how you react after it's departed.

Froome keeps pedalling. But he's not desperate and he doesn't waste energy wondering why the team hasn't been better today. Most of all he lives to fight another day. Ventoux is ahead, looming ominously in the schedule. If he can get to Ventoux with as much energy as possible, then he can be the pied piper and others will dance to his tune.

And the accountant in him knows that on flat stages like this one, a minute only seems like a long time. In the mountains, a minute is what you lose riding from one hairpin to the next. When we speak a few days later he won't deny the loss he and the team have suffered but neither will he see it for more than it's worth.

'The way Contador and his team rode shows you can't let your guard down. Before yesterday I thought Valverde was my biggest rival but he was knocked out of contention, and Contador is now the most dangerous. In the mountains and the time trial, I will be okay. When there's crosswinds and any team lining up near the front, I've got to be on their wheels. End of story.'

Notably he didn't say, 'We've got to be on their wheels.' The more I see of Froome, the more I warm to him.

Into Saint-Amand-Montrond Mark Cavendish takes his win. His twenty-fifth in an outstanding career. He points his fingers at the skies. One day they toss urine at you, the next day it is laurels. Chris Froome rolls over the line 1'09" behind. His advantage in the General Classification has had a big lump taken from it but he lives. The yellow jersey is still his. He even allows himself just a razor thin smile when receiving it. He is just 2'28" ahead of Mollema in the GC. Contador is third at 2'45". Valverde has vanished.

This evening I travel from the finish with Ellingworth and Kerrison. They're talking about how they've seen the day.

Ellingworth says it's been a hard day for everyone in the team.

'I worry a little bit about G and Ian and Pete because they fucking nailed themselves out there.'

TK: 'Day like today, you miss Kiry [Vasil Kiryienka]. And a good Kosta [Kanstantsin Siutsou] . . . I don't know that we can be so confident about what's to come but we will know if we have a good Chris. It's so hard because when you look at him, he always looks so fucked after the stage.'

RE: 'I think the Ventoux is perfect for Chris. I don't think he wanted to empty the tank today.'

TK: 'We have said that for the second time trial he can bury himself, but he needs to be a bit careful, given the next three stages are hard, and how he felt after the last time trial. But I think he needs to be a bit careful on the next time trial, certainly not lose time, try to take time. The difference between ninety-nine per cent and one hundred per cent is small in relation to time but can be a lot in fatigue.'

RE: 'The Annecy stage is going to be so hard, you could have a three-and-a-half-minute lead on that stage and still lose.'

TK: 'But that's Stage Twenty [of twenty-one].'

RE: 'What I mean is he's going to have to be calculating.'

TK: 'We have the best climber and the best time trialler in the race, with a time trial and three mountain top finishes to come. It's not over yet.'

I sit silently, letting two of the best brains in the business air their thoughts, hopes and nerves without interruption. As I look out upon Auvergne's hills and pastures, post-stage analysis as my soundtrack, I am acutely aware of the access I am enjoying. Other journalists will now return to their hotels for another round of dinner, sleep and breakfast with only their speculations to cling on to between stages and press events. Instead, I live among the riders, coaches, managers, mechanics and carers that keep this team in the yellow jersey, following the Tour from inside Team Sky.

Julich solved the mystery of Chris Froome like a veteran detective working a complex case. Brailsford's old adage about a £900,000 rider with a coach would be proved true. Froome says that one of the greatest misapprehensions people have about him is that he is naturally skinny, that he could live on a diet of Big Mac meals and not gain a pound. The truth is that he is obsessive about food, snacks on nothing more fattening than bean sprouts, and has to work at his conditioning.

His tutelage under Julich coincided with the growing influence of Tim Kerrison's ideas. Bradley Wiggins, somewhat envious himself of Froome's build, has noted that when he got serious about road racing his weight fell away. He was between 81-82kg at the Beijing Games in 2008 but weighed 73kg the following summer in France. For Froome it was a similar story as he adopted the regime of no breakfast rides. In the spring of 2011 he weighed 73kg. In September he weighed 68kg. Consider that the UCI imposes a minimum weight limit of 6.8kg for bikes used in the Tour. Froome shed almost the weight of a bike from his 6 foot 1 inch body.

Finally he was ready for the road.

The bilharzia persists. Eggs can get trapped in the liver, the lungs, even the brain, and the difficulty with treatment is that they can't eradicate eggs trapped within tissues and organs during lengthy infection. Sometimes in rare cases the long-term avoidance of organ damage requires chemotherapy, a detail which has occasionally been seized upon to bolster the accusation that Froome has hugely exaggerated the problems associated with bilharzia. He hasn't. Froome has never had anything but conventional treatment and has never claimed to have suffered anything from treatments beyond the usual week of feeling bad. He had a third dose after the Critérium

International in 2012 and in early 2013 tests showed that the condition persisted. He has no Therapeutic Use Exemptions (TUEs) for any drugs concerning bilharzia or anything else.

Head doctor Alan Farrell consults regularly with the doctors in South Africa who deal with Froome's condition, and the team has no problem with the treatment taking place so far away from Europe because of the greater understanding of bilharzia in Africa. My feeling with this condition is that it's a case of move along folks, there's nothing to see here.

So. Imagine if Team Sky signed Chris Froome for his immense potential, if backroom members of Team Sky saw that potential even before there was a Team Sky. They didn't hire him because he rode like a comical marionette. They didn't hire him for the fun of inventing a whole whacky back story for you to swallow.

In fact, they pay him a huge amount of money so that they can enjoy his potential as it is realised. And they have spent many, many hours polishing the roughness off him, putting him together after crashes or naïve tactical errors, telling him not to ride when sick, poring over books to learn what exactly bilharzia is. Many, many hours.

If you were going to make up a story with which to fool the world, Chris Froome's would have been too much trouble and demanded too much colour. You already have within the ranks Bradley Wiggins, with his long history on track and on road, his rough charm and huge likeability, his marketable face furniture and his salty tongue. He is story enough. And you had a team around Bradley in 2012 who could escort him to a Tour de France victory while reading magazines and making small talk as they rode.

Why would you want a Froome, a bean-sprout oddball with an English passport and an African heart? Why split your team into the Wiggos and the Froomeys, cycling's Mods and Rockers? Why have two top dogs? Why, when you answered all the questions in 2012 about Wiggins, would you step up and beg the world's indulgence because you have an even better yarn to spin this year?

In the house of Team Sky I have looked around. I have asked the questions. Done the journalism I came to do. Nobody has given me a secret handshake or password signifying membership of the Masonic Lodge of Supreme Wizard Murdoch. Nobody has slammed doors in my face. And I have concluded that Chris Froome exists within Team Sky because he is an almost unstoppable force, one of those freak talents which, against all the odds, somehow bubbles to the top.

A white, shy middle-class kid in a gentle suburb of Nairobi gets left to play with the black kids in the township? It's almost too cinematic. He gets whipped away to South Africa for his schooling but goes back to Kenya every summer and every holiday. Back to Kenya and his bike and his friends. He learns Swahili. He gets chased by a hippo. He collects snakes and scorpions.

Bradley Wiggins used to say that winning the Tour de France doesn't happen to kids from Kilburn. Getting to hear of the Tour de France doesn't happen to kids in the township. But Froome is irrepressible. He turns up in Europe at a UCI meeting as the manager, administrator and sole competitor of the Kenyan team. He hustles. He crashes. He does stupid things. He loses one race by 1'25", having lost 1'20" of that time crashing.

Anytime he is in the last chance saloon he gives an exhibition of his derring-do. The main thing they had to teach him was to ride with a little less swash to his buckle.

He made it because nothing was going to stop him making it. He came late, very late; he saw, he learned, he conquered. He brought bilharzia with him and it almost sent him home again. His condition and the way people respond to it are almost emblematic of his whole story.

And here he is on the podium, still in yellow at the end of Stage Thirteen. Today he has looked human, and in doing so we have seen the determination and the intelligence which have underscored his flashier performances. It's no great stretch to imagine that those qualities have informed his long journey from the township to here.

This evening our home is Hotel du Pont Neuf at the village of Le Veurdre in the Auvergne. At the last count 544 people lived in this village and there is no indication that much has changed since. There are approximately sixty tourists tonight, thirty from Sky and thirty from Saxo. If there was one evening on the Tour that Sky doesn't want Saxos for company, this is it.

In the restaurant at the Pont Neuf, Froome and Richie Porte are shooting the breeze with Geraint Thomas who is complaining about the lack of support from other riders when the Saxos went. 'I went to Dan Martin [Garmin] and said, "You know it's your Tour as well," but he didn't want to work. None of them did.'

Only 68 seconds were lost but the cleverness of Saxo's manoeuvre and Sky's failure to cover it sent ripples of excitement skipping across the surface of the race. 'I was there when it went,' Thomas is saying, 'but I was caught in a bad position, blocked in.'

Froome listens and nods his agreement, his calmness as unwavering as the Tour is unrelenting. While he listens to Thomas, the last of the Saxo riders walk past. They are taking their meals in an extension to the restaurant, separated by a thin partition.

Beyond the divide, the Saxo boys are in fine fettle. Staff at one end of the table, riders at the other end. In this little partitioned extension to the restaurant, Sky's staff take their evening meal, seeing all but pretending not to notice. Service is slow, partially because so many of the Saxo group must be served first. Among Sky's staffers, the mood is subdued. Each speaks to the man alongside, quiet conversations that are normal when it's been a tough day at the office. Then Saxo's riders raise and touch their glasses, Alberto Contador says something and they all drink.

A toast to their success earlier in the day.

The mood among Sky's carers and mechanics isn't brightened by this.

And the ultra-slow service isn't helping. Eventually, food begins to arrive but not yet to the ravenous Sky carer Christian Alonso.

Then there is the crash of plates on the wooden floor, a bang so loud it almost makes you jump. Alonso stays sitting, and just says in an unheard message to the waiter, 'If that's my steak, I kill you.'

Next morning I walk with Froome to the team bus as we're ready to leave the Pont Neuf.

'Yesterday was tough?' I say.

'I'm feeling much better this morning, a very good night's sleep does that. Slept really well last night.'

'Is the calmness more apparent than real?'

'I think there have been times when I have been panicking a little inside but I'm fully aware that this is a three-week race and I don't think there's any one moment that you can throw away the whole race. Yesterday we were put under pressure by Saxo. I just missed it, but didn't want to spend too much energy riding in no-man's-land. Better to sit up and wait for teammates to regroup and then start to chase. Knowing I had a buffer of almost four minutes was a factor in my decision. Definitely.'

These mature and considered race calculations place him closer to his brothers' professions than he might like to accept. Perhaps he did choose the life of accountancy after all. But his dreams are on these roads, working in the outdoors, feeling the wind on his face.

He would be the first to admit that in the narrative of this Tour de France, Alberto Contador and his Saxo teammates delivered some good lines on the road to Saint-Amand-Montrond. But the accountant in him would curtly remind them that there is only one line that matters. The bottom one.

CHAPTER TWELVE

'I had a farm in Africa, at the foot of the Ngong Hills. The Equator runs across these highlands, a hundred miles to the north, and the farm lay at an altitude of over six thousand feet. In the day-time you felt that you had got high up, near to the sun, but the early mornings and evenings were limpid and restful, and the nights were cold.'

Karen Blixen, *Out of Africa*

Once I asked Chris Froome what he would do if the world was ending and he could have one last bike ride before the curtain came down.

He didn't have to pause. He'd take his bike to the Ngong Hills, the range of four knuckles which wrap around one part of the Great Rift Valley. It was between these lush summits, in this world teeming with buffalo, rhino, hogs, snakes, wildebeest and other creatures missing from the peloton, that he fell in love.

His love was the bike, the place. A skinny, diffident white boy tagging along after a gang of local kids as they hauled ass from Mai-a-Ihii, a Kikuyu township, to the highest Ngong

197

peak Lamwia, 2460m above sea level. This was but one part of an adolescence that was half *Huckleberry Finn* and half *Tom Brown's Schooldays* but played out under the canopy of African skies.

He was the only white kid, the *mzungu*, in a bunch led by a former pro David Kinjah. Kenyans like to run. These kids liked to cycle. Kinjah led them like a pied piper. Froome chased him down every time once he grew into his strength. They took a thousand tumbles on the narrow pathways, gasped for air on a hundred summits.

The heart never leaves home. Chris Froome carries a British passport and tells people that he grew up in a British home in the heart of Africa. Yes, it's true, he turned the blade of his knife inwards and paired it with his fork after eating, and asked to be excused before leaving the table. The licence under which he now races bears the stamp of the United Kingdom and when he races in the Olympics, it is for Team GB.

But does this make a man British?

I asked him too if on his travels between countries and continents there ever comes a moment when he thinks, 'Yes, I'm home now.'

Again, he didn't need time to consider.

'That comes when I land at Nairobi Airport and I hand my passport to the official as I'm going through. He looks at it and grins, I grin too. He hands me the passport, I walk on and that's when I think, "I'm home now."'

Africa is in his soul. His heart never left the place.

Bastille Day!

One rule of Tour de France coverage is that Bastille Day

clichés aren't on the banned list. The day is so fragranced with wafts of epic heroism and Gallic liberation, so full of native pomp and splendour, that it sometimes seems that the Tour de France was designed around it. We are licensed in perpetuity to reach into the sack of history and find whatever we can to make 14 July on the Tour more than a national holiday.

Today, though, brings a special gift. The peloton tackles Mont Ventoux, the immense and ghostly mountain of Provence where Tom Simpson died and from which legends have been born. So many that it is hard to believe that Ventoux is in fact an infrequently visited icon of the Tour. Yet the place is instantly recognisable. The Tour's other showpiece summits hunker with their neighbours on mountain ranges and conceal their weaponry until you try to conquer them. Ventoux just sits there on the rolling plains of Provence, staring down on the Rhone Valley. A brooding, half-dressed sentinel.

Its nickname, Mont Baldy, diminishes its dignity but the top of the mountain is nude limestone without stubble of vegetation or trees. Even in the summer sun the bare limestone gives the impression from a distance that the summit is snow-capped. It is eerie and impressive, and as you gaze up from the plains you recall a second fact from 1967 and Ventoux. In February of that year, months before Simpson keeled over with heat exhaustion and a pocket full of amphetamines, a wind gust of 198 miles per hour was recorded atop Ventoux – 198 miles per hour!

The Tour, when it snakes through its native turf, has no corporate boxes or premium levels. It is raucously democratic. Those who want a close-up of the superstars along the *parcours* will drive, ride or walk up Ventoux till the road is lined either side by what look like refugee camps for the middle classes. Cars, camper vans and picnic tables. Flags and banners. Men strutting in ridiculous mankinis. Women tanning. It is a ramshackle guard of honour composed by hundreds of thousands, some of whom will spend days waiting to see which rider can spend the least time on the mountain.

It is Sunday and Ventoux looms at the end of a mixed week for Team Sky. After the heroics of Froome on Ax 3 Domaines, it became increasingly clear that the team weren't working with the ominous efficiency of 2012. Stage Nine was a disaster and just two days ago Froome had lost a minute to Mollema and Contador on the stage from Tours to Saint-Amand-Montrond. The boys in black were dispersed through the field being buffeted and disheartened by crosswinds which didn't seem to take the same toll out of their rivals from Saxo and Belkin.

Today the pack will want to isolate Froome again, make him think that he can't keep doing this on his own. Pick off his lieutenants and see if their general has a breaking point.

Gary Blem's shoulder-length hair distinguishes him straight off from the clipped military neatness of his Team Sky colleagues. So too does the South African accent. Team Sky's lead mechanic is part of what seems, from a distance, to be the new Africa. He travels to Europe to work while his wife, a Scot, and children stay behind in Pretoria.

He doesn't have either the guilt or the arrogance of the old colonialists but gives off an intense pride about the continent. He came to the team because in 2011 Mark Cavendish told Dave Brailsford there was only one man he wanted messing with his bikes, and that man was Blem. A year later, the sprinter moved on to Omega Pharma-Quick step, Blem was supposed to follow but it couldn't get tied down in time and, though he loves Cavendish, Blem was happy to stay on at Sky. Now the kinship he feels is with Chris Froome.

'Froomey, to me, he is Kenyan, a hundred per cent Kenyan, and I would love to tell everybody. I've discussed this with him. You know I've said to him, "Listen, well done, this is great for African cycling."'

When Froome rode his first Tour in 2008 he did so with a little Kenyan flag stitched into his *dossard*. Last year when Bradley Wiggins conquered France he had a small mod symbol stuck to his bike. Blem wanted something which would personalise his friend's bike and maybe even inspire him a little.

'I wanted to let him know that there is actually a whole continent that is supporting him, you know; apart from the UK and the British ties to the team, he's got a whole continent that's actually supporting him out there. And that's why I had a few little inspirational stickers made, I know it's small but it's, it's just something that if he looks down and he's suffering he can remember, maybe his mother even, in a sense. Or his roots. It's just small things, you know, you never know if it will do anything for him or not but . . .'

He settled for symbols rather than words. The centre of the Kenyan flag bears a Masai shield with spears. Giving more thought to the gesture than the average mechanic would give to a Christmas present for a spouse, Blem had a sticker made first of the shield and spears in the colours which appear on the Kenyan flag. He then had a shield and spears made predominantly in the colour yellow for when Chris Froome's jersey colour inevitably changed during the Tour. He also had a little sticker made up in the colours of the Kenyan flag, but in the shape of the nation itself.

Froome was moved but wondered about such an expression of individuality within a team which discourages it.

'Don't you think I might get into shit for this, you know?'

Gary Blem told his friend that if he had any doubts the bike would be stripped of its new decoration instantly.

Froome shook his head.

'Ah no, screw it, leave it, I'll keep it on my bike.'

So today Chris Froome – reared in Kenya, educated in South Africa, resident in Monaco, and passport holder of Britain – rides up Mont Ventoux with a Masai shield and spears on his bike, reminding him of where the story began. He is the boy from the Ngong Hills. The pale *mzungu* on the bike too small for his spidery legs.

It is a still, oven-hot Provençal day. The peloton has learned the hard way that Team Sky like to ride at high tempo and drop challengers off the back with accelerated bursts. There is only one response. To do the same. Or die trying. To string the black jerseys out, isolating them, letting each Sky rider do his own hard toting to nobody's benefit but his own.

So they leave Givors at a furious pace, about fifteen minutes before eleven in the morning. There are breaks from the start. Philippe Gilbert [BMC] and Lieuwe Westra [VCD] are hauled back after a few kilometres. Three more race ahead without saying goodbye at 16km. Nothing doing. Katusha, the Russian team, are bullying the peloton along at top speed and the breakaways flare briefly before dying.

An escape committee of ten gets away; a disparate group of individuals, a talented *rouleur*, a few useful *équipiers*, but no one worries the big guns keen to keep their powder dry in the peloton. So the gap stays at just over a minute for a time; the elastic between the escapees and the pack taut. Then it snaps and the lead is 7 minutes.

Dave Brailsford travels on this 242km stage on the team bus, as does the doctor Alan Farrell and the physiotherapist Dan Guillemette. They watch the race on the decent-sized television at the front which will be replaced by the big screen pulled from the ceiling once the bus has stopped.

The first hour of the race has been ridden at an average speed of 48.2kmh, the second at an even more punishing 50.4kmh. For a day which is going to take almost six hours and finish with the ascent of Ventoux, this is too fast. So when the ten breakaways begin to increase their advantage, Brailsford kicks back.

'We can relax a little bit now, let those guys build up a lead before reeling them in as we get closer to the beginning of the climb. What we didn't want was for this attacking and counter-attacking to continue, and then some dangerous people getting in breaks.'

But on Bastille Day, order can't be maintained for long. For this is *le quatorze Juillet*, the day the French must show themselves. No one expects a home winner of the Centenary Tour de France but, perhaps today, there can be a local hero. Five of the twenty-two teams in the race are French but only three are represented in the breakaway group. *Quel dommage* for Europcar and Cofidis!

They have missed out and, of course, they then try to

salvage the wreck of their day. Europcar's best rider, Pierre Rolland, counter-attacks with the German Marcus Burghardt. They are in turn chased by Cofidis's Christophe Le Mével. Wearing the polka-dot jersey of mountains leader, Rolland chases for a long time, and gets to within 15 seconds of the breakaways.

Brailsford has a vested interest in the outcome of this race-within-a-race, and from his seat at the front of the team bus, he leans forward, animated. On days like this his chimp can feel he's back in the zoo at feeding time. 'Go on, Rolland, you're there, just one more bit.' But the final bit is the hardest. Rolland can't close and the gap begins to widen again.

'Shit,' says Brailsford. 'Rolland will sit up now, wait for his team and they will start chasing the break which is what we don't want. But this is fairly typical of Europcar, they miss their opportunity, they then try to get the break back and they piss off a lot of people. What we want is for the leaders to stay away, with our guys chipping away at the lead until it all comes together at the foot of Ventoux. Then let the strong guys sort themselves out.'

Rolland does sit up, the pack devours him and then Europcar's green jerseys are massed at the front, trying to save their honour. Brailsford thinks it's all a waste of time, which it is, but he lived in St Etienne for three years and learned to understand the mentality and the culture. So despite the protestations, he knows.

On Bastille Day, no Frenchman takes defeat lying down.

This is how to behave, Gary Blem believes. With respect and consideration. The way that Chris Froome behaves. Guy like that, with his politeness and his steel always wrapped in velvet? Men will walk the line for him.

Gary with his shoulder-length hair. When you see him first you wonder if perhaps he won't be the rebel digit in Dave Brailsford's complex equation for success, but his loyalty runs deep. There are things he likes and dislikes about the environment he is in, but the big picture never eludes him. Today he has watched young Pete Kennaugh put in a tough, tough shift and he admires him for it. Kennaugh is young and he still wants to tackle the world and wrestle it to the floor. Søren Kristiansen, the team chef, complains that Kennaugh has been short and disrespectful towards him, but Søren, a Dane, has never lived on the Isle of Man.

And Kennaugh has that thing, that edge his fellow Manxman, Mark Cavendish has, a belief that he is the best and the strongest. And by the way, everybody else is wrong.

Blem watches and tolerates. But there is a line he doesn't like to see crossed.

'There's a point you know, I leave them in the race because in the race they always stress, but, after the race if the rider's still got the same attitude, straight away I'll put them in their place. But in a nice way. I'll speak to them and say, "Look, what is your issue? If you have a problem with me, tell me straight and I can always organise someone else to look after you or whatever, but at the end of the day we need to work together." It's about respect.'

And that's how he gets through the long days. Team Sky isn't an outfit that does high fives. Certainly not without cleaning their hands with alcohol rub immediately afterwards. The idea is to keep the emotion in check. Let the computer run the race. The chimp inside you can celebrate in Paris.

So this Chris Froome. He's the guy who came with his girl-friend Michelle to Gary's barbecue back in Pretoria last November. The guy who played with Gary's baby daughter Hannah and who never spoke about cycling.

'An average human being. Nothing special. You know?'

As Ventoux looms, the affairs of the breakaways become less relevant. Their expiry date comes in the trees of the foothills, reeled in like a fish on the end of a line. This doesn't happen without a last nervous twitch from the dying French chal-lenge. Sylvain Chavanel counter-attacks from the fragmenting lead group, as if somehow he can stay ahead of the tidal wave surging towards him. Futile.

The serious business will go down in the group surrounding Froome and his yellow jersey. There he has Richie Porte and Pete Kennaugh for protection and another twenty-three riders eyeing his top like vultures. Among them: 2011 champion Cadel Evans; the two Saxo-Tinkoff riders Alberto Contador and his sidekick Roman Kreuziger; the two Movistars Alejandro Valverde and Nairo Quintana; the Belkins Bauke Mollema and Laurens ten Dam; and Garmin's Dan Martin.

The plan to isolate and exhaust Froome before Mont Ventoux has not been a success. It is time for Plan B. Ventoux's first 5km are cruelly gentle, because the 16km of climbing that follow are murderously steep. Much of the middle section, with its 8 to 10 per cent gradients, is lined with trees that offer protection from the sun. But then you leave the forest and come out onto the famous scree slopes, with the weather tower on top and the micro climate which makes this place different from most places on earth.

With more than 200km in their legs, even the modest early slopes claim good men. Rolland who had fought so valiantly for Europcar drops like a stone, as does the talented young American Tejay van Garderen, who should be doing better. Also feeling the hard tug of gravity is Andy Schleck, who enjoyed greater success on this climb four years ago when he and his brother Frank slugged it out with Contador on the penultimate stage of the race.

The first sign of a Plan B comes from the precocious young Colombian Quintana. It's an oddity of Tour coverage that any Colombian doing anything impressive on the mountain stages is beyond question, because like some sort of exotic species they are bred at altitude. Froome's life at altitude in Nairobi and the Ngong Hills will not buy him any such exemption from suspicion. Few even realise he was nurtured at altitude.

Anyway, with the smooth acceleration we will become accustomed to, Quintana breaks away with 10km to go. At this point Team Sky's tough young Manx Pete Kennaugh is just about to clock off his shift of hauling Froome through the early inclines.

Froome is a quiet and reserved man addicted to his pleases and thank yous, but through this terrain he needs tough cookies. Kennaugh is four years younger than Richie Porte, but climbs well and isn't afraid to get to the front of this elite group on one of the most brutal mountains and push on. Some of the guys complain he's too headstrong and too lippy, but they know he's worth the effort.

Porte, the Tasmanian (or 'the angry little man' of the Tour, as Froome occasionally refers to his friend in jest), takes over at this point. He ups the tempo. Riders fall off the back, but it is still the Sky way, chipping away at the breakaway's advantage without going into the red zone to do so.

Froome has such an air of formality about him sometimes that you almost expect him to stop the bike to shake Kennaugh's hand, thank him for his sterling work and wish him a safe journey to the top, but instead he and Porte maintain the same relentless tempo. So strong, that now every other member of their elite group has been burned off. It's the two of them bearing down on the Colombian.

There are moments in any Tour de France that are pivotal and this is one of them. Froome isn't making a swashbuckling solo pursuit of the Colombian. His comrade Porte is calmly leading him to his prey. 'Froomey, I will bring you to him, then you deal with him.'

Soon Quintana is in their sights, the picture of his back and behind growing bigger with each pedal stroke. They join up and take a little breather, giving Contador an opportunity to come from a little behind and make the leaders a group of four. Buoyed by this little victory, the Spaniard will think that maybe he can do something now, but Froome knows Quintana is the greater threat.

There is an arresting theatrical drama about Ventoux when the riders get to the top of the tree line and come out into the blinding light of the moonscape beyond. It is a mountain built to stage final acts.

This final act begins with Froome attacking and leaving everybody for dead except Quintana. Tactically it is a master class, and illustrates how much wisdom Team Sky have been able to plant in Froome's head these past few years. The younger, straight out of Africa, Froome would have chased down every break of the day before finding himself out of gas.

Or on another day from the early years he would have looked around him, taking in all the big names, and decided his only chance was to attack from far out, when they weren't paying much attention. They would think he was mad and do what bike riders have done since 1903: give him enough rope to hang himself. He would often get a good placing on the stage but would have emptied his tank to do so. The next day, he would sleep with the fishes.

But here on Ventoux, he is calculating, waiting for the right moment. And his understanding of the perfect strategic climb is no coincidence. Froome has climbed Ventoux before. Twice.

Back in May, Chris came to the mountain to film an episode of *The Ride*, organised by Eurosport and Oakley. One amateur, a Norwegian competition winner named Jonas, would climb with two pros: Sean Kelly, former Irish pro cyclist and 1982 Tour de France stage winner; and this year's hot favourite, the Kenyan man of the mountains.

Along the route Sean recalled his experiences on the inclines, where he attacked and where he struggled. The pace was steady despite Sean attacking from a little way out and a valiant attack in the final stages by the Norwegian amateur on the year's most hotly tipped pro. Still, Froome yearned for a harder ride, for a proper go at the climb he would have to repeat in the Tour just two months away.

So what did he do? What could you do after reaching the top of one France's toughest climbs?

'I went and rode it myself again afterwards, just on my own. At a faster pace.'

The fun ride was over. Now time for the serious stuff. This time, without nostalgic flashbacks rehearsed for the cameras and no one to worry about leaving behind, he could get a proper feel for the slopes. Although alone on two wheels, he had his professional, and personal, support following him on four, in the form of *directeur sportif* Nicolas Portal and girl-friend Michelle Cound. With his head down but his eyes open, he started plotting the perfect climb.

When Chris Froome hits Ventoux and closes down Quintana like a lion about to make lunch of an antelope, Gary Blem shifts his head into neutral. If he thinks about what is happening, his closeness to it all, he'll feel intimidated and awestruck.

He will make a point of not watching this on television later. Then his thoughts might wander to the size of the audience he is part of. He might begin to notice the fanatics who press forward, narrowing the path for Froome and Quintana to race up. The fact that this is a mad and crazy phenomenon for which, in his own little way, he is responsible might just dawn on him.

'So long as I don't see television, they're just another rider wearing cycling kit, and I treat them like a normal, an average human being, nothing special, you know?'

Froome and Quintana soar past a *stèle* at the side of the road. It is the monument to British rider Tom Simpson whose life, forty-six years and one day previously, was claimed by this mountain while riding on a cocktail of alcohol and amphetamines. It is a monument which marks a different time.

Does Blem ever wonder if the men he serves are part of the brotherhood of the needle? He has thought about it. No man who has been around cycling for years hasn't. No way, he thinks.

'As a rider you'd have to be an absolute fool to dope in this team. It's the wrong team for you if you want to dope. Chris did this last year as well. But what's nice is it's consistent now. It's not erratic, it's not like he's coming up to this thing going bam, and then disappearing. He's been really, really, really consistent.'

Nairo Quintana won't go away. Every time Froome tries to leave him behind, the Colombian finds another air pocket which gives him enough energy to live off. Froome has one tactic left and it's not a surprising one. He burned Contador off with 6.5km to go by injecting a short burst of acceleration into the climb. At the end of a long day, it is a deadly weapon.

He uses it on Quintana again and again, and is beginning to reconcile himself to not taking the stage win today when the youngster runs out of responses. For the last 1.5km the gap grows and Froome wins by 29 seconds. Afterwards people will say he should have let the Colombian win the stage for it was his attack that ignited the race. And after his victory in the Pyrenees, Froome didn't need it.

But the argument is not logical and owes something to the general tiredness with Team Sky's dominance. Froome didn't need the victory on Ventoux, though it is the greatest of his career so far, but he may need the extra time that his final acceleration has gained on all rivals. He was prepared to let Quintana have the stage, but unprepared to wait for him.

As Froome crosses the line, he throws his right arm into the air and allows his left hand to rest close to his heart. Had he been listening carefully he would have heard, in the midst of the cheering, the noise of people booing. Almost six hours have passed since leaving Givors; the attacking, the counter-attacking, the chess-like plays on the mountain that foretold the final surge, and when you arrive? The sound of disapproval.

Froome hears but is not listening. Some don't believe, others don't like Sky. Always suspicion hangs in the air and his aggressive style of racing causes the clouds to thicken. When he breaks clear of Quintana, he seems unnaturally strong but nothing he does on the mountain is much different from what he does in training.

Christophe Bassons, the clean French rider in the Festina team of the 1990s, used to say he never had any problem climbing with Richard Virenque on training rides. It was just in the races that Virenque was a different animal, transformed by the stuff he was taking. When Brailsford and Kerrison examine Froome's numbers after Ventoux, they will agree they were good but not as good as some of the training numbers.

Doping is not the sole cause of disaffection.

Consider this from a French point of view. Twenty-eight years have passed since Bernard Hinault's victory in the 1985 Tour. With the exception of Laurent Fignon in 1989, no French rider has worn a yellow jersey anywhere near the

Champs-Elysées since then. Along comes an Englishman in 2009, sets up a team that he enters in the 2010 Tour and three years later his team is about to win the race for a second time.

Two weeks of the Tour have passed. Froome is trying to roll with the punches. Nothing for it but to wait by the finish for his rivals to make their weary way to the summit of Ventoux before the end of day rituals of media bites, podium presentations and doping control.

In the scant moments of calm he gets a chance to think back to the race as he dreamed it two months ago, as he rode alone up the now conquered peak. How similar was the race stage, peloton and all, to May's battle plan?

'I'd sort of pictured it to be pretty similar to how it panned out. I had planned to hit the bottom with the whole team pulling at the front, so that we were in prime position. But then once we were on the climb, I'd envisaged that it would be easier then to back off a little bit, and let other teams take it up. Which is exactly what happened and I was left with Richie and Pete, who then, later on on the climb, came and started working. And setting a really hard pace, so, I'd sort of seen the bottom really steep part, I'd figured out that other teams were going to take that up anyway, and it didn't really matter if it was us or someone else pulling at that point, but I thought it was better to try and save the guys for a little bit later on.'

So far so good. But what about that ambitious solo attack from 8km out?

'Yeah. I had thought Richie would be there until the final sort of two or three Ks, but given that it was so hard up until

213

that halfway point and he was already in pieces I thought, okay, here. I can really gain big time if I go here and the guys are left chasing for the last eight K, could open up some big gaps.'

But all in all a successful recce?

'Yeah, it wasn't far off.'

Chris Froome is in the A-Team, and he loves it when a plan comes together.

He smiles broadly and thanks his confederates. It has been a long day but he has taken time on everyone, and has extended his overall lead to more than 4 minutes on Mollema and Contador.

Gary Blem knows there is a week of racing to go, and a tough one at that, but the likelihood now is that he will be back home in Pretoria next Tuesday in time for little Hannah's birthday, and that he will return home as part of the Tour de France winning team. The nice man who came to their house for the barbecue will be champion.

And tomorrow, Monday, is a rest day. He might look forward to that, but there is a record-breaking gust about to hit Ventoux. Accusations and insinuations flying at 198mph. The questions will come by reflex, thrown in the knowledge that anybody who loves cycling has a right to ask questions, but thrown without much constructive thought as to how to move the discussion or the inquiry forward.

Froome has hardly stepped off his bike, but the humming wires of the social media universe can be heard conveying the doubt and outrage of the armchair jury. The doubts which had been festering all season and through the first week of the

Kanstantsin Siutsou takes some refreshment during the Tour. Detailed planning even goes in to the composition of the drinks bottles on his back.

Head of operations Carsten Jeppesen would often work with Rod Ellingworth to provide advance information on the state of the roads and the wind conditions before the cyclists got there to ensure as little was left to chance as possible.

Chris Froome gives Geraint Thomas a helping hand during Stage Thirteen of the Tour.

Froome had learned much of his cycling from David Kinjah, growing up in the Ngong Hills in Kenya. But this was the day he really showed how he had become a master tactician.

Chris Froome tucks in behind Nairo Quintana on the desolate, windswept Mont Ventoux.

With the crowd urging them on, Froome would eventually secure the stage win by 29 seconds from Quintana.

Dave Brailsford, physio
Dan Guillemette and
team doctor Alan Farrell
pose next to the Tom
Simpson memorial on
Mont Ventoux.

Chris Froome toasts the
rest of Team Sky after his
success on Mont Ventoux.

After success come
yet more questions
about doping. Froome
and Dave Brailsford
try to find the answers
that will convince a
sceptical world.

The Team Sky bus, designed with the help of Formula 1 teams, which is set up to provide maximum comfort for the cyclists.

Alberto Contador's smile seems genuine enough, but he has just lost out to Chris Froome on the final time trial of the Tour.

The crowds for Stage Eighteen gave Chris Froome a mixed response, with some cheering him on, while others were more hostile.

His teammates made sure that Froome was well protected on his ride up Alpe d'Huez, and at the end of it all he had increased his grip on the race.

Chris Froome is accompanied by press officer Dario Cioni after the end of Stage Twenty, which ensured he would be riding into Paris the next day as the winner of the race.

Accompanied by his teammates, Froome celebrates as he crosses the finish line.

Jonathan Tiernan-Locke has his time-trialling position analysed during Team Sky's pre-season training camp in Mallorca, but the year would end with questions being asked about some anomalous readings in his biological passport data.

Lead carer Mario Pafundi is the oil on the wheel for Team Sky.

Tour about Team Sky and their collective strength vanished after the team's collapse in the Pyrenees. Now it's just the yellow jersey they worry about.

Nobody could do what we have just seen Chris Froome do and sleep soundly at night.

Why not? They just couldn't.

Coming down the mountain, the forest echoes with the sound of statistics being fired in anger. The Ngong Hills are very far away indeed.

CHAPTER THIRTEEN

'Facts are stubborn things, but statistics are more pliable.'

Mark Twain

A few nights before Ventoux I had a fascinating evening in the company of Dave Brailsford and Tim Kerrison. The men were discussing an email that Dave had received from Antoine Vayer, the French sports scientist who, with his co-author Frédéric Portoleau, has created a model that allows them to estimate the power output of riders on the climbs of the Tour de France.

They compare these power outputs to what they believe is possible without doping and then, depending upon the extent to which a rider exceeds this limit, he is deemed suspicious or even more. In *Le Monde* the previous day, Monday, Vayer wrote that Froome's performance on the 7.8km climb to Ax 3 Domaines was beyond the limit of what's possible clean. He had more or less accused Froome of having doped.

Because of his sports science background and his refusal to be involved in doping when working with the notorious Festina team in the 1990s, Vayer has credibility on the subject of doping. So much so that some see him as a Breton Caesar, sitting in the tribune and delivering a thumbs up or a thumbs down to what he sees. A coach and teacher in physical education, Vayer writes for *Le Monde* during the Tour and his take on the race is generally interesting and hard-hitting.

Just before the Tour he'd published a magazine, *Not Normal*, which examined the performances of twenty-one of the most successful modern riders – a range running approximately from Greg LeMond to Cadel Evans, with a large slice of Lance in between. Having examined the performances Vayer then ranked them in an index of suspicion.

He came up with three categories of performance, the names of which are redolent of the old-school codes which the peloton would put on surprising performances.

Suspicious – A ride showing a power output of 410 watts at threshold.

Miraculous – A ride with a power output above 430 watts.

Mutant – A ride with a power output above 450 watts.

(He standardises the performances of riders against an 'average' rider weight of 70kg to allow him to compare the performances of heavier and lighter riders in the same way.)

After Froome's climb on Ax 3 Domaines, Antoine pronounced a power output of 446 watts according to his calculations. (Scaled to a 70kg rider; the equivalent of 6.4 w/kg for Froome.)

Miraculous.

After Ventoux, the situation looked like Vayer standing in

a small room and berating Froome for being a cheat. Antoine says, though, that all he is doing is letting people decide for themselves.

So on the Tuesday of this week, Vayer emailed Brailsford and asked to meet him. A totally off-the-record, no-journal-ists-present meeting. He hoped Brailsford would be able to give him the information that could, perhaps, allow Vayer to believe in Froome.

Antoine Vayer and I go back to the 1999 Tour and a clan-destine meeting in the Gobelen bar of those journalists who weren't buying the romance of a cancer survivor winning the Tour de France clean. Back then he coached Christophe Bassons, cycling's Mr Clean, and condemned in unambigu-ous terms the culture of doping that was destroying the sport.

He was what cycling needed then: a breath of clean air.

Now, I'm not so sure. Froome's power at Ax 3 Domaines was deemed beyond suspicious but, in wanting to meet Brailsford and Kerrison, it seemed he was open to being per-suaded that the Team Sky leader was clean. It seemed to me there was a disconnect between the post Ax 3 Domaines con-clusion and the possibility of being persuaded that it wasn't miraculous at all.

Brailsford is inclined to meet him because he knows that Vayer's figures on power output in the Tour de France are the basis for others' calculations. Kerrison, too, because whatever his reservations, he recognises the attempt to factor in many of the variables makes Vayer's model better than most people's. These calculations are this year's craze.

Brailsford believes totally and passionately that Froome is clean. He wants to help Vayer to understand this. He asks

Kerrison if he would come along to the meeting with Vayer as he believes it would be helpful to have his sports scientist along – a man who understands completely the significance and the limitations of measuring power output.

Kerrison says he would like to go along because he disputes the idea of drawing a line and saying, 'Beyond this is not possible without doping' as a starting point. 'In ten years' time people would look at that line and laugh because things will have moved on so much,' he says. Both Brailsford and Kerrison have yet to see a model which would satisfy them as being acceptably accurate. This frustrates them.

Brailsford asks me if I know Antoine.

I say I do. Antoine and I are friends and I add that his anti-doping stance while working for Festina was seriously admirable. He and two of his sons, Titoine and Benjamin, have come and stayed at our home in England.

'Is his mind made up about this?'

'Hmmm,' I say, 'that's something you will have to discover for yourself.'

All in good time.

It is the morning after Froome has won the stage up Ventoux and the air hangs thick with accusation as Brailsford sits down to Froome's right at the head of the press conference. Froome has a *bidon* of Gatorade which he sips from occasionally. Brailsford looks slightly bemused.

Not all the questions concern doping. It just seems like that. A lot of the questions are framed with that nervy intro journalists use when asking a question but not wanting to get offside. 'What do you say to those who ask you . . .?'

Brailsford and Froome are patient and strong on the issues. Froome asserts yet again that he is not cheating. There isn't much more he can say. 'I can only be open and say to people, I know within myself that I've trained extremely hard to get here. All the results I get I know are my own results . . . Outside of that, I can't talk about that; I can't talk about that other stuff. I know what I've done to get here and I'm extremely proud of what I've done.'

Somebody tosses up a comparison with Lance Armstrong and Froome raises his shotgun and fires. 'Lance won those races but that aside, to compare me with Lance . . . I mean Lance cheated, I'm not cheating. End of story.'

Brailsford, as ever, has been having a walk and a think outside the box. He asks reporters to tell him what it would take to convince them, an acknowledgement that what has been tried so far hasn't worked. He asks them if they might not sit down collectively and discuss what would be a satisfactory outcome.

'You're asking me, how can I prove to you that we are not doping? You're all asking the same questions. We wrack our brains every day.'

Brailsford stresses his reluctance in a competitive environment to release his team's power stats willy-nilly, but suggests that perhaps monitoring riders using the conventions of the biological passport process would be feasible.

'We've been thinking about the biological passport and how that works with an appointed panel of experts . . . If you extrapolate that thinking forward I think we'd be quite happy, we'd actually encourage maybe the World Anti-Doping Agency (WADA) to appoint an expert and they could have everything that we've got. They could come and live with us, they could have all of our information, see all of our data, have access to every single training file we've got. We could then compare the training files to the blood data, to weight . . . All of that type of information they could capture on a consistent basis.

'And it seems to me WADA are a good body to sit and analyse all that data. And they then could tell the world, and you, whether they think this is credible or not.'

It seemed to me at the time, and still seems to me, that:

Say you've decided that Brailsford is the evil godfather of a sophisticated doping programme. A doping programme going down in an era still reeling from the carnage of Lance Armstrong's bio-physical racketeering. If you are the master-mind of this scam, which would surely end cycling forever, well, this is a pretty big thing to offer. He has a sceptical jour-nalist living with the team at the moment. A scientist from WADA is a step further.

Then he displays a charming lack of understanding of the way the media operates.

'Rather than asking us all the time to come up with some creative way to prove that we're innocent, why couldn't you . . . get yourselves together . . . and you tell me, what would prove it for you, what could we do? . . . Get your heads together and come to me and say, "Well this is what we think we would like in order to prove to us beyond reasonable doubt that you are not doping."

'Bottom line is, it's a rest day, it's ten o' clock in the morn-ing and I'm trying to defend somebody who's doing nothing wrong. I'm quite happy to do it, and I'm more than happy to try to convince you guys that we're not doing anything wrong, but I need a little bit of help, I think, in coming up with a way about how the hell we do it.'

Some hope.

Froome, by his own standards of chill and cool, has become a little agitated as the press conference has worn on. His last words have an edge to them. Still, he manages to keep a hold of his tongue.

'I just think it's quite sad that we're sitting here the day after the biggest victory of my life yesterday, quite a historic win, talking about doping. And quite frankly, I mean, my team-mates and I, we've slept on volcanoes to get ready for this, we've been away from home for months, training together, just working our arses off to get here, and here I am, basically being accused of being a cheat and a liar and ... that's not cool.'

A year ago on the Tour, Bradley Wiggins snapped and then railed against the faceless peloton of tweeters and bloggers. By comparison, Froome's quiet hurt and frustration and Brailsford's cerebral response to the intractable problem of proof seem quite eloquent. There is a recognition that a sport which has suckered and short-changed its customers for so many decades has no right to instant redemption. There is hurt there also, however.

As they get up to leave, their faces suggest that restraint and grace will bring them no respite. Outside, the TV crews are waiting at the Team Sky bus to continue the inquisition.

Today is for resting. Tomorrow is for racing. Oddly, the racing brings more peace than the resting.

Two days later, at breakfast at the Hotel Les Bartavellas in Embrun, I meet Dave Brailsford. He tells me about his television appearance on the France 2 post-race discussion in Gap. He was invited because Cedric Vasseur, a studio pundit for France 2 during the Tour, had said two days earlier that Froome's feat on Ventoux was unachievable without drugs. That he didn't believe it.

Brailsford was seriously annoyed over what Vasseur had said, and in retaliation accepted the invitation to go on the show and speak about doping. He had hoped Vasseur would be present and gave serious thought to how he would respond to his challenger. As it turned out, Vasseur wasn't there and, though Brailsford had done well on the show and received plenty of support from Jean-René Godart, a broadcaster who has covered Team GB on the track, and had argued convincingly that Sky were clean, he was disappointed not to get his moment with Vasseur.

'I was going to pretend and say to him that I'd heard from different people in different teams that he had doped, but hadn't admitted it. I'd also heard that his name would come out in the list of the forty-four positives from retrospective testing at the 1998 Tour de France.

'I reckoned he would deny it, say he had never doped and he would not be named in the AFLD positives from ninety-eight. And that I had accused him without having any evidence. Then I was going to say, "So now you know what it's like to be falsely accused, which is exactly what you have done to Chris Froome." But sadly, he wasn't there and I didn't get my chance.'

It's a visceral response from a cerebral man. And pinpoints the deficiencies in the media approach to this issue.

So. The Miracle of Mont Ventoux?

I'm neither a great fan nor avid student of statistics. When we wrote together in the Lance era, my writing partner Pierre Ballester and I divided up the work as follows: he did the doctor, I did the massage therapist. So Pierre met haematologists and oncologists, wrangled the scientific stuff, and was both scrupulous and discerning about what he believed and what he used.

Nevertheless a cottage industry has grown up in recent years, supplying the blogosphere with statistics which are supposed to 'prove' or 'disprove' whether a cyclist is guilty. I don't believe the statisticians themselves set out to be conclusive, but their stats draw the rapt attention of scholars of the University of Wikipedia. If the exchanges between these crowd-sourced academics are any indication of the general comprehension of the stats, then it's all a bit depressing.

Lies. Damned lies. Statistics. You get rabid takers for each.

When *L'Equipe* analysed eighteen climbs of Froome's from the previous two years they discovered what, for me, was the most relevant statistic in the debate. What Froome did on Ventoux is what Froome does best. He has the ability not just to maintain tempo but to insert five-minute bursts of maximum power output.

Why pay attention to just one statistic? Well, *L'Equipe* were comparing the performances of a single rider and isolating a small component of that rider's performances on hills. The variables are not eliminated but they are minimised, and there is enough baseline data to make a general conclusion viable.

Fred Grappe, who did the analysis, didn't provide a ticker-tape parade proclaiming Froome's conclusive innocence. That wasn't his job and he hadn't enough data for that.

Grappe limited himself to a modest conclusion from the figures he was given.

After Dave Brailsford's attempt to think out loud about a solution during the rest-day press conference, it was a pity that WADA felt unable to help, but understandable as this is not their brief. Nor was it Brailsford's fault that *L'Equipe* chose Grappe to do their analysis. Many were quick to point out that in 2001, 'Grappe said the exact same thing about Armstrong.'

He didn't. He provided a general impression of the benefits of training smarter and came to an overly optimistic conclusion about Armstrong. I am sure it was an embarrassment for the man and it was certainly an irritation for those of us trying to investigate Armstrong, but there is no reason to think that, having been humiliated for reaching a broad and erroneous conclusion twelve years ago, Grappe was going to deliberately err in the same direction again.

Grappe got caught in the crossfire anyway, and Brailsford's attempt at transparency provided little protection. Talking to the Team Sky people before and during the race, they were more than a little alarmed that even the grasp of so-called 'experts' of the science of performance was years behind what teams were using. The calls for VO Max results were a case in point: 'We have to have the VO Max results. Have to know them. What!? What do you mean VO Max testing is no longer done? Oh ... Regardless, we must be the jury on all scientific data!'

I thought that Ross Tucker of the Sports Scientists site, a man who I have met and respect, got it right when he spoke about what we were seeing this year, the new craze for science to feed extreme conclusions.

'It doesn't deserve outright dismissal and it doesn't warrant embracing as conclusive proof of anything,' Tucker said.

He also recommends that we use our other senses if we feel the absolute necessity to come to conclusions. To me this is called journalism. You go into the background, test the transparency, test the substance of the people involved, find out what they do when we are not looking. When Bradley Wiggins speaks to me about doping in the context of letting his children down, when he speaks as the child of a man and doper who let *him* down, I hear somebody who has weighed the cost of cheating and found it excessive. That doesn't end my curiosity but it informs my conclusions.

Elsewhere, the blizzard of statistics just limits our visibility.

The other day I was speaking to Tim Kerrison about the new data. He was pointing out that measuring power and measuring physiology just aren't the same thing. Then he said:

'So power is torque, which is basically force, but circular force. Torque multiplied by angular velocity – basically the speed at which the crank's moving. So power is force times velocity if you're talking about linear, or when you're talking about circular it's torque, which is the equivalent of force, times angular velocity. So the SRM measures the torque two hundred times a second. So at every point around the pedal stroke. But it only measures the angular velocity once every revolution. So there's a magnet that basically measures cadence, and so assumes a constant velocity each revolution. But because on the oval rings you go from, say on a fifty-six oval ring, you go from the equivalent of a fifty-eight at the big point, and fifty-four at the smaller point. A big variation, and one of the whole ideas of the oval rings is that through that dead spot, you can get through that dead spot much quicker. So then your velocity's slower through one part of the revolution, and faster through the other part. And the mathematics of it is, if you were to measure it correctly, you'd measure the angular velocity at the same frequency that you're measuring the torque. And multiply the two of them together. But the way it calculates it, which is absolutely fine for circular rings, because the angular velocity is much more constant, it just multiplies each of those torques by the average angular velocity for that revolution. So that's where the error creeps in.'

Funny, that's exactly what I was about to say . . .

I understand the appeal of the new approach. Statistics give the illusion of being as emphatic and decisive as a gun fired during a heated discussion in a pub. In this argument they are an illusion. Forgive me if this sounds too intuitive for those who speak in numbers, but no estimate of power output has ever made me as suspicious as Johan Bruyneel railing against blood tests in an interview before the 1999 Tour de France.

I don't fully grasp the maths but am willing to accept Brailsford's charge of pseudo-science on the basis that the limitations of the data seem very obvious to me. As they used to teach accountants years ago: GIGO. Garbage in, garbage out.

Garbage, I grasp.

Take Ventoux, for instance. Different sites take their stats from different starting points. It is worth mentioning that these times themselves are taken from television coverage, not systematically and reliably harvested. Is that exactly where the climb starts? Was the stage winner at the front or the back of the peloton when they went past the start point?

One source measures times from a distance of 21.5km out, quoting an average 7.5 per cent gradient. The stats here include performances on Ventoux from both the Critérium du Dauphiné and the Tour. By this measure, Froome's climb of Mont Ventoux comes in twenty-third.

Iban Mayo's ride in the 2004 Dauphiné was delivered at an apparent pace of 23.10kmh while Froome rode at a more sedate 21.86kmh. That's quite a difference. However, this collection of times omits data from the Dauphiné of 1998, 2000, 2002, 2005 and 2007 because there wasn't any data.

Another site measures Tour rides only over just the final 15.65km, that is from the hairpin of le Virage de St Estève to the summit – 1368ft of elevation with an average gradient of 8.7 per cent. By this reckoning, Lance Armstrong's ride in 2002 was the fastest ever at 48.33, with Froome coming in second at 48.35 mins.

Five of the top ten times by this measure came in 2009, when Ventoux marked the last day of racing before Paris. The stage winner Juan Manual Garáte had a breakaway lead hitting Ventoux. He clung to that and his time isn't among the top ten.

Garáte commented at the time, though, that 'It was very hard on the final climb, there was a lot of headwinds.' Those winds were timed at 25kmh. Behind him a massive battle unfolded, however, with Armstrong, Contador, Andy and Frank Schleck and Roman Kreuziger all in the mix. Contrast that with 2013 when Team Sky's high tempo on the climb, broken up by sudden accelerations, saw them catch Nairo

Quintana who, having done so much to break away, was vulnerable to Froome's last surge.

The 2013 stage to Ventoux was longer than the 2009 version, but the four climbs preceding Ventoux were gentle – three of them category four. In 2009, Ventoux was again the fifth and final ascent as the stage approached from Montelimar but three of the four preceding climbs were category three.

So the foundation for the statistics is notoriously unsteady to begin with, before we start adding twists.

The newest twist on time stats has been to submit them to various equations depending on when they occurred: 2002-2008 is the doping era, 2008 onwards is for some reason (well, the biological passport) deemed to be the clean era (it is not worth asking about Armstrong and Contador in 2009).

Now, to me, if you are going to compare statistics with any sort of academic rigour, you have to eliminate the variables, or else all the baseline data is faulty. The variables are considerable.

First, the weather:

Wind is the key factor. We are told that a 10kmh tailwind can give 40 watts of extra power. Both weather reports and riders' testimonies suggest mainly tailwinds and crosswinds on Ventoux in 2013. In the inevitable deconstruction of the stage after the finish, Francesco Gavazzi [Astana] claims, 'We had a tailwind from the start and this made the pace very high when we came to the base of Ventoux.' Greg Henderson [Lotto-Belisol] even modestly admits, 'Tailwind up the whole climb helped my watts per kilo, guys, so don't get too impressed with my time up Ventoux.' But these times *are* getting people impressed. Because they are being compared to times posted in 2009, done riding into a strong headwind in the 'clean era'. Again in 2000, reports suggest Pantani and Lance racing into a headwind.

And what about the man himself? Did Froome feel a tail-wind delivering him to the top that day?

'Everyone talked about this front wind from the left, front crosswind, that you normally get once you go out of the forest there. But we went up there, I certainly didn't feel any of that, so I've got to assume it was a tailwind.'

So it's the case, I ask, that you feel a disruptive wind but not a charitable one? That if you don't feel a thing it's probably because you're getting a little help?

'That's it. That's it, one hundred per cent.'

We know from the rider in question that in 2004 Iban Mayo had a side/tailwind for most of the final 6.5km of his record-breaking climb. Wind is a massive variable but so too is humidity. Where is the reliable measure of the humidity down on the plains as the peloton pounds towards Ventoux?

If you want to run the forensics over the dry dust of statistics it is best not to try it on a mountain named for its susceptibility to winds. Ventoux (from *venteux*, meaning windy) is defined by the mistrals which rake over its scalp all day and all night, giving the mountain its own micro climate. The plains of Provence down below may slumber and swelter in a heat so still and intense that it weighs upon the shoulders, while at the same time, up high on Ventoux, the winds and rains can feel like you have ridden into another season or another planet.

Energy levels:

Everybody hits the mountain feeling differently. These are humans, not machines. Team Sky, with their usual attention to detail, arranged for a feeding station at the base of Ventoux for their riders. Nobody else did.

Schedule:

Where in the race does a particular ascent come? How many stages, how many miles, and how many ascents have riders had in their legs before they get there?

Tactics:

Has a rider been left on his own all day, or protected and drafted to within sight of the finish line. Has it been a day of persistent breaks? What were the team orders? How do you assess the contribution of Porte and Kennaugh in a scientific analysis of Froome's performance?

Strength of the peloton:

In 2013 the previous year's winner (Wiggins) and third place finisher (Nibali) weren't present. Jurgen Van den Broeck (fourth in 2012) crashed out after five stages. Tejay van Garderen (fifth in 2012) lost 13 minutes on the first climb of the Tour. Other 'contenders' Valverde and Contador didn't have the strength many thought they would.

You don't have to have graduated from the University of Wikipedia to figure that one out.

Manufacturing science:

Are all bikes and equipment created equal? No. Is the rolling resistance of all tyres the same? No? Is the drag exerted on every rider the same or even constant? No. Do these things change between riders and between the years in which the stats are taken? Yes.

Doping:

There is a certain attraction in saying that all figures in a certain timespan are to be considered 'doping' figures, but the assumption that all dopers consumed the same PEDs (Performance-Enhancing Drugs) at the same times with identical physiologies, therefore experiencing the same effects, undermines the whole business. If Lance has a nice big blood transfusion the night before a big climb but Jan just has a little testosterone patch applied, do we attach the same statistical weightings to their rides? Discuss.

Genetic outliers and geniuses:

Are we to eliminate the possibility that cycling can produce a Federer, a Messi, a Woods or a Bolt? Froome grew up in Kenya for instance, at altitude, cycling mountains for fun. We have never had a Kenyan ride the Tour before. The pool from which we are finding cyclists grows. Is it strange to expect better riders if the nets are cast more widely?

At the end of the day, all we know is that Chris Froome wasn't the fastest man ever up Mont Ventoux. It wasn't the greatest performance ever seen. He wasn't selling 'shock and awe' as Paul Kimmage suggested.

If we want statistics which will survive argument and dispute, we need lab conditions, identical equipment, riders of same weight and body fat composition, same bike set-up and saddle angle, riding in a controlled environment, etc.

Until then, accusing a rider of being guilty according to stats is as valid as pronouncing him clean because he hasn't failed a drug test.

The easiest part of investigating Lance Armstrong was to say that he was very fast and therefore there was a chance he was very dirty. The hard part was all the rest: establishing the connections and visits to Ferrari, the pattern of payments, the witness evidence from his admission to an Indianapolis hospital in 1996, evidence from those who shared the same toxic environment, the background to his failed test in 1999, his payments to the UCI, the habits and attitudes of those he surrounded himself with, his weak responses when being asked about these things, the pattern of his movements (abandoning France to live in Girona when the French police stepped up their interest in doping matters), his attitude to outspoken clean riders, the background of those advising him and guiding him, and on, and on, *ad infinitum*.

I spent a good portion of 2013 living with Team Sky and applying those questions to them. I was aware that their reputations weren't the only ones at stake. My reputation was impugned from the time I decided to see what was on the inside. But, on the inside, I found nothing that sent alarm bells ringing. I found no doors locked.

I used my senses. And more importantly I used some sense. I had a lot to lose, so I needed to.

At the Park Inn Hotel on the evening of 14 July the mood in Team Sky is buoyant. Alan Farrell stands outside on this balmy French evening looking for someone to relive the day with. Chris Haynes keeps an eye out for the return of the yellow butterfly. Gary Blem loves this evening because tomorrow's rest day means he and the team of mechanics will have time to draw breath and prepare mentally for the final push through the Alps and on to Paris.

Bikes, of course, are still being washed and cleaned. In the rooms, carers are reviving tired bodies. Mont Ventoux has taken its toll. If you eavesdrop on the conversation between

Brailsford and Tim Kerrison, the race that matters is their own race up Ventoux the following day.

They ride together during the Tour, mostly very early in the morning but on rest days they go for a proper ride. Staying in Orange, they will retrace the steps of Froome, Quintana, Porte and the others up Mont Ventoux, and there is much teasing and banter about how this *mano à mano* will pan out. The smart money says Kerrison.

Mechanic Igor Turk is from Slovenia, and at first I couldn't fathom him. A big man, with big arms and eyes that seem to see more than the face revealed. For a few days, I had the impression he viewed me as you would a zebra on a working farm – exotic, but not contributing much to productivity.

Then one evening in a hotel where the rooms were particularly hard to locate, I asked if he knew where 302 was and, rather than try to explain, he took me there. This invited conversation and I asked if he was enjoying being on the Tour. Not really, he said, because he didn't like being away from his family and he liked to draw a line through each day as it passed.

'It's another day closer to home,' he said.

That broke the ice and from that moment I could see Igor as everyone in the team saw him. A strong man, mentally as well as physically, who liked to laugh. As the Tour wore on, that laugh became more noticeable and I understood: another day closer to home.

Here in Orange on this Sunday evening, every Sky staffer is smiling.

'Did you see Froomey when he accelerated away from Quintana?'

'Richie did some ride; see how the group disintegrated when he went to the front?'

This is a day to celebrate, for it leaves Froome with a vice-like grip on the race and only something unforeseen can stop him. But Sky isn't good at celebrating. 'At HTC [his previous team],' Gary Blem told me during the Giro, 'we were smaller, had less resources, were less organised but we had a lot of fun. This [Team Sky] feels more corporate.'

This is something they've spoken about and, in keeping with the team's commitment to trying to improve, there's been a conscious effort to celebrate the good moments this year.

When Rigoberto Urán won the tenth stage of the Giro d'Italia at Altopiano del Montasio in the Apennines, riders and staff members gathered for a glass of champagne before supper. Dave Brailsford said a few words and there were calls for the popular Urán to speak. He is a good rider but it's not often he gets to stand in that section of limelight occupied by Froome and Wiggins.

So, he began his victory speech thus: 'My name is Rigoberto Urán, I am a rider with Team Sky ...' everyone laughed and understood, Wiggins enjoying the joke as much as anyone. When Urán finished, someone shouted, 'Now in English, please?'

But here at the Park Inn at Orange on this Bastille evening, there is cause for greater celebration. Froome's win on Ventoux is the team's best day of the year so far, for it has been a spectacular victory and it's now hard to see how he can lose the Tour. That the good times arrive when the team has camped for two days at a decent hotel in a pretty and historic town adds to the occasion.

Team Sky eat in a room specially set aside for them. Riders sit at one table, the staff are at two others, and bottles of champagne and glasses are laid out on a fourth table. Igor and fellow mechanic Richard Lambert have been asked to serve the bubbly, a touch that reflects the attention given to the smaller details.

Froome then thanks everyone, staff and teammates, for the help he's received. He speaks for less than a minute but looks from one member of staff to another, his eyes conveying as much gratitude as his words. Such is his status within the team that it is incumbent upon Brailsford to speak at times like this.

It is not a duty he either takes lightly or that weighs heavily.

'Since the last rest day, we've had some real challenging days, no? I think we've faced more challenges in this race than we have probably in the last couple of years put together, really. And I think the way that you're coping, and the way that you're handling it, and the way we're riding, pulling together as a team, is phenomenal. Absolutely phenomenal.

'Froomey, you're leading the lads brilliantly, you're doing a fantastic job. But equally, all of you guys, each one of you has your own little story along the way. You know, G [Thomas] won't stop moaning about his broken pelvis; we've seen the X-ray photo, G, we've seen it! Honestly, we've all seen it.

'Pete threw himself down a ditch, Ian was on his arse and hurt his back, David's fighting his heart out, Kosta's doing a brilliant job, and Richie today you, once again, you were phenomenal. Once you put your foot on the gas after Pete went, boom, they all disappear.

'And then it's up to Froomey to do the rest. So you're all

doing a brilliant job, and from a staffing point of view, it's not easy when other teams give us some shit, as they have been doing. You can go one way or another, you can either let it really bother you, and crumble.

'Or, you put your backs against the wall and you come out fighting, and you pull together. And we stick together and look after each other and tell 'em all to fuck off basically. And show them what we're made of. And I think credit to you all, thanks ever so much because you're doing a fantastic job.

'Froomey, just keep doing what you're doing, let's stay calm. Let's not get over excited. We've got some tough days coming up and if we can just keep doing what we're doing now, you're gonna win this race, mate. For sure. So let's stick together, let's look after each other and also, let's enjoy this evening because it's not often you get a guy, a British guy, on the top of Mont Ventoux, not far from the Tom Simpson memorial.'

This heartfelt tribute is interrupted by a heckler from the riders' table.

'Kenyan. A Kenyan guy,' G Thomas says.

Brailsford recognises the voice.

'British. British, British,' says the team boss who then tries to come over all hurt, 'I expected a little bit more than that, G.'

Thomas is laughing, unrepentant. 'And all them British people who will see him wear that thing he wears to massage,' he says, referring to Froome's *kikoy*, a sarong-like piece of clothing traditionally worn by men in East Africa.

Not winning against Thomas, Brailsford returns to safer terrain.

'But Mont Ventoux. Centenary Tour. Yellow jersey. To win like that at the top of Mont Ventoux – fuck me, that is an incredible, incredible performance, you know? And that'll last for years and years. Legendary stuff. So well done everybody, but let's stay on it.

'Ready, ready Pete? You start it.'

The last sentiment is a request to Pete Kennaugh to initiate Team Sky's celebratory chant. Kennaugh passes it on to the second *directeur sportif* Servais Knaven. 'He's better than me at this, he's my inspiration.' Knaven stands holding his glass in the air and begins: 'Oooohhhhhhh.' Then everyone joins in: 'AaaaaaaaaaahhhhhhhhhhhhhhhhHHHHHHHHHHH.'

It lasts for seven or eight seconds but with every voice contributing to the rising volume, the effect is stunning. And here, not far from the scene of Froome's triumph on Ventoux, the team shows it is getting the hang of celebrations. Everyone sits down and smilingly drains their champagne. Nineteen days on the Tour, this is a high point.

But then the spell is broken.

He walks in unannounced, a youngish man, mid-thirties, medium height. Before anyone realises who he is or why he's come, he goes straight to Froome. They speak for a minute or so and then this young man walks back towards the door, pulls up a chair and sits alone, facing the riders' table.

By now everyone gets it. He is a doping control officer and has come for a sample of Froome's blood. One of his colleagues had come to the hotel that morning, another blood test, and Froome had done the post-race urine test, an obligation for the wearer of the yellow jersey.

Three tests in one day but there isn't a hint of disapproval. Not a scintilla of resentment towards the one who killed the music. He's got his job to do. As for the celebration, it was like a cow's tail. All it lacked was length to reach the moon.

CHAPTER FOURTEEN

'When you're climbing at high altitudes, life can get pretty miserable.'

Sir Edmund Hillary

Before the sun goes down on any particular day Team Sky are already preparing for what will happen when the sun comes up again the next.

If it is too cold or too hot, the mechanics are in a special climate-controlled truck washing the bikes and checking the tyres. Every bike. Every tyre. The physios and *soigneurs* are performing a similar service on the riders. Neil Thompson, the mechanic from Jaguar, is checking the fleet of cars. Provisions are being prepared.

Tomorrow is Alpe d'Huez. A special circumstance. Rod Ellingworth and Mario Pafundi have already talked it through. The logistics of getting the Team Sky armada to the top of the Tour's most famous climb while that climb is temporary residence to the population of a decent city are too much. The bus won't be seeing the summit.

This sounds like a small thing. It isn't. The aftermath of a stage is key to recovery. The bus is key to the aftermath. Team Sky own two of the celebrated Volvo 9700 buses. They are maybe the symbol of how Team Sky do things. Getting ready to launch in January 2010, and having completed the controversial and expensive signing of Bradley Wiggins from Garmin-Sharp, the team needed a chariot to bear him in.

Not content with merely looking like a Decepticon waiting to transform, the Volvo has even played a part in claiming the scalp of one of Sky's original Autobots.

There were many reasons why it didn't work out between Team Sky and its first 'senior' *directeur sportif* Scott Sunderland. For a start, Scott liked the word 'senior' before his job title. Big mistake. An Australian, Sunderland had enjoyed a long career in the European peloton and knew his way around. There was much he felt he could teach the fledgling Team Sky, but he didn't seem to get it that Dave Brailsford didn't want his team to be a newer version of the old continental European model.

Brailsford dreamt of something very different. For example, when Sunderland thought the team should have more or less the same team bus as the best European teams, he unwittingly insulted Brailsford's intelligence. Why, thought Brailsford, would we do that when every time he stepped on board a traditional team bus, he was struck by how badly designed they were on the inside? What Brailsford saw was an interior designed by people who saw riders as just one part of the team, not the central part.

So he employed designers who had worked with Formula 1 teams Honda and Benetton to create a bespoke high-spec performance vehicle in which to convey his prize assets. The buses were refitted from scratch over a period of four months. It's not, however, so easy to refit humans from scratch and midway through his first full season with the team, Scott Sunderland departed. As he'd signed a three-year contract, there was a financial settlement and an agreement that ensured both parties would in the future speak glowingly of the other.

Brailsford had ideas that Sunderland would never have conceived, and certainly had never seen during his racing days. Team Sky's psychiatrist Dr Steve Peters was commissioned to design mood-lighting to help the riders relax. The front of the bus carries the riders in large comfortable seats which swivel and recline, just nine seats because there will never be more than nine riders at one race. The rear of the bus is a meeting room cum treatment room cum work area. It is here, on long flat stages of the Tour, that Brailsford will catch up on lost sleep.

Each rider has a personal WiFi, and a fold-away table for laptops, a socket panel containing charging docks. And of course there are Sky Boxes. On the ride back to a team hotel or the journey to a stage, riders can Skype, surf the net, watch a movie, listen to music or just sleep.

Energy drinks and food are on their seats when they board the bus. There are showers, toilets and fridges, and a washing machine and drier so that gear can be washed on the road. Open the fridge you've got an assortment of chilled drinks, freshly made tuna pasta dishes, yoghurts. Everyone swears by the coffee-maker.

That coffee-maker won't be making it to the summit of Alpe d'Huez tomorrow, but preparations must go on regardless.

As one by one the staff finish their tasks and turn in, I watch Mark Dzalo and David Rozman, two Slovenian carers, complete their final job of the night – filling the big cooler box in the team cars with ice. Through this Tour, these guys have handled more ice than a gang of workers in a fish factory. The Alpe tomorrow. Biggest day of all. They are ahead of themselves. In the morning they can top the bag up with more ice. Bring it on.

There are 177 riders left and for those who have hung in there through sheer bloody-mindedness or just to defy their broken pelvises, today is a perverse reward of sorts. You'd have to be a cyclist to love this place. Alpe d'Huez! The mountain put on this earth to break men. You pass two churches on the way up, just in case you feel like it's time to make your peace with the Man above.

If you are riding out today though, this is the climb you tell the grandchildren about. And some day when you are dandling them on your lap, they will brace themselves well for the story of this particular day. The Tour has channelled Levi Roots for this year's stage planning – Alpe d'Huez is so nice you'll climb it twice.

Here is the gnarled spiritual heart of the Tour de France. The first summit to host a finish, back in 1952. Before that, mountains were just obstacles on the way to finishes on the flat. Each of those draining switchback hairpin bends is named after a stage winner on l'Alpe. Today the estimates of the crowd lining the twenty-one hairpin bends range from 750,000 to double that. People claimed the best spots a week ago. The climb is 13.8km with an average gradient of more than 8 per cent. It starts with a few kilometres at 10 per cent. Just as a meet and greet.

At the summit we will be at an altitude of 1,850m. We will also be in a car. For this much, thanks.

Of course it would be too easy if the riders just rode up l'Alpe twice in an afternoon. Far too easy ... Instead, the final climb will come at the end of a gruelling 172km stage with a series of four lesser climbs and a spin up l'Alpe along the way. That's more like it. All that and fans pushing and pulling at riders in the afternoon sun. This is cycling's waterboarding.

From the start the pace is hectic. Jens Voigt, one of the peloton's breakaway addicts, is restless. He makes an early break, gets caught, and then surfs the wave created by Saxo-Tinkoff's early aggression. Good old Jens. Who said that the Germans don't do optimism?

Eventually an escape group of nine establishes itself and pushes on down the road, hoping for the best. After 60km they have a decent lead of nearly 6'30", but they know that when the peloton wants to it can reel them back in at a rate of one minute every 10km. Doing the maths has never been more depressing.

It would seem Saxo-Tinkoff have had a hearty breakfast and an inspiring team talk. They are full of ideas and gambits. Just a week ago these boys made a little theatrical production out of toasting themselves following a modest success on Stage Thirteen.

Since then all has not gone well for Saxo-Tinkoff. Yesterday was another setback. Froome won the time trial, with Contador second. Sport can be brutal. By this point in the race, Contador knows he can't take Froome's yellow jersey and he's just trying to get something for himself, one victory he can look back on and think, 'Yeah, that was a good day.'

The time trial from Embrun to Chorges was that opportunity for Contador. At 32km, with two second category climbs and a weather forecast that made slippery descents likely, it favoured Contador more than Froome. After all, the Team Sky rider had 4'30" cushion and mentally he geared himself up to ride conservatively and limit the time losses to his rivals.

Contador went for it, as did the other Spaniard, Joaquim Rodríguez, and when the Saxo rider beat his compatriot's time by a single second, it seemed certain he would claim a stage victory after all. Froome was the only one who could beat him and as the roads dried through the final third of the race, the Sky rider changed bikes to allow him to take better advantage of the flatter final section of the course.

At the finish line Contador waited, knowing he was ahead of Froome at all of the intermediate time checks but fearing the race leader would keep on keeping on. He did, and by finishing strongly, he bettered Contador's time by 9 seconds. In Chorges that evening Alberto Contador was the picture of misery.

Commenting on the achievement of Contador and his teammate Roman Kreuziger leap-frogging over Bauke Mollema and claiming second and third in the overall standings, Saxo's *directeur sportif* said he was glad that his riders had 'conquered the two lesser places on the podium'. With three Alpine stages to come, his talk of conquering podium places seemed as premature as the little dinner-table celebration in Le Veurdre five days before.

Back at the Team Sky hotel in Embrun, Brailsford slept

through most of the time trial, waking in time to watch the finish on television.

'Chris has always been a good time-triallist,' he said afterwards, 'that's where I first saw him, in Melbourne in the Commonwealth Games in 2006, first time I set eyes on him. Nathan O'Neill won that time trial, we had Steve Cummings and the usual suspects. I was there with Doug Dailey and Shane [Sutton]. Shane's saying [in Brailsford's best Australian twang], "You're not going to believe this, some bloke's turned up in sand shoes, jumped on his bike and look what he's done. In a pair of fucking sand shoes!"

'We all looked and thought bloody hell that guy is impressive. He wasn't up there, but it was impressive, you know, he caught the eye. And he was completely unknown. And then Doug, being Doug, said, "Ah, I might have a word with him, lads," they got in touch, and the rest . . . was history really.'

Arising from Contador's gut-wrenching loss in the time trial is the likelihood of further disappointment. He gave that time trial everything he had, but it wasn't enough and he knows he can't match Froome in the mountains. Who'd want two ascents of the Alpe after that? He came here expecting to duke it out with Froome. Instead he is being badly beaten and has been denied the one victory that would have softened his fall.

Two of his Saxo comrades, Sérgio Paulinho and Nicolas Roche, are sent ahead of the main bunch, not so much to chase down the leaders but to be in a position to help Contador when the race gets serious. Looking sprightly, they head off into the great unknown.

The nine men in the break hit the halfway mark of the stage with a lead of 7'15". There are 88.5km remaining. Too early for anybody to get excited. By this point Paulinho and Roche are still on their own somewhere between the escapees and the main field. Though they are racing, they are also waiting for the moment when their services will be needed.

It is the kind of tactic a team uses when its main man is on the ropes.

At around half past one, lunch is done with and the riders sit up straight in their saddles and contemplate. Fed and watered, Team Sky lead the peloton. The break is still ongoing, but no one there worries Froome. All are too far back. Contador is waiting, waiting, lurking behind Sky. He's got one foot in the grave but he keeps pedalling with the other one.

At just after two o'clock the first five of the fragmented breakaway group hits l'Alpe for the first time. Chris Froome and Team Sky are still at the front of the peloton, winding their way through the twenty-one hairpin bends that will take them to the summit. Ian Stannard has done his job and dropped back. Kosta Siutsou takes a shift driving the rhythm. Nicolas Roche gets caught by the peloton.

The mountain is a world of chaos and a house of pain. The riders' progress is impeded on each side of the road by the seething masses of fans. Hairpin corners offer the best observation posts and attract the densest crowds. There is a 'Dutch corner' which has drawn a huge number of fans from the Netherlands that fill almost a kilometre of road.

There is also an Irish corner for the first time, less populous than its Dutch equivalent, but with enough green and raucous cheering to distinguish it. Every group has its favourites among the cyclists. It isn't a universal feeling, but if there were to be a referendum for which team are getting it in the neck, Team Sky would have a second yellow jersey.

Coming through the tiny little village of Chantelouve back down the road, somebody has taken the trouble to hang a curiously inquisitive banner. Simply: 'FROOME?'

Now on the corner where the Irish have gathered hangs another banner. 'FROOME DOPÉ'. A camper van with four Frenchmen in it is reckoned to be responsible. They fixed it to the bare rock, just over four Irish tricolours. The first time the cyclists come up this corner three of the occupants run towards Froome and squirt water at him from large toy syringes. He assumes it's water, but he doesn't know. It is fired at pressure and mostly what he wants is to keep it out of his mouth on the chance that there is a contaminant lurking in there.

The yellow jersey instinctively strikes out with its right sleeve and punches the assailant in the face, an act of physical violence utterly at odds with the character of its inhabitant. 'Some of the stuff went into my mouth, it might have been beer but I was conscious of not wanting to swallow even a drop and just kept spitting out. I was thinking, "What if there's some product in that stuff?"'

All the way up to the top some fans scream at Sky riders while miming shooting up. Eggs smash against the cars, beer too, and when a car slows enough for the jeering mob to rock it from side to side, that's what they do. The abuse is worse on some parts of the climb than others.

Froome is used to some interaction with the gallery. He often tells the story of how, on Stage Seventeen of the Vuelta in 2011, a spectator ran up to him and put a proposition to him. 'You win. I kill you.' He dismissed the guy as a lone crazy but three more showed up with the same message before the finish line. This, though, in its own way, has more ugliness to it. This felt like a siege.

The race rolls on. Upwards and onwards. This is just the first climb. The pandemonium can only grow.

The American rider Tejay van Garderen is out on his own at the front of the race now, 7'45" ahead of the peloton, with 56km left. Christophe Riblon is the closest man to Van Garderen, about 15 seconds back. Riblon is French so this is major excitement. Behind them, the field continues to thin out and 2011 winner Cadel Evans gets dropped again. It has been a tough Tour for the Australian. They battle to the summit. Van Garderen first, Christophe Riblon next. For the French it would be the best day of the Tour if Riblon could win. So he will be excused the left hook he swings towards an over-enthusiastic countryman who almost blocks his way up the hill.

Crazy scenes now, fans spilling everywhere. Sérgio Paulinho who made that odd break with Roche is finally caught and almost immediately gets spat out the back of the peloton. That was one tactical gambit which didn't work.

Froome and four Team Sky riders are still battling through the multitudes as they hold position near the front of the peloton. Up ahead, Moreno Moser of Italy catches van Garderen and has the moderate thrill of being first over l'Alpe this time round. It's him, van Garderen and Riblon for the descent down Col de Sarenne, which is either very tricky or very crazy depending on who you speak with. Or depending on the weather.

Five minutes later the Team Sky guys roll over the summit.

Shadowed still by Contador, Roman Kreuziger, Nairo Quintana and Joaquim Rodríguez, the race is now less about the yellow jersey but the places alongside him on the podium. Sure, if Froome weakens the others are ready, but no one expects it and his lead is big enough to allow for a relatively bad day. Better for the others to fight for what they believe is winnable.

Behind, in the convoy of cars, Team Sky have unexpected problems. The two *soigneurs*, Marko and David, who last night packed the cooler with ice, had duly topped up with more ice this morning. Unbeknown to them the previous evening's ice had begun to melt at the bottom of the cooler and on the descent from the Col d'Ornon, 15km before the first of two ascents of Alpe d'Huez, Gary Blem was sitting in the back of the team car when he heard water sloshing about in the cooler.

Not good. Around the tight corners on the descent, the water crashed against the sides of the cooler, some spilling out into the boot of the car and, from there, into the electronics.

This was the Number One team car, driven by the *directeur sportif*, Nicolas Portal, but also carrying News Corp's James Murdoch and Blem. They just about got the car to the top of Alpe d'Huez. A stop-start-stop business through the hairpins even on a good day, Portal knew something wasn't right with the car. Then the dashboard panel began to light up like a fruit machine. Flashing warning lights everywhere. Blem reached back and saw the water, all over the boot, causing the electrical carnage that foretold the day's disaster.

Things are starting to happen on the bikes too. Out ahead on the descent Moser has been left behind ... until van

Garderen's chain goes, leaving Riblon clear, until . . . Riblon misjudges a turn at speed and leaves the road to explore ditch and stream . . . leaving Moser to reclaim the lead.

Meanwhile, at the top of the descent, Alberto Contador surveys what's ahead, takes a deep breath and launches an attack. Chris Froome surveys Alberto Contador, takes a deep breath and says 'Off you go.' Froome, the calculator, works it out instinctively. If Contador attacks on the descent it is because he knows he cannot do anything on the climb.

With 21km to go (nearly 14km of that is another climb of Alpe d'Huez), Contador finds himself 20 seconds ahead of Froome and 90 seconds behind Moser and Riblon. At this point he is second overall and still feels he has a chance to win the day.

Meanwhile . . .

On the bumpy descent from the Col de Sarenne which Contador has just hurtled down, the Team Sky Number One car just cuts out. The riders are pushing ahead for the second climb of Alpe d'Huez, but here on the downslope the car has cut out. They give quiet thanks that this has happened on the loneliness of a descent and not amid the wild multitudes on the way up Alpe d'Huez.

Chris Froome will later comment that those scenes between the walls of fanatics reminded him of being stuck in a car in Kenya once with his mother as a riot went on outside. A broken-down Team Sky Jaguar might have been stripped for parts in seconds as the mob turned to piranhas.

On the Col de Sarenne, Gary Blem gets out and coaxes the battery into renewed life. The reprieve, however, lasts only minutes, so they wait on the side of the road for the second team car to come. Seven minutes that seemed to stretch towards eternity. The back-up arrives. They switch cars and head off trying to recover their number one place in the cavalcade.

It was close to hopeless, for by now the leaders were climbing Alpe d'Huez for a second time and, on a road filled with fans, overtaking was dangerous and difficult. Needing to feed before Alpe d'Huez, Froome got teammate Pete Kennaugh to go back to the team car.

'Car's not there,' said Kennaugh on his return.

And if Chris Froome was into his country and western, he might have hummed Kenny Rogers: 'You picked a fine time to leave me, Lucille.'

Froome was hungry, he needed some sugar and soon.

And so they hit Alpe d'Huez for the second time. The leading trinity have been reunited. Moser, Riblon and van Garderen will battle it out for the stage.

On the corner where the 'FROOME DOPÉ' libel hangs, there is yet more chaos. The first Team Sky car squeezes through the mob. The syringe gang have entered their camper van and changed into medical scrubs ready to cause more chaos when Team Sky come past. Somebody takes the rather brave decision to throw themselves against the door of the camper van, trapping the phoney medics inside. The one escaping member of the group is running around outside with a bucket of water.

The second Team Sky car approaches through the churning sea of people. Dave Brailsford is inside. People are shouting to shut the windows. People are shouting abuse. People are shouting. The bucket of water comes through the window.

252

The car goes on. There are scuffles on the road behind. The gendarmerie begin to take an interest.

Contador has been hauled back to the bunch which is really pushing on now. Richie Porte takes a turn at the front. Froome is behind him. Then Froome attacks.

He doesn't go with a swoosh, though. Just grinds it out and the serious men behind him are having none of it. Contador, Quintana and Joaquim Rodríguez go with him. Now, now, Mr Froome.

Mr Froome is undeterred. He hopes his little attack has seduced his rivals into thinking he is still going well, and that he can leave them whenever he wishes. Bluffing isn't just for the poker table. No one reads that Froome isn't himself; he's not going to hold up a sign that says glycogen depletion.

A roar is building up ahead and rolling down the mountain like a wave so that the whole climb is one big noise. The roar is for the battle for the stage. Van Garderen is ahead again. Jens Voigt, forty-one, the heroic old breakaway lad of the Tour, is second! Riblon and Moser haven't given up.

And Froome goes again. Maybe the noise is sucking the judgement from his brain or maybe he reacts to the need to do it to them before they do it to him. If he attacks, they can't know how weak he feels. This time he loses Contador, but Quintana won't be shaken. The Colombian seems the most comfortable of all on this second ascent of l'Alpe.

This is the sport of our childhood, the Tour as told around the fireside on a winter's evening. Contador is crumbling before our eyes. Richie Porte and Alejandro Valverde are trying to get across to join Froome and Quintana. Joaquim Rodríguez has succeeded in that already.

Froome is now looking as he feels. Wasted. Porte makes it across, which cheers Froome because he's going to need his friend. Up the road nearer the summit van Garderen is pushing on for the stage.

At this point amid the heave, Nico Portal in the team car is too far from Froome for their two-way radio to work. Having missed an opportunity to refuel, the race leader is becoming hypoglycaemic – extremely low on sugar. Seven kilometres from the summit, Portal had worked his way through some of the race cars when he hears Froome's voice on the radio.

'Nico. Sugar, sugar, I need sugar.'

Portal still has some more overtaking to do and by the time he gets into position behind Froome, it is too late to legally give the rider the sugar-rich gels he needs.

Froome makes lots of mistakes but he seldom makes the same mistake twice. Five years ago he arrived at the foot of Alpe d'Huez in his first Tour, a race for which he had only a ten-day crash course to prepare. The weeks before the Tour started, being quite sure he wasn't going to be selected anyway, Froome had gone home to Africa following the death of his mother, Jane. He hadn't been home in some time and he stayed a while after the funeral. When he came back to Europe he got the word. 'Prepare.'

He was riding for Barloworld, a South African team which was disintegrating by the mile. Their leader, Moisés Dueñas, had tested positive for EPO after the Stage Four time trial and as soon as the result was announced the French police raided his room in Tarbes in the Pyrenees. They found a one-man pharmacy and took Dueñas away in handcuffs.

Froome commented that it was best if he never saw Dueñas again as he would risk getting arrested for assault if he did. Then two other Barloworld riders crashed into each other and withdrew. By the time the Tour hit Alpe d'Huez, Barloworld were four.

Still, Alpe d'Huez. Froome isn't steeped in the lore of the Tour but he knows the places where a man might leave his mark. Froome tucked himself in ambitiously behind a group containing many of the race favourites including the eventual winner, Carlos Sastre. At the bottom of l'Alpe Sastre went for it with a sudden and aggressive attack. Froome was on the wheel of Denis Menchov, but when it all went off Froome found he had no response.

He had seen Alpe d'Huez as a venue where he might make a name for himself. He'd latched onto the leaders' group ready to take up the gauntlet. In the thrill of it all, he had forgotten to take food on board. In fact when the team car beckoned him with a fistful of energy gels he waved them away politely.

'I blew completely. I had no sugars left and lost a lot of time. That taught me a lesson.'

This isn't like that, but it's still not good. Froome and Richie Porte have an exchange now. Greater love hath no *domestique* than that which will slow down on Alpe d'Huez, wait for the team car to come alongside and get some food for his leader who has just, to use the term favoured by academic nutrionists, 'bonked'. Porte gets the energy gels. While he is delivering Froome service, Quintana attacks.

Can a gentleman not have his afternoon tea?

Froome doesn't panic. This was to be expected. Letting Richie Porte drop back as Nairo Quintana burst forward was a game of percentages which Froome got exactly right. He remembered the lesson.

Ahead it is all delirium. Riblon is closing on van Garderen as they grind it out. They pass the two-kilometres-to-go sign. A little way up the road the Frenchman heroically overtakes the American. Not bad for a cheese-eating surrender monkey, cry thousands of his countrymen. Riblon just keeps getting faster. Or van Garderen keeps getting slower. Either way it's going to be a French win on l'Alpe.

Van Garderen comes in second. Moser third, and Quintana takes fourth after a mature display of climbing nous. Joaquim Rodríguez, then Froome and Richie Porte come home together. Froome and Porte will be docked 20 seconds each for the energy gel business.

Nico Portal wants to appeal the penalty because the team were victim to such bad luck with the car. Froome tells him to drop it, explaining that if Richie hadn't broken the rule, the time loss might have been a minute or a minute and a half. Twenty seconds was a price worth paying. Portal shakes his head in wonder, for such maturity is not common in an athlete, let alone one bearing the pressure of the yellow jersey in the Tour.

This has been a strange Tour. The Clouded Yellow butterfly that Team Sky's media chief Chris Haynes had seen in Corsica had followed us all the way to the Alps. On this pivotal stage, Froome had really struggled, yet he climbed off his bike at the finish on Alpe d'Huez with his lead extended. Contador is over five minutes behind now.

Two stages left before the ride to Paris.

*

There were no recriminations about the accident that fried the electronics in the team car and could have hurt the team even more than it did. Mario Pafundi felt it was his responsibility because he hadn't done enough to help David Rozman and Marko Dzalo make a better decision about the ice.

'On a day when everyone says it's going to rain on Alpe d'Huez, you don't need ten thousand ice cubes. But it's my responsibility, I should have given them that information.'

That evening, Neil Thompson, the mechanic provided by Jaguar to be there if anything should go wrong with any of the cars, worked on the messed-up electronics from 6pm to midnight. 'If you can imagine pouring a litre of water down the back of your television while it is on, that's the problem I was trying to sort out.'

This is Thompson's second Tour with Sky. Before this, he had no interest in cycling. Football is probably his game. He manages his son's team and when he says they went through last season without winning, he wants you to understand he could never see sport as a matter of life and death. But this car, he badly wanted it back on the road. Thought he had it, all those flashing lights went away, but then late in the night, a warning light for the air-suspension system came back to haunt him and he knew he was struggling. He went to bed worried, woke up worried, and when he went to the car first thing in the morning, he threw up, anxiety churning away until his stomach could take no more.

'I know it shouldn't matter so much, but I want this team

to win. We needed the car back in the race and now I'm probably going to have to pull it out.'

You can tell the man's heart is breaking. These are people he never wants to let down.

CHAPTER FIFTEEN

*'At Team GB, Rod Ellingworth was his [Cav's] coach
and confidant and had worked with him since he had
been a teenager on the national team. Rod's a moral and
ethical rock, immune to celebrity or wealth, and I have
no doubt in my mind that he is one of the main reasons
for his success.'*

David Millar, *Racing Through the Dark*

This will be the third and final time on this Tour that Dave
Brailsford will address a general assembly of the team.

On the evening before the first stage in Corsica, he gathered
the staff on the team bus. He spoke to them, photographed
them and asked what they wanted to be able to say when
looking back on the photo in six months' time. Two weeks on,
he spoke in the team hotel at Orange after Chris Froome's
spectacular victory on Mont Ventoux. Now it is the evening
before the ceremonial ride into Paris. The riders and staff are
gathered outside the Hotel Novel La Mamma in Annecy and
Brailsford once again has the floor.

Respect from staff transcends the fact that he is boss. Through the near four weeks of the race, he has spoken easily to everyone and is perhaps the most up-beat person in the team. Any doubts he has had about the team or about the way the support staff were doing their jobs were never expressed loosely. More importantly in terms of the ambience in the team, his authority is never used to create fear and tension. Everyone understands that if someone is not doing their job, they won't be with the team the following season. Gone before anyone even realised they were in trouble. This isn't a problem, just a fact of life in Team Sky.

Anyway, now is not the time to worry about that. The job has been done. Again. Two Tour victories in four years. Not bad for a man who said his ambition for the team was to win the race within five. Back then the target seemed too ambitious. But here he is, making another victory speech to staff and riders. The intention had been to have this celebration before dinner but, it was pointed out, the mechanics were still working on the bikes outside.

Rather than the mechanics leaving their station, everyone is directed outside onto Avenue de France and glasses of champagne are passed around on the pavement. While cars whizz past, it somehow seems right that Brailsford's second Tour de France victory speech is delivered not only among the riders, and those who care for them, but the mechanics' labours of love as well, the carbon-fibre steeds that have rolled all this way.

'For you to come here as the favourite,' he says, directing his first comments towards the champion-elect, 'and to build yourself up from last November to the point where you've come into the race as favourite, was a pretty special thing to do. But I think then to arrive as a favourite, put extra pressure on you; the way that you've handled that throughout this last three weeks, has been immense, you know. And credit to you.

'But also I think the fact that you decided to take a dive in the neutralised section of the first stage. I thought, "Fucking hell, they haven't started racing yet" and "*Chute! Chute! Chute!* Froome. Froome." That was a bit of a worry.

'And I think from there, going through Corsica, I think we obviously had G [Thomas] and Yogi [Ian Stannard], who had both crashed, which was a big worry. And G got a photograph of his fracture, don't know if anybody's seen it? He's a bit shy about it all, but if you ask him nicely he will show you!*

'But, you know, credit to you two obviously for battling through and I think when it came into Nice, and I think the team time trial was a brilliant performance from everybody, it really was a fantastic performance. And for you [Thomas] to get your arse from that start ramp down to the Promenade [des Anglais]. That performance set us up. It really did. A brilliant performance.

'Onto Ax 3 Domaines, Pete [Kennaugh] your first mountain stage in a Grand Tour. You know that day, I thought as

---

*The pride and eagerness with which G Thomas foisted the X-ray of his pelvic fracture upon anyone and everyone quickly became a running joke within the team. Some claimed to have seen the photo many times and were still getting accosted by Thomas most mornings: 'Have you seen my X-ray? Look, there's my fractured pelvis.' Of course, the frequency of these was soon more than doubled by the other riders' mickey taking and sarcasm: 'Hey G, how's your pelvis? I heard you might have a picture of it on your phone. That sounds really interesting, can I have a look?' Thomas could take the ribbing and return it with interest.

a team, was probably one of the best team performances we've ever had. It was an absolutely textbook performance. The way that you took it over that Col de Pailhères, the way that Richie [Porte] then took it up, you brought Quintana back and then the way that you took over from there, it was off the scale. That was phenomenal.

'And then of course the next day, I think Pete decides to chuck himself down a ditch in the morning. And that pretty much changed, in many respects, I think that morning the way that, you weren't there, and then Richie you were there having to do that little bit more, and then Froomey finds himself isolated on his own. I think it's the first time in eighteen months that any team, or any rival in this race, has gone, "Actually, it's only a little chance, but we might have a chance," you know? And I think your performance on that day, Froomey, was unbelievable. And Pete diving down the ditch I think changed the nature of this race for the rest of the race. Because from that day on, this race . . .'

'He lost his Oakleys, did he tell you about that?' chimes in G Thomas, to cackles of laughter. 'His Oakleys, he still hasn't got them back.'

Brailsford resumes: 'If you hadn't scrambled back up that ditch, quick as you did, the whole race would have gone on past without knowing you were down there, and while it would have been a real shame for the team it would have been a bit quieter. But actually when you think about it, everybody started attacking from that point on, and where we're thinking [five days later], we've got to the crosswind section. And I think Froomey, you made the decision, to me the decision of this race, when you were caught in no-man's-land, where Cav got the hand-sling to get onto the group in front, instead of going you sat up and you went back to the group, and, okay, you lost a minute, but actually going back to the group and riding with the team, and all of you lot sticking together, that was the decision of the Tour for me.

'Because if you'd tried to go and blown there, we could have been in big trouble. And I think that day, more than anything, showed that if we stick together as a team, and yes you manage your efforts . . . You know it wasn't a great situation, but actually it was a brilliant decision that we made there. As you guys said, it showed what we can do when we stick together as a team.

'So moving on from there, I think then you got stronger and stronger and stronger. I think, David [López], you got much, much stronger through this race, and credit to you. And where's Kosta? Kosta, you've been the same, you've been great through the Alps. I think we were all thinking about the Alps going, "Phwoar, it's going to be full on here." We came into it and actually through the Alps you've been the strongest team. By far. Contador, you've reduced him to attacking on descents. And that was because you stuck together as a team; you know, it was an absolute privilege to watch.

'Richie, your individual time trial, on the first individual time-trial day, to run third having had a bit of a setback on one day and then come out and shown everybody where you're at. To me you're a . . . Obviously Froomey won the race, but in actual fact you're the second best rider in this race, and everybody can see that, you know? Credit to you, anyway. And of course then it's all made possible by everybody, all the staff, we all know how hard they work. To all the staff, well done. Nico, thirty-four years old, youngest DS [*directeur sportif*] ever to win the Tour de France. That takes some doing, you know.'

'And the best looking,' says Kennaugh.

Brailsford again, 'And he promises next year he's gonna speak English! But anyway, where's Servais? Do your thing. Here we go, Froomey.'

Servais Knaven, the second *directeur sportif*, takes over.

'READY? One . . . Two . . . All together.'

Everyone joins in: 'OoooooOOOOOOOOOOOOHHH-HHHHHHH!!!!!!!!!'

One afternoon, Dave Brailsford had tried to explain to me the particular, almost unique, contribution Rod Ellingworth made to Team Sky. He spoke of the three hands of a clock: the hour hand, the minute hand and the second hand. Most plans are based on the second hand – what do I need to do this evening/tomorrow? Some people can also make plans for the short to medium term, the minute hand. 'This is where I will be six weeks from now.' And a few work off the hour hand. 'This is what I'm planning to do twelve months from now.'

'What is very difficult,' said Brailsford, 'is to find someone who can work off the three hands at the same time and plan for the short, medium and long term. Especially when you're at the Tour de France, because this race just consumes you and you're thinking, "What do we need to do now? How long is Froomey going to have to spend at the finish today, how long before he's back at the team hotel?"

'Rod can be in the middle of this race, dealing with all he

has to deal with and he's still planning for the medium and long term. Very few people can do this, especially when they're in the middle of something as demanding as the Tour de France.'

I thought it was a generous tribute to Ellingworth but found it hard to believe. Whose mind is not consumed by this race to the exclusion of everything else? Ellingworth's. For, once Brailsford had drawn attention to it, I couldn't stop noticing how Rod's mind worked.

On the first rest day, a week and a half into the race, I encountered him as he walked by the sea at La Baule in Brittany. 'I've just been thinking about Pete [Kennaugh],' he said. 'I mean he's young, in his first Tour, he's been brilliant for the team so far. And I've been looking at his programme for after the Tour. It's too hard. We need to change it and put him in less demanding races, because this race is going to take a lot out of him and if he's pushed too hard after the Tour, we could do more damage than good.'

At that moment Vasil Kiryienka had already departed, G Thomas was struggling with his pelvis, López and Siutsou weren't performing in the mountains, and with Mont Ventoux and three tough Alpine stages remaining, young Kennaugh was needed more than should ever have been the case. But Ellingworth was able to see beyond that and plan for an easier end-of-season campaign for him.

Another evening – at dinner people were discussing the start of the 2014 Tour which takes place over two days in Yorkshire and one in the South-East. The British public would be turning up in their hundreds of thousands, it was said. Ellingworth saw this purely from a planning point of view: 'It's going to be particularly difficult for us, because many of our riders are British and their family members will come to Yorkshire and want to meet up with the guys. That's natural and it's not something you would discourage.

'But we must plan for it and I thought Team GB's Hospitality House worked really well during the London Olympics, and that "Nearest and Dearest" suite was a clever idea, a place where the athletes could meet their family and closest friends in private. We should really think about doing something similar in Yorkshire, close to where we're staying, so we can control what's going to be a crazy situation.'

This was Ellingworth, the planner. Yet he's more than that to this team.

This is Rod Ellingworth. Busy.

'How's it going?' you say.

Rod Ellingworth always pauses and says, 'Good, thank you.'

Then he will inquire of your wellbeing. The day he stops doing that he won't be Rod Ellingworth. He will never become a fat cat.

Hush.

A deathly still French morning. The heat laying everything to rest.

And if you listened to Rod Ellingworth's chest with a stethoscope, you'd catch the beat of a cycling man. Get your ear closer and you'll hear the whirr the cranks make when turning, the clunk of the derailleur dropping chain on cassette, the muffled fizz of rubber tyres rolling on asphalt, the telling rhythm of a rider's breath.

I picture him sitting in a bar, sipping a coffee and shooting the breeze with two old Belgians on the morning of the Tour of Flanders. Rod is asking them about Roger De Vlaeminck and what made him so good. Their memories and their passion are music to his ears, for no matter the size of their love for this sport, it is not greater than his.

We ended up spending a lot of time together, sharing many car journeys from race finish to the hotel. He reminded me of Belcher in Frank O'Connor's compelling short story 'Guests of the Nation'. A British soldier in Ireland, Belcher was captured by the IRA and taken to a safe house where he awaited his fate. His captors couldn't stop themselves from liking him.

It was a treat to see how Belcher got off with the old woman in the house where we were staying. She was a great warrant to scold, and cranky even with us, but before ever she had a chance of giving our guests, as I may call them, a lick of her tongue, Belcher had made her his friend for life. She was breaking sticks, and Belcher, who had not been more than ten minutes in the house, jumped up and went over to her. "Allow me, madam," he said, smiling his queer little smile. "Please allow me," and he took the hatchet from her. She was too surprised to speak, and after that, Belcher would be at her heels, carrying a bucket, a basket or a load of turf. As Noble said, he got into looking before she leapt, and hot water, or any little thing she wanted, Belcher would have ready for her.

Ellingworth has the same straightforwardness, the same easy humility, the same readiness to help whoever he meets along the way. There is a perception abroad that the English are arrogant, and Team Sky, with their '*veni vidi vici*' mentality haven't exactly dispelled the thought.

But come around the back of the bus after a stage has ended, sidle up to Rod Ellingworth and ask him how the lads are. He will make as much time for you as he would for a BSkyB bigwig flown in for the event, and speak more frankly than you'd ever expect. Because if you love cycling you are his friend. No one spending a moment in his company would come away thinking Team Sky arrogant.

On those car journeys we got to talking about anything and everything. He told me where he came from, born in Burnley in the industrial North-West, raised in Lincoln in the part of England that God forgot.

Look.

You can create a team like this, a team which lives in a black bus on the cold cutting edge of everything, but somewhere within the team you have to have a beating heart, a bloodline of warmth that sways back and forth like the Gulf Stream. Sometimes you need a down-to-earth man who talks tough and shoots straight but who loves what he does without a hint of scientific detachment. You need a Rod Ellingworth.

Boy to man. The back story is modest and uncomplicated. After leaving Burnley, he settled in Margaret Thatcher's Grantham and young Rod Ellingworth began riding for the Witham Wheelers when he was a boy. No matter what he has achieved in cycling in the years since, when the local papers write about Rod he is always 'former Witham Wheelers rider Rod Ellingworth'. He likes that.

He progressed to Cherry Valley RT and his life seemed like a journey from race to race, sometimes on the road, occasionally on grass, and every dream for the future had Rod making a living doing what he loved. He turned pro and rode with Team Ambrosia and later the French outfit UV Aube. And that was it folks, a couple of years as an honest pro in the late nineties. Nowt fancy.

He fell into coaching naturally though, realising quickly that his hard-fisted rules could make tough road men out of soft BMX boys. His first serious project was a tough nut. An eighteen-year-old kid from the Isle of Man who came to the velodrome in Manchester one day for an informal interview about becoming part of the new wave. Mark Cavendish had a reputation for being mouthy and headstrong, and for losing races that he might have won due to scattiness or lack of concentration.

He sat down and Ellingworth asked him merely to recount everything he remembered of the journey that day from the Isle of Man to Manchester. Cavendish did so in almost cinematic detail. Every turn, every diversion, every roundabout. He had a brain to match his talent and the awareness to match his brain. Ellingworth knew he could work with him and knew he could be the voice that told Cavendish what he was doing wrong, without being the ear that had to suffer the consequences.

They had great times together. Eight years of success. When Cav moved on from Team Sky last year, he wanted Rod to go with him. Rod didn't want to do it. He is a team man. He talks sometimes about the problems of *soigneurs* getting too close to top riders. It creates resentment among the other *soigneurs*. An accidental hierarchy. What happens if the rider drops out? Does his *soigneur* mope about having to lower himself to massage so-called lesser riders? Many problems.

He loves Cav and there would have been more money in the move, but he decided to stay. 'If Cav has a major crash, do I have a job? What's the chances of him having a big crash? Fairly high. I'm with a team which is consistent and has a long future.'

In a sport pedalled by big egos, Rod Ellingworth is happy to hew some wood and draw some water.

There is a story I like about Rod and Cav. The story tells you where Rod's heart is. The 2011 World Road Race Championships were held in Copenhagen in September of that year. Mark Cavendish won, adding another line to his *palmarès*. Rod had started planning this coup back in 2008. It was called 'Project Rainbow', and the plot to steal the World Championship had its beginning one quiet night when a few key figures were invited for a meeting.

When they got there, an old woolly cycling jersey was hanging in the room, a jersey with the rainbow hoops of the World Champion. Feel the weight of it, how the poor bastards must have sweated wearing those things. Whose is it, Rod?

It belonged to Tom Simpson, who had been the last British rider to win the Worlds back in 1965, two years before his tragic death on Mont Ventoux. Rod had gone to the Simpson museum in Nottinghamshire to borrow the jersey for the evening. Tom Simpson was almost there in the room with Rod, the man planning for a race years in the future by paying his respects to a ghost of the past. As Brailsford said, this planner does every hand on the clock, especially the hour hand.

And this Tour, the British nook of it, is testimony to the quiet and relentless influence Rod has had over the past decade.

Cav is here of course, though no longer with Team Sky, but so too are lads who came through the house in Tuscany during the same era: Pete Kennaugh, Geraint Thomas and Ian Stannard. They give a strong Ellingworth influence to Team Sky. They are the team's transfusion of tough.

And then there is Chris Froome. You argue that he came from nowhere, that he was teleported from obscurity to the yellow jersey by some alchemy? Hang on.

Back in 2006, Rod was living in Tuscany running the Team GB Under-23 Team out of a modest house on the Via Madonna in Quarrata near Florence. As such, he had a special interest in the Giro delle Regioni. He had a few of his lads riding the race – Geraint Thomas, Ian Stannard, Ben Swift – all good riders and they didn't win a single stage. But they were all curious and talkative about some guy from Kenya who had won two uphill finishes.

'You don't win them races and not be good. If you look at Joe Dombrowski, you look at Pete Kennaugh, you know they both were first and second, not in the same year, in the baby Giro. It's like a rider who's done well at the Tour de l'Avenir, they've got that quality. So it's not like Chris has just gone, "Well here we go." And while Under-23 he won some bloody good bike races.'

And then one evening during the Regioni there was a knock on Rod's door. There he was. The guy, this length of string from Kenya.

'Hi, I'm Chris Froome.'

Rod knew who he was talking to, of course. Not a sparrow falls ... The guy just asked if he might have a chat. So he came in and he sat down, quiet and confident. They talked.

What would happen if I did do this? Or that? All hypotheticals. How would it work within British cycling? Rod explained where he was with the Under-23 project in Italy and what was being done and the young guy nodded a lot and said yeah, yeah this is all good.

'He could see what we were doing in 2006, so there was that group of young road riders; Cav was already kind of starting, wasn't full pro then, but he was winning, we were winning races. We'd won a few races here and there. And it was building and I think he could see that.'

When Froome left he continued to think. He kept in touch with Doug Dailey from British cycling. An acorn had been planted in Froome's mind. Ellingworth would never claim the oak, though.

Of all the people in this team, Rod is the most enjoyable perhaps to stop and spin a yarn with. He talks about people in a way that explains as much about himself as the subjects he describes:

A guy he's thinking might be a good staff member –

'He is emotionally intelligent, great with people, as for the other stuff, the more technical bits, well the sort of planning we do, if I can do it, he can do it.'

Pete Kennaugh and his diversions, as predicted, from Rod's reduced post-Tour schedule –

'I've started now texting him in big, bold letters, capital letters, "STOP, DON'T DO THIS. STICK TO THE PLAN, because ..."'

A Sky rider who he worries might be taking defeat a little too much in his stride –

'Yeah. Is there enough fight in him? Has he got that mean

bastard about him? Which Pete Kennaugh has. Froomey has that edge, you know, as much as he's a nice chap but bloody hell, can he let you have it when he wants to.'

Within Team Sky, Rod is the flesh and blood counterbalance to the science and the technology. Tim Kerrison speaks of how important it is to rely not just on numbers but on the words and thoughts of the riders. Rod Ellingworth likes the science and sees the benefits, he likes and he appreciates a Kerrison or a Steve Peters, but like most great coaches he believes in a little of everything and not too much of anything.

Chris Froome is going to win this Tour de France and it doesn't surprise Rod Ellingworth greatly. He sees guys come and go, riders who get a lot of money quickly in this new cycling world and they are soft before they have won a thing. Froome, for all his politeness and manners, is a tough bastard underneath. Ellingworth knows the need for tough. The British boys have stories that will testify to that.

Rod, with Team GB, was mulling over the team's disappointing showing at the Athens Olympics. Ellingworth took a cold look at every aspect of the team's preparation. He was starting the Under-23 operation in Tuscany with very specific goals in mind. Tuscany, he realised, may have sounded glamorous to some of the kids dreaming of breaking away to *La Grande Boucle*. Ellingworth took care of that notion first. He got everybody together and poured them some cups of reality.

Young cyclists at the time received a flat annual grant of £10,000. Ellingworth cut it to £6000, requiring the kids to live on a budget of £58 a week. If they picked up ten or twenty pounds winning a bonus sprint on a Sunday morning, fine, they could buy their teammates a cup of coffee – but the life of the young cyclist didn't involve much else than stoicism and self-denial.

And before Tuscany? He instituted the Manchester boot camp. Up at 6am, boys, then work from 7am to 7pm. Six weeks of this before you felt one ray of Italian sun warm your face. The young lads had been tagged as elite riders. Ellingworth chalked them down to the more modest category of First. They got cheaper bikes. If they weren't in the gym, on the road or on the track they were learning French or Italian and getting educated. They'd arrive back in the evenings too exhausted to move and would have to prepare their own evening meal. When they got to Tuscany it wasn't much different. They learned that the life of the pro rider is many degrees different from that, say, of the pro footballer.

Rod himself tells a story which, inadvertently I think, defines him. He is a key part of a team which does things differently. Team Sky do things differently in both small ways and in big conspicuous ways. They have a lack of self-consciousness which is sometimes frightening. Rod is old school. You imagine some part of the clockwork nature of Team Sky must run against his grain.

He is speaking about the set-up which the team have used for several years before the World Team Time Trial Championships (the team time trials at the Worlds are not contested by nations but by pro teams). Team Sky like to put down some flooring, erect some clocks, place panelling around the area that they are allotted. Every other team just cordons off an area to work in and starts to get ready.

So, from the very the first year, Team Sky were laughed at. People came by specifically to scoff. Rod jutted the jaw, though. He was adamant that they had to do it like this. 'Ignore everybody,' he would say as the wiseacres leaned over the panelling, asking if it came in a nice pine finish and where was the best place to put the sofa, etc.

'We wanted flooring down so whether you were on a gravel car park or in a grass field or on the side of the road, the flooring gives it the same feel every single time. The surrounding around the rider is the same. There's only one or two of the guys who will be getting into the zone. But it's for them you are doing it.'

Still, it's not a nice job. Highly paid men crawling around on their hands and knees assembling this stuff until they are sweaty, clammy, dirty and red in the face. Tired of hearing the jokes coming at them.

So one day they were setting up for another World Team Time Trial Championships. This time they were the first there. They got a jump putting the stuff together. Bobby Julich, the American coach, was working with Rod. In Team Sky there is no standing upon your rank or pay grade. If there is work to be done, roll up your sleeves, son.

So Rod and Bobby got everything put together in record time.

'There we were on the bus washing our hands and Bobby said, "Whoah, got away with it again, thank God for that."

Rod said, 'What do you mean?'

'Nobody saw me.'

'Nobody saw you what, Bobby?'

'Nobody saw me down on my hands and knees.'

'Bobby, you should be proud that you got down on your hands and knees, you are rolling up your sleeves, showing the other people you are prepared to do the job. You shouldn't worry what other people think. What does it matter what other people think?'

That is Rod Ellingworth.

It must be the upbringing, but he has a constant suspicion of glamour. No fat cat ever impresses him. In the morning of a rest day when the riders take a spin to stretch their limbs, it is often suggested to Rod that he go along with them. There are good reasons for it and it would make a nice snap or news clip: Rod Ellingworth, former Witham Wheeler, out between the superstars and the sunflowers yesterday . . .

He stays behind, though. He feels part of his job is to be around; if there are ten things people need to know or twenty questions they need to ask, he will be around and the team's day will move forward a little bit easier.

'Anyway, I like to get down for breakfast with the mechanics and the carers, not every morning but most mornings, because if somebody from the management team isn't there, it doesn't send out the right message. They should see that you are doing just as much as they are.'

One evening when we arrive at the team hotel they are three beds short for the Team Sky group. That's three people who'll have to drive half an hour up the road to get their kip and half an hour back at the crack of dawn. Rod is first to put his hand up.

These days are long and he talks sometimes to Dave Brailsford about how much the team asks of everybody. Everybody here works harder than they would on any other team. Harder and longer. They are a young team but Rod knows so much is being asked that good people will start falling away, just burnt off the surface. He's thinking about a way of making sure that Sky holds on to its best people.

Often in the car we spoke about doping and at one point he pondered his own career. He wasn't making a fuss about it but he hadn't doped and, like everyone else rowing a boat against the blokes with outboard engines, he didn't get very far. 'I was the same era, more or less, as guys like George Hincapie, Bobby Julich and even David Millar.

'They were good riders, but I felt I trained as hard as they did, I wanted it as much as they did, but they went on to have great careers. I thought about it a lot, why they went so far and why I went nowhere. What I believed is that they were much smarter than me. They trained better, they were cleverer in races and I felt I just wasn't bright enough.'

Rod was filled with doubt over his own intelligence for years. To meet Rod now, who has traditional intelligence to rival his emotional intelligence, this is almost unthinkable. But until the true cause for his competitors getting so much more out of their training and races came to light, his self-confidence was shaken.

Cycling's ultimate short-cut is pharmaceutical. When others took that route fifteen years ago, it hurt Ellingworth. Now, just one Team Sky rider taking that short-cut and getting caught could destroy the team and leave people like Ellingworth wondering what they wanted to do with the rest of their lives. You know Rod's answers on the subject, but you want to torture him anyway because on a Tour with so many ghosts and bad memories you can never have enough reassurance.

'It would be absolutely gut-wrenching, wouldn't it, you know?' he says. 'That's always the fear, isn't it? Oh we've had a few conversations about somebody doing something on their own, and it coming out and it's just, just everything you do or have done it's just . . . ah . . . it'd just be . . .'

Chris Froome once said that he couldn't be left in a room with a teammate who had cheated. Assault charges would follow. He left the rest to your imagination. Rod is more specific. A baseball bat, if you were wondering.

Meanwhile, it's summer and it's France and the former Witham Wheeler has miles to go and promises to keep. When it all ends he has more work to get into, but holidays beckon.

The Isle of Wight. Hitting it at 9am of a morning, taking in a small music festival that will be going on down there. Himself and Jane and their little Robin, Rob Hayles and his wife and their two kids, and a few more friends. A few days of camping and chilling.

You'd never see a fat cat under canvas.

How is it going, Rod? Good, thank you.

They really tried with the post-Tour party this year.

And by Team Sky's standards, it was deemed a notable success. 'Definitely, the best we've ever had,' said Rod Ellingworth.

An upstairs bar in the team hotel was taken over and drinks and very fancy canapés and chocolates were served. I'd been a reluctant participant as the party seemed an occasion best left to those who were genuinely part of the team. But in the end, the Slovenian *soigneurs* Marko Dzalo and David Rozman thrust a bottle of beer into my hand and ensured a late night became a very late one.

Rozman told me again about how highly he regarded Froome and that it wasn't just because he was a damn good cyclist. In Froome he saw a fine human being. We had spoken one day on the Tour and I'd asked Rozman if he believed Team Sky was clean and if he did, what convinced him.

'A small thing,' he said. 'I have worked with cycling teams before this one and I would walk into a room and two riders would just stop talking. That happened many times. In this team, that has never happened. There aren't conversations going on that people need to stop just because you've walked into the room.'

Gary Blem was looking forward to getting back to South Africa and seeing his family. He reminded me one more time about what defines and distinguishes Mark Cavendish. They were working together at the Tour de France for the first time and Cav had just finished second in a bunch sprint.

'Well done,' said Gary, acknowledging a decent effort.

'Gary,' said Cavendish with the kind of post-race passion that is exclusively his, 'don't ever, *ever*, congratulate me on finishing second.'

You live and you learn.

At the nightclub the riders were there with their partners and G Thomas was talking rugby. 'Gatland was right to pick Jonathan Davies before Brian O'Driscoll for that final Lions test in Australia,' he said, and then seemed disappointed that the Irishman in his company was agreeing with him. More than likely just happy G wasn't reaching for that X-ray photo he's convinced no one has seen yet! For almost three weeks, this has been a fountain for banter and you might almost forget that he's shown unimaginable courage in not just finishing this Tour but making a significant contribution to the team. Whatever he earns in his career, he deserves.

Then there's Richie Porte who once examined himself and diagnosed 'small man syndrome'. This condition isn't always helped by alcohol and by the time Richie gets to me, he's several to the wind. It's like his index finger has fallen in love with my sternum. 'You know when people spit at me on a climb and call me a doper, I think of all the journos who accuse me and I get so pissed. I've never done anything wrong. Why should I have to put up with that shit?'

When that first wave of outrage crashes against the sand, Richie's waters go still and conversation flows in a different direction. He's amusing, engaging, fun to be around, and it's not hard to work out why Froome would rather share a room with 'small man syndrome' than bunk alone.

Celebrations are not Dave Brailsford's tipple, for it is the process, not the result, that excites him. If you feel too good about the victory, you lessen your chances of repeating it. So, to get through this long night, he has more than a few drinks.

Some dance to remember, some to forget.

CHAPTER SIXTEEN

'He said the world was an inferno full of darkness and evil, and that there were only two ways of dealing with it. The first was easy and wrong: to accept it and become part of it. The second way was harder and right: you fight it, and recognise those who aren't evil, and help them endure.'

Scheherezade, Arabian Nights

Months after the Tour de France, with the Wiggins–Froome cold war all but forgotten, the two stars made nice to each other at a press conference before the World Road Race Championships in Italy. That was just the public show of *rapprochement*. There was a more meaningful coming together on a Team GB training ride that, despite him being nowhere in sight, had a distinct ring of Brailsford about it.

Back in July, Dave Brailsford decided to accompany the Sky riders out on a rest day training ride in an attempt to pick up the pieces of his team that had been strewn across the Pyrenees the day before. One by one, the riders dropped back to Brailsford for a more honest discussion of their feelings than they ever could have managed out of their saddles. Now, months on, a morning ride was again generating more than just sweat, hunger and leg ache, in the shape of much-needed communication. Only this time, instead of dropping back to get things off their own chests, the riders left the heavy-chested together at the front. One by one, the riders splintered from the eight-man group until only the two golden boys remained, no one to talk to but each other.

'Now, guys you've got to talk,' was the collective message to Froome and Wiggins from the group and, finally, talk they did. It was a step forward on the road to reconciliation, but no one was getting carried away. Such had been the enmity since the 2012 Tour that one harmonious week in Tuscany wasn't going to blow away more than a year's worth of accumulated mistrust. Still, some seeds were sprinkled on what had seemed to be barren ground that week.

Froome will return to the 2014 Tour de France as defending champion and favourite. He will encounter tougher opposition than he did in 2013, not least because Vincenzo Nibali, the Sicilian, has targeted the 2014 race. However, Team Sky believe that they can be far stronger as a team than they were this year. But not without Wiggins.

After the breakdown in relations in the second half of 2012, Team Sky thought the best way forward was to allow them to ride more or less separate programmes. Through the first seven months of 2013 they rode together only once, at the relatively low-profile Tour of Oman. Wiggins dutifully helped Froome to record his first victory of the year; Froome dutifully thanked him. Nothing changed.

Thereafter, they went their separate ways. Froome raced the

Tirreno–Adriatico, Critérium International, Tour de Romandie and Critérium du Dauphiné before tackling the Tour. Wiggins had won Romandie and the Dauphiné the year before, but this year he chose a different route and asked to ride the Giro d'Italia as well. He imagined riding well in the Giro and then showing up for the Tour de France five weeks later in good form.

Injury, sickness and a loss of confidence on wet and dangerous descents destroyed his Giro and, back at home, he needed to rest his sore knee for five days before starting back. He felt he wouldn't be able to get himself 100 per cent fit for the Tour. And that was that. The champion would not be defending his title. Though there was some sympathy for Wiggins, there was also relief within Team Sky because relations between the two leaders were still chilly.

During the Tour, there were many occasions when Wiggins's absence was felt – most keenly at the team time trial in Nice when a narrow defeat would have been a convincing victory had Wiggins been there. That evening on the Promenade des Anglais, the lament around the Sky bus had a recurring theme: 'We could have done with Brad today.' Had he been on his best form, Wiggins would have been alongside Richie Porte in the mountains, helping to control things for Froome.

Once a season begins, everything moves at a frantic pace and there isn't much time for conciliation talks. Once the Tour de France starts, no one, certainly not Brailsford, would have been keen on having such talks during the race.

In the immediate aftermath of Froome's win in Paris,

Wiggins didn't publicly congratulate him and, given the frostiness, that wasn't a surprise. Two weeks later he did, however, acknowledge that Froome had earned the right to lead the team into the 2014 Tour, which was his way of expressing admiration for Froome's performance in winning the race.

They are both stubborn, and Froome wasn't going to read that comment and think everything could now be hunky dory between them. There was a problem, though, that neither seemed able or even inclined to address.

They needed each other.

Froome needs Wiggins in the team for the 2014 Tour because his inclusion will make the team stronger and give Froome a better chance of winning again. Wiggins needs Froome because a man on a Tour de France winner's salary (£3-4 million) can justify his wages only if he actually rides the world's greatest race. Furthermore, Wiggins's targeting of the Giro didn't work out due, in part, to bad weather but that is always more likely to occur in May than during the Tour in July.

Team Sky also learned something about the Giro. After Wiggins departed, Rigoberto Urán was made leader and he rode an excellent race, won a mountain stage and climbed to second place overall in 2013. Few even noticed how well Urán and the team had done in Wiggins's absence. The Giro was just the Giro and second was nowhere.

That experience in Italy would have confirmed for Brailsford something he already sensed. If Wiggins was to do his job properly for the team in 2014, he must ride the Tour de France. And so the diplomatic mission began. Brailsford went to see Wiggins and they spoke about his relationship with Froome and how 2014 might pan out.

Cycling has been Wiggins's life and, in becoming Britain's most decorated rider, he has been a highly dedicated athlete. In the past, however, the dedication was always for himself. That didn't make it easy and because he would have been hurting himself, he didn't take shortcuts. It was true he found it hard to forgive Froome for what he saw as betrayal at the 2012 Tour, but his difficulty in adapting to the role of team rider wasn't solely down to that animosity.

Wiggins wasn't sure he could make all the sacrifices necessary to get himself to peak condition just to help someone else. A year of gruelling training rides day after day after day? Taking yourself to the brink of exhaustion come wind, rain or shine? All that to help somebody else fulfil their dreams while yours remain buckled in your pannier bags? It's a tough ask for anybody, let alone a proud, stubborn, former champion of the Tour de France.

But that still left Brailsford with the question of how the team could get value for the money they were paying Wiggins. Without the Tour de France, it would be impossible. Wiggins then went to Verbier in the French Alps to train at altitude and Brailsford made sure he was there. Given how much he is being paid, Wiggins should, perhaps, just do what he's told. Brailsford's bosses at News Corp would almost certainly subscribe to this view. But Brailsford has a keener understanding of how highly strung the best athletes can be and coercion wasn't going to work with Wiggins. If forced to simply turn up at the Tour and ride for Froome, he might not find the motivation to prepare as thoroughly as he would need to.

They spoke at length and tried to find a way forward.

When it comes to problem-solving, Brailsford doesn't get

wound up by others taking a difficult or even unreasonable position. Instead, he reminds himself that the ultimate goal is not winning the argument, it's winning the Tour de France. The focus is on doing everything to make that more likely to happen. Team Sky need Wiggins in the 2014 team riding for Froome, and doing so of his own volition.

Brailsford gets on well with Wiggins and usually when they talk, they can work things out. The appeal needed to be to Wiggins's intelligence and his sense of fair play and, after Verbier, the Sky boss felt he was getting there. In his discussions with Wiggins, he would have pointed out that the money he'd not given Froome after the 2012 Tour needed to be paid in full. Without that happening, there would never be resolution.

Verbier helped Wiggins get into good shape and he rode at the Tour of Britain to record his victory of the season. That was an important week, as Brailsford brought along Wiggins's old sidekick and mentor Shane Sutton in the hope that the naturally funny Aussie could help the mood within the team. That played to Sutton's strength, and his gentle and not-so-gentle banter got everyone laughing and Brailsford thought it one of the most enjoyable weeks of the season. More importantly, Brad was back in the fold.

Brailsford then went to Monaco to discuss things with Froome. On the surface you might imagine this was the less complicated part of the jigsaw, because Froome is clear headed and fair minded. But he can also be obstinate and he wasn't prepared to accept that everything was suddenly okay just because Wiggins was feeling better. Brailsford appealed to Froome's calculating spirit. What's the ambition? To win the

Tour in 2014. Who would be leader? Chris Froome. Would Froome's chances be helped by having Wiggins as willing *équipier*? Of course.

Froome thought it wrong that he hadn't had his cut from the 2012 prize money.

The money was paid.

The World Championship Road Race was down for the Sunday, but the main event was happening in the meeting rooms of an old Florence building in which Machiavelli once lived. Brian Cookson was taking on Pat McQuaid for the presidency of the UCI. Much had been made of Machiavelli's distinction between politics and morality. The campaign had been vitriolic and stained with carelessly flung battery acid. Both men promised a new beginning for the UCI. In the end, Cookson convinced more people that he was the man to deliver that new beginning.

Once upon a time . . .

Whether a fresh start would be at all possible was a moot point. Cycling has many stakeholders and few are willing to loosen their grip in the name of progress.

The Tour de France and several other races are run by the Amaury Sports Organisation (ASO) and they cut their own deals and make their own rules. The sport has several layers of professional activity and a calendar which is poorly designed and full of silly overlaps and bad planning. Team owners and team sponsors are constantly looking for a fairer shake of the proceeds and better rewards for their riders' success. And the entire caravan travels under the cloud of doping. So when the cycling world gathered to find a World Champion and to elect a new president, it was always likely to come away with more questions than answers.

For Team Sky, though, a third factor was intersecting with the election and the race in Tuscany that weekend. Between the vote and the race the word leaked out about the Jonathan Tiernan-Locke case.

Jonathan Tiernan-Locke, a Team Sky rider, had been sent a letter by the UCI requesting an explanation for anomalous readings in his biological passport data. The readings under question were from a blood sample taken after Tiernan-Locke won the Tour of Britain in 2012, soon before signing for Team Sky. The nitty-gritty facts of the Tiernan-Locke business would be compelling in their own right, but in one key sense they didn't matter at the time. This was Team Sky. This was the wrong sort of drama for a team which proclaims to be at the vanguard of cycling's reform. He was given a period in which to make his response to the request, with a British Cycling official stating that no comment would be made until the case was resolved.

There had been plenty of noise around Tiernan-Locke's reputation before he joined the team and, when it emerged that Sky and Brailsford hadn't properly explored reservations expressed seven months before, sympathy for Brailsford and company was muted. No one was saying Tiernan-Locke was guilty, but Sky should have spent more time working out why some of his rivals at the Tour Méditerranéen considered his performance suspicious.

Geert Leinders had been a mistake, a costly one, but the cycling world expected the centurions at the gate would prevent such a thing happening again. One imagined Team Sky would now vet everybody like vice-presidential candidates in an American election. The timing was almost darkly comic. Here was Brailsford fighting a rearguard action just as cycling was talking about its new beginning.

Once upon a time indeed . . .

The case would be a considerable embarrassment for Team Sky and for Brailsford, but more critically it would come at a time when cycling stood at a crossroads. The sport needed to reform itself in all sorts of ways. If Team Sky could gather the respect and admiration to match their success, they would be big players in determining the future of cycling. If Team Sky kept shooting themselves in the foot, that future might not happen at all. So Team Sky had come to Tuscany with two things in mind. The World Championships was one, of course. But also more media massaging.

In January 2013 in Mallorca the team had entertained a large swathe of the British media. The key element of the trip as far as Sky were concerned was a three-hour media presentation on what the team were about. The first question asked was by Dave Brailsford himself as he began the PowerPoint presentation.

'How are you going to succeed in winning admiration, if people can't be sure you are clean?'

That established the theme for the next 179 minutes. How would Team Sky become the most admired sports team in the world? One imagined that the first thing they needed to do was stop talking about becoming the most admired sports team in the world, but there is something almost endearing about the manner in which Brailsford wears his ambition on his sleeve. 'Call me naïve, but . . .' he says occasionally, and there have been plenty of times when he has been.

So the PowerPoint presentation aimed to hose down that chorus of overheated former pros who pronounce on everything from their media talking shops without actually being familiar with the scientific approach the sport has now taken. This was a particular bugbear of Tim Kerrison's. Sky talked of the philosophy of marginal gains and how it worked. Click, next slide. Their faith and investment in sports science. Click. The benefits of state-of-the-art equipment. Click. Coaches that know the human body as much as they do the sport. Click. The injustice of the growing tendency to establish guilt by performance. Click, click, click. Over three hours Team Sky placed themselves front and centre of cycling's battle to escape the past.

Upon review, Brailsford and company felt that the session had worked well. So in Tuscany in September 2013 it was planned to offer a similar session to the Italian media, who are among the most caustically critical of the Team Sky operation. After Froome's victory on Mont Ventoux, Italy's foremost sports daily, *La Gazzetta dello Sport*, had its physiology expert proclaiming Froome's power output incredibly high and lacking credibility.

Sky has a sister station in Italy (and another in Germany), so bringing the Italians around wasn't going to be purely an academic exercise. Team Sky's ownership is as follows: 60 per cent is owned by BSkyB, the British broadcasting arm of News Corp, 25 per cent is owned by Sky Italia and the remaining 15 per cent belongs to News Corp itself.

Cycling is an unusual sport. It clearly doesn't have the mass casual following that Premiership football enjoys. For many people, cycling at an elite level barely even exists beyond the three weeks when the Tour de France generates its pretty images and epic narrative for millions of viewers. Yet it is a sport with huge grassroots participation and those who take an interest often do so with a passion that means opinions aren't merely expressed. They are fired as bullets.

Sky Broadcasting would be the first to concede that they get a good deal commercially with their finger in the cycling pie. Their involvement in city-centre Sky Rides is estimated to have put 750,000 people back on bikes in the first two years of operation alone. Coupling these with a pro cycling team is a branding master class. The popular success of the GB track cycling team has been matched on the roads. If people can believe the story then the possible returns are huge and Sky could find itself at the popular heart of a major sport – certainly a change from perceptions of it as the sugar daddy enabler to the corrupt Babylon of Premiership football.

But every time the word doping gets mentioned in a media report or suggested by Google after just about any cycling search term, the value of cycling as a business takes a hit. When the Tiernan-Locke story broke, Sky's bosses wanted to know how this story could have got into the public domain when it was just a preliminary letter sent by the UCI to its rider. Cycling is cycling. Tyres puncture and stories leak. They had bigger problems than sourcing the leak. Their anxiety confirmed the weight of the story, though. Rule number one in such cases: mind your back.

In that sense Sky are no different from so many other

sponsors in the game. There is a bottom line. There must be a return. No matter how much people at the upper echelons of the company like cycling and enjoy it, if the tainted elite cycling world continues to contaminate Sky's brand image, well, perhaps the experiment will have to finish.

For example, the German and Italian spin-offs are welcomed by Sky. But, if coverage in Italy is always to be coupled with the sort of colourful accusations which the domestic media specialises in, then Brailsford's challenge of becoming the most admired sports team in the world is doomed. Tiernan-Locke had received only an enquiring letter but he'd provided the media with another big stick with which to beat Team Sky, thus turning himself into something more than the small fish he really was.

The patience of sponsors, any sponsors, will always be finite. And cycling lives off the generosity of its sponsors.

Those sponsors get their money's worth. For less than £10 million a year you can give a pro team the same name as your company. The Team Sky deal represents excellent value. Estimates of Sky's broadcasting contribution to the team in 2011 put the figure at about £6 million. The annual report and accounts for that year suggest that BSkyB spent a total of £1.2 billion on marketing. The involvement in Team Sky represented considerably less than 1 per cent of that outlay.

The deals come at a discount because cycling is a minefield of scandal and cynicism. What happens if a team with your firm's name becomes synonymous with cheating?

Cycling's difficulty is cynicism as much as it is drugs. When 2013 produces a winner like Chris Froome, a healthy sport should be looking at pushing its market into Africa.

When a teammate of Froome's is asked about irregularities in his blood passport, though, people think it is 1999 all over again. In 1998 cycling had the Festina affair. It promised 1999 was the new beginning. It was. It was the beginning of the Armstrong machine, the most cynical doping operation any sport has ever seen.

In 2012, the Armstrong Report opened everybody's eyes to what a noxious sham all that talk of reform had been. Was 2013 a mirror image of 1999? I don't think so, but it would be hard to blame fans and sponsors for standing back from cycling.

What was the financial impact of the Lance years? Well, Lance did very well for himself but the sport as a whole has been retarded in terms of its own potential. Sponsorship is vital to top-level cycling teams, but because reputable brands suffer the risk of fire damage if associated with a scandal, they pay less than they would otherwise do. Interestingly, major global brands like Nike and Budweiser who backed Armstrong as an individual never got seriously involved in the sport in Europe – the cockpit where Armstrong made his name.

They still got burned in the end but their instincts were probably correct.

In 2013 Rabobank, a long-standing team sponsor, announced that they'd had enough. 'International cycling is rotten, including some of its highest institutions,' said Rabobank's chief financial officer Bert Bruggink, bringing to an end a seventeen-year association with the sport.

Rabobank had long spoken about zero tolerance in their team. It emerged, though, that in 2007 the team had purchased a brand spanking new Sysmex XE–2100 machine, the same as that used by anti-doping authorities, to measure their own blood cell counts. Testimony given by Michael Rasmussen, a former Rabobank rider, suggested that Geert Leinders had used the machine and that Leinders had, among other things, stored Dynepo – a form of pharmaceutical EPO – in the fridge on the team bus.

Leinders is still under investigation by Belgian authorities.

Cycling was fortunate that the Californian consumer goods manufacturer Belkin eventually stepped into the breach after Rabobank's exit, but it won't always be like that unless reform is visible and effective. Belkin began their connection with cycling by talking about zero tolerance. Now though, all of a sudden, the market leaders in zero tolerance are struggling to explain themselves.

The news about Tiernan-Locke came when team owners were campaigning for radical changes to what is a conservative business environment. Ideally this would involve simplifying the racing calendar at World Tour level, so the three Grand Tours and a selection of other races would attract the top teams and give the season some continuity. There would also be revenue sharing to make pay structures more competitive.

As it is, cycling works in a peculiar way. Teams are beholden to major sponsors for most of their income. As payback, teams operate under the names of sponsors. This in turn means that when the sponsor changes, goes broke or withdraws because of a fresh scandal, the team virtually ceases to exist to the fans.

Those teams, despite raising the bulk of their cash from sponsors, receive a very small slice of the big pie in return for success. Chris Froome won €450,000 for coming home first in the Tour de France in 2013. By the standard of major world sporting events that is small beer. Factor in that this is a uniquely gruelling event and that Froome has to share the money out with his riders and staff, and the system seems distinctly feudal. Of course, Froome's contract with Team Sky will allow reward for success but in broad picture terms, Froome will be paid less than many Premiership footballers.

He received less than half what a golfer gets for winning a middle-ranking event on the PGA Tour in America. Then his team will receive little financial reward for his success. The appearance fee for a team in the Tour de France is €55,000.

The total prize money pool for the Tour de France comes to roughly €2 million, a sum which includes payments to the various jersey winners and €8000 a day for the stage winner and so on. Eight thousand euros for winning a stage is derisory. The other Grand Tours – the Giro d'Italia and the Vuelta a España – dangle prize money of €1.38 million and €1.1 million respectively, so the derision is at least multilingual. According to the Australian Financial Review, writing in the summer of 2013, the Tour includes a paltry further €1.6 million in allowances for participating teams.

Even in macro terms, cycling continues to underperform as a business. The Tour de France, for instance, takes in just €200 million for global broadcasting rights for a three-week race which bills itself as the third biggest sporting event in the world. Analysts place that figure at a fraction of the Tour's earning potential. The Tour is beamed to 190 out of all 196 countries. These rights fees account for 60 per cent of the Tour's income. By comparison the 2011–12 cycle of Olympic activity generated $3.91 billion in rights income.

The total budget for Team Sky, considered to be the Manchester City of the game but probably more fairly bracketed within the top four or five teams in terms of budget, is estimated to be in the £25-30 million mark. That sort of money would buy a single half-decent Premiership footballer, but not a player from the very top echelon. In cycling it makes Team Sky the envy of most other outfits.

Again, compare. Sky's modest sponsorship has brought two Tour de France wins. To be one of the sponsors in The Olympic Partner (TOP) programme for a winter games/summer games cycle costs about $100 million. Eleven TOP sponsors generated $957 million for London. There are a further three tiers of sponsors beneath the TOP strand. That's forty-four more companies squeezing their corporate logos into the picture.

So for cycling's sponsors and teams, the payback is as modest as the input. So the spin had better be good. Cycling, however, has a perverse and contrary constituency.

On the Tour in 2013, one of Froome's principal rivals was Alberto Contador – former winner of the Tour who had since served a ban for discrepancies in his biological passport. One of the oddities of the spite shown against Froome was the general tolerance shown for Contador – the Barabbas Syndrome. In the Bible when the crowd are offered the choice to free Jesus or Barabbas – a known criminal – their resentment of Jesus causes them to cry, 'No, not him! Give us Barabbas!' The Tour creates an unlikely rerun. The mob were absolving Contador, the known sinner, while calling for Froome's crucifixion. (Contador's boss is the Dane, Bjarne Riis, who has admitted to having won the 1996 Tour de France while on EPO and other drugs, but who remains a leading figure in the sport.)

Contador rode for Saxo–Tinkoff in 2013. Soon after the Tour ended, the second part of that sponsorship arrangement broke down when Oleg Tinkoff took his cheque book away. More confusion for the casual fan.

Dave Brailsford's burden goes beyond the corridors of the velodrome in Manchester and the team's house and office on the Promenade du Soleil in Nice. By advertising his team's virtue so aggressively, he seemed set to put Sky (the team and the business) at the centre of the reform and growth of the sport. When Brailsford fails, however, he doesn't get credit for his efforts and his ambitions. He gets crucified.

Nail Brailsford. Give us Riis!

Though he tries not to show it, this gets to Brailsford. He knows his record in the sport and insists he is 100 per cent clean. There is no evidence, not a scintilla, to counter that. Yet he can often feel the vibe of resentment rippling towards him and the team. Call him naïve, but he doesn't understand it.

I imagine Dr Steve Peters talking to him, asking him to consider where this resentment comes from. Of course, most of those who work in the sport have links to its past. Ex-riders who once doped or team bosses who, if they didn't organise the blood transfusions, looked the other way when someone else did. When Geert Leinders got into trouble because of his time at Rabobank, and UCI asked Tiernan-Locke some accusatory questions, this was manna from heaven to many traditionalists in the sport.

In public his bosses at BSkyB speak glowingly of the environment Brailsford has created at Team Sky, but they continue to demand a return on their investment. Namely, success. And they like their success neat; that is, without any contaminated mixer. They understand scepticism goes with the territory, but when a Leinders happens or when they are told that the UCI wants an explanation from Tiernan-Locke, they are not so understanding. It is Brailsford who then feels the heat.

Having set themselves as the most zealous zero tolerance unit in the game, Team Sky have unwittingly fallen into a rivalry with the Garmin team – who spearhead the truth and reconciliation movement within cycling. Jonathan Vaughters, Garmin's Brailsford, has been a leading voice in calling for cycling reform and it is fair to say that Vaughters has occasionally got under Brailsford's skin more than a little.

The difficulty for Team Sky is that every failure of the zero tolerance policy gets written up in larger print than a failure in an environment which says let's forgive and ... not forget ... but learn and move on.

At the end of 2013, Team Sky, despite their ambition and their success on the road, had a reputation that was all shot through by snipers. They had two very highly paid stars and a roster of ambitious young men behind them. Keeping all those plates spinning was going to be impossible. The team had lost ground and lost influence in the battle to reform cycling both financially and ethically. They were no nearer to becoming the most admired sports team on earth.

They had won two Tour de France titles back to back within four years of becoming a team, a monumental achievement. The great smoking slag-heap of cycling's decades of failure and mistrust loomed over that monument, though. There is no public relations spin which will shift that dark mountain. It's a job for shovels and backbone, a job that will take years.

Cycling's problem has always been the search for something

easier than getting the hands blistered by the shovel. There are no shortcuts and lots of backsliding on the road to reform.

It's not certain that the job can ever be completed. Cycling on the old continent has its past but, more than that, there is an ambivalence to doping. I have read and re-read the thoughts of Antoine Blondin – the late French novelist and sports columnist for *L'Équipe* – on how traditional fans of the sport respond to those who dope:

'In a rider's life there are moments and places where circumstances require that he transcend himself. Each struggles to face up to that obligation. As sports fans we prefer to dream about angels on wheels, Simon Pures somehow immune to the uppers and downers of our own pill-popping society.

'My own opinion is that there is, all the same, a certain nobility in those who have gone down into lord knows what hell in quest of the best of themselves. We might feel tempted to tell them that they should not have done it. But we can remain, nevertheless, secretly proud of what they have done. Their wan, haggard looks are, for us, an offering.'

The new beginning, hopefully, is arriving. Maybe not quite 'Once upon a time . . .', but a consensus is forming. Doping is wrong and it will not be tolerated. Testing is better. Many teams are ethical, and Sky certainly is part of this group. But there are dissenters, some of whom could be inside your tent, and while others take the long road to full reform, they still seek shortcuts.

Team Sky have the appetite for success. That's been proven.

Only time will tell if they have the hunger for anything beyond that.

CHAPTER SEVENTEEN

'A phone call should be a convenience to the caller, not an inconvenience to the called.'

Mokokoma Mokhonoana

Alarms don't just ring in the morning.

It was a Thursday afternoon, late in September, three days before the World Championship Road Race in Tuscany, and the press agency report was nondescript in every respect but one. Jonathan Tiernan-Locke, one of the Team Sky riders selected for Team GB for Sunday's road race, had pulled out of the team and would be replaced by another Sky rider, Luke Rowe. According to the first agency report, Tiernan-Locke's withdrawal was for an 'unspecified reason'.

Some PR person had messed up. Unspecified? That was a bit cryptic. Why unspecified? Unspecified to whom? By whom? He wasn't a footballer who had played badly in a training five-a-side or strained his groin the day before the game. He wasn't Lord Lucan, he hadn't just vanished. After a few hours there would be a corrective update, some hidden hand trying to erase suspicion. Tiernan-Locke had pulled out because he wasn't riding well enough to help Chris Froome win the rainbow jersey of world champion. The rider posted a tweet.

'Was sorry I had to withdraw from the worlds line up, just don't have the form to help the lads there. Good luck to team GB though.'

Hmmm. Too late. The alarm had sounded. You can't unring that bell.

This new version was just about plausible because Tiernan-Locke had endured a terrible first season with Team Sky. Within the team his name was rarely mentioned. Like the aunt hidden away in the attic, no one let on he was part of the family. But why hadn't this poor form been mentioned in the first instance? He didn't lose his form after learning of his selection. He never had it. Why did Tiernan-Locke wait until so late in the day to decide that this poor form, which had coloured his entire season, meant he wouldn't be able to do himself justice in Tuscany? Unspecified. That was the word of the day. The petard upon which the PR exercise was hoisted.

That Thursday evening I was in London speaking with a group of cycling fans, mostly corporate guys working in the City. Three of them in turn asked about Tiernan-Locke and the unspecified reason for his withdrawal from Team GB. They thought something was up. As the Inspector Clouseau of cycling, I felt I should have had an answer for them. I didn't, but at least mine wasn't the only suspicious mind. The more I thought about it, the more I sensed that this smelt more fishy than an anchovy's armpit.

Next day I rang Dave Brailsford. He was in Tuscany. He

didn't pick up. Slight relief for me, as this was going to be a tough call. I left a message saying there was something I needed to check. I knew things would have been fraught in Italy with the Cookson/McQuaid shootout cum election going down the following day and the ongoing Froome/Wiggins peace process still at a delicate stage, but it was still unusual for Brailsford not to return the call.

Time spent on the Armstrong case had led to relationships with people committed to anti-doping. People with the inside track. Drugs wonks. Deep Throats. They continue to be helpful. Calls are picked up. Questions are answered.

Curiouser and curiouser, as we often say while exploring the shady wonderland of doping. I called people in other teams, sources close to the dark heart of the Union Cycliste Internationale (UCI) and people involved in the anti-doping movement. There *was* a story behind Tiernan-Locke's withdrawal.

According to one source, the rider had been sent a letter by the UCI asking him to explain an irregularity in his biological passport. Another source simply knew that a Team Sky rider had some kind of issue related to a discrepancy in his biological passport. Some anti-doping people feared the case was being used as a political tool in the UCI presidential election.*

Here's what I put together.

Earlier that week a letter had been sent from the UCI's headquarters in Aigle, Switzerland, to Tiernan-Locke.

---

*The thinking was that as Jonathan Tiernan-Locke was a British cyclist riding for a British team, an anti-doping case against him would destroy the notion that Brian Cookson came from a country (GB) with no link to cycling's doping culture. The sources said 'political tool'. They meant 'ice pick to Cookson's skull'.

Because he had ridden in a lower-tier continental team, Endura, he had not been part of the biological passport system for most of 2012. This changed after he won the Tour of Britain in September, when it was public knowledge he would ride with Team Sky in 2013.

He was tested in Manchester towards the end of the year. Systematic blood testing started from 1 January 2013, when he officially joined Team Sky and became a WorldTour rider. These tests would establish his baseline values and allow him to be part of the bio-passport system. Towards the end of 2013, a panel of three experts came to the conclusion there was a discrepancy in Tiernan-Locke's values. Hence the letter.

Such a letter reflects serious concern and can be sent only when all three members of the panel, each assessing the blood values independently of the other two, agree the results are suspicious. If one analyst disagrees then there's no letter. It may be that the panel decide to 'target test' the rider whose blood values give rise for concern but are not sufficiently irregular for the panel to need an explanation.

Ironically, the outlier blood value for which an explanation was needed came from a test undergone in late 2012. That is, when it was known that Tiernan-Locke would be joining Team Sky but had not yet done so. Only by establishing base-line values for Tiernan-Locke through 2013 were the UCI panel able to deem the 2012 result suspicious. Furthermore, his race results during 2013 were not those of a rider bene-fiting from performance-enhancing drugs. If he had doped he was entitled to a refund.

In one important respect, I was in a difficult position. The letter to Tiernan-Locke was the first step in a drawn-out process. After receiving it, he had three weeks to provide an explanation for the discrepancy. His explanation would then be considered by the three-man panel who had sent the original letter. They could accept his explanation and that would be it. No further action necessary. Or they could choose not to accept it and then the case would go before a panel of eleven experts who would decide whether or not the rider deserved to be sanctioned.

There have been many cases of riders asked to explain a discrepancy similar to Tiernan-Locke's and, because the explanation was accepted, the case never became public. According to the UCI's protocols, the initial letter is a private matter between the governing body and the rider, and only in the event of the three-man panel not accepting the rider's explanation will he be charged and a case initiated against him. Then it will become public.

But the UCI's protocols were their business, not my concern. Their policy back in the dark days, to warn riders about suspicious tests or blood values, as they did most notoriously in the cases of Lance Armstrong and Tyler Hamilton, was one I despised. What did it achieve, other than to alert cheats they were sailing close to the wind? 'Thanks, guys,' and off the dopers went to plot a new course.

So much for the UCI and protocol.

My concern was journalism.

For sure, there was the question of fairness to Tiernan-Locke and I understood the argument that his reputation could be damaged by a story which in the end might not result in an investigation. The fight for a clean sport, though, is a fight for transparency. For me this was a story that should be told and it wasn't just about Jonathan Tiernan-Locke. If and when he got the all clear, the story would become a footnote and a testament to a more enlightened system.

As important as it is was to discover whether the UCI believed he'd competed clean in 2012, the case also had ramifications for Team Sky. Simply put, did the team have the wherewithal to run a clean programme? After Geert Leinders, how had Sky got itself into this position? For many of us in the cheap seats, Leinders hovered behind Team Sky like Banquo's ghost. For the principals, however, it often seemed like they were too busy to notice.

In his meeting with staff members on the night before the Tour began in Corsica, Dave Brailsford spoke briefly about how the team should deal with the media. The important thing was for everyone to sing from the same hymn sheet and this would be best achieved by the boss himself handling most of the enquiries. What often happens, he said, is that the journalists not getting change out of him go to Tim [Kerrison] or Rod [Ellingworth] in search of satisfaction. So, to avoid unpleasantness, Brailsford thought it better that he did most of the talking.

Of course, at the end of a race, journalists would naturally go to the *directeur sportif* about how things had unfolded on the road and that was fine. The *DS* was best placed to answer those questions. Brailsford asked his men to be polite in their dealings with the media and said he wanted the team to be open and transparent. But then the proviso: he wanted the team to stay in control.

Perhaps no one else on the team bus that evening paid

much attention to that little piece of advice, but it sent a small shiver down my spine. What was I doing on this side of the fence, listening to these Clintonesque definitions of openness and transparency? Had I become part of the Team Sky's world of controlled controllables? There was no shortage of advice on this question from those on social media. All I had to do was tap the Twitter icon on my iPhone and feel the warmth of human kindness.

> July 10: @SlapshotJC wrote – What was the price for David Walsh to sell out. How can the most insistent and vocal Journo of the last 20 years not see what's going on?
> July 10: @smnb – that's because David Walsh got what he always wanted, an invite to the inner circle.
> July 14: @mikkber – @DavidWalshST Do you still believe this fairytale? Or maybe Murdoch tells you to.
> July 15: @phanley55 – David you've become Sky's bitch. Seriously thought you had more sense.
> July 15: @Digger_Forum – In order for Walsh to have any doubts, Froome would need to wheelie up Alpe d'Huez while signing breasts and on his mobile.
> July 23: @eamonolenin – So D Walsh of the Sunday Times (prop. R Murdoch) investigated Team Sky (prop. R Murdoch) and gave them the OK? #laughter.
> August 14: @Mackannovic – @DavidWalshST is @SkySportsWTS tv slot your reward for doing the PR job for Team Sky over the past months #companyman.

Before accepting the invitation to live and look within Team Sky, I imagined there would be this reaction from some quarters (above is just a brief sample of the thoughts of my correspondents) but I never really saw the difficulty. If the organisation I work for thought that I was that easily purchased and influenced, I would never have been employed by them in the first place. If I sensed that such was their view I would have resigned and gone elsewhere long ago. We are adults and professionals, though. If – after a lifetime of fighting for transparency and honesty in cycling – the top team in the sport was inviting me to come in and look wherever I wanted to look, I would be failing as a journalist not to pick up my magnifying glass and deerstalker and join them.

The most frightening thing, ironically, was the prospect of not finding anything. To take the abuse and the insults to my integrity and then give Team Sky a broadly clean bill of health was going to be grist to the mill of the online detractors. That's how it panned out however, and I had finished the coverage of the Tour de France with a long piece in the *Sunday Times* expressing my view that Chris Froome was a winner in whom we could believe. For some, this expression of belief in Froome was treachery.

Now on the Saturday, the day before the World Championship Road Race, I called Dave Brailsford who was still in Tuscany. Again he didn't pick up. This time the message conveyed a lot more urgency. Deadlines have a habit of curing awkwardness or embarrassment.

'Dave, I need to speak to you about something really important. I'm writing a story for tomorrow's *Sunday Times* and it's vital I get a reaction from you.'

Not long after that he called me back. I told him what I knew. He was calm but unhappy that I'd found out. I had the sense that how I had found out might be a significant issue within Team Sky. 'How did you come to hear this? As far as I know, this process is supposed to be totally confidential at this point.' Such is the way of damage limitation exercises, they begin with witch hunts.

Brailsford was shocked that the Tiernan-Locke letter was quite common knowledge among those with a passing awareness of the UCI's political corridors.

'Okay,' he said, 'officially Jonathan Tiernan-Locke withdrew himself. And obviously we brought Luke [Rowe] in, and carried on, so I can't really comment any further than that. So I think probably the best port of call would be Andrew McQuaid [Tiernan-Locke's agent].'

I asked him if he knew the reason for the rider's withdrawal.

'Well, I can't comment at the minute. Let's put it that way.'

'Why can't you comment?'

'Well, the process here is that an individual would be informed there was a reason for suspicion, and they would be informed personally and it wouldn't be public. At that point, an individual has the right to explain themselves in confidence. And the way the system works, if the explanation is accepted, it's "Okay, fair enough, we accept that reasoning, thanks very much, carry on." And there is no issue. On the other hand if the explanation is not accepted and there is a case to answer, then the other stakeholders and the press would be informed.

'Our society is based on the presumption of innocence, and beyond that I don't want to comment.'

I put it to Brailsford that if the information I'd received

about the letter to Tiernan-Locke was false he would tell me. He agreed he would, leaving it at that. It was true: the letter had been sent.

This was Saturday. The story would stand up. On Sunday things only got worse for Team Sky however.

In foul conditions, the team riders performed dismally in the World Road Race. Josh Edmondson and Steve Cummings crashed on roads slickened by relentless rain. They at least had some excuse. After giving the impression that he would welcome an offer of marriage from Chris Froome at the midweek press conference, Bradley Wiggins left Froome standing at the altar in the rain. Wiggins struggled at the back of the pack for some time before abandoning soon after the halfway mark. He headed for the team bus like a bride going home to mother. His only bit of luck was that he wasn't injured in the stampede.

The rest of the team surrendered one after another and the bus filled quickly with sodden cyclists. The early efforts had taken a toll, and so too had the conditions. Froome gave up the fight with 100km of the 270km race still remaining. 'I think the only two guys who actually did anything on the GB side were Cav and Luke Rowe,' he said. 'I'd say they were the only ones who pulled their weight, myself included.'

Team GB manager Rod Ellingworth was brutally frank. The willingness of his troops to dismount and take shelter from the storm troubled him.

'We should be very disappointed. The lads' attitude wasn't where it needs to be, to be honest. I'm not sure they really took this on thinking it was going to be as hard as it actually was. Chris said he struggled with the cold and the rain, but it is the same for everybody. That's what makes the Worlds what it is.

'All of them sat on the bus with a hundred kilometres to go is very disappointing. Luke [Rowe] and Cav [Mark Cavendish] were average, the other guys were well below average. I'm sure Brad will be disappointed with his performance. It is not as if he didn't have the form. He had the same problem as he had in the Giro: he couldn't get down the hill, went out the back and was gone.'

After the bikes were washed down, the cars loaded up and everyone in Team GB went their separate ways, there was still the problem of what to do about Jonathan.

Born in Devon, Tiernan-Locke was first noticed riding mountain bikes. He achieved some success and became part of a new generation of riders reaching the professional level via this new form of the sport. At eighteen he switched to the road and like so many aspiring professionals, he took himself off to France, and rode for the amateur team UV Aube. His results were enough to earn him a place on the British U23 team at the World Championships.

After UV Aube, he rode for another French team, CC Etupes, and achieved decent results. This was 2005 but after making a strong start at CC Etupes in eastern France, Tiernan-Locke's career was derailed by illness. He fell victim to what seemed a nasty strain of Epstein-Barr virus, a condition whose mildly exotic name hides the fact that most adults suffer from it at some point or other.

'One day I started coming down with a cold,' Tiernan-Locke told *Cyclingnews*. 'That turned into flu and then it became the worst strain of flu I'd ever had. It just got worse. Then my immune system broke down. I had a skin disease. I was literally falling apart.'

The team wanted him to continue racing but he was in no condition to do so and after a month of misery he returned to England. 'I turned my back on the sport. I went to university [Bristol] and thought about another career. I put on two stone, drank, partied and didn't touch my bike. Keeping active for me was walking home from the pub pissed.'

For three years he rode his luck in college and surfed on sofas and lived the life but cycling crooked its finger to him eventually. He got a job in Colin Lewis Cycles shop in Paignton, Devon and in the July of 2007, he stood with colleagues and customers and watched the Tour de France unfold on television. Tiernan-Locke saw himself as a climber and he watched in wonder as riders he'd once competed against rode the Tour's great mountain stages. He wanted to get back. He'd train over the winter and be back in shape for the start of the new season.

He was as good as his word.

In March 2008 the *Bristol Evening Post* carried an unobtrusive report on cycling. It was noted among other things that Bristol University student Jonathan Tiernan-Locke, riding for the Plowman Craven team, had won the second springtime pursuit race of the season. That encouraged him, but the gods were just toying with him. Soon after, Plowman Craven went bust. To continue his comeback, he switched to the Sport Beans Wilier team and finished a creditable ninth in the Abstraction Lincoln Grand Prix. Then there was an accident with a horse that set him back. You get the drift.

But on the deck of this sinking vessel stood John Herety, a former European pro. He was *directeur sportif* at the Rapha Condor team and he remembered Tiernan-Locke back when the young rider from Devon had made the British U23 team. He offered him a place in the Rapha team for 2011 and at the age of 25, the rider at last had the opportunity to show he could compete against pros. Rapha was a relatively small team but well enough organised and they could get into some of the better races.

At the end of season, Tiernan-Locke won the mountains jersey and finished fifth overall in the Tour of Britain. That won him a place on the stronger Endura team who would campaign in Europe and offered him a bigger stage. It didn't take long for Tiernan-Locke to show he could compete successfully at a higher level. On the second weekend of February 2012, Tiernan-Locke won two stages and overall victory in the Tour Méditerranéen. A week later he won the second stage and overall victory at the Tour du Haut Var, a race he had won as an amateur seven years before.

Through the eyes of his fellow riders in those two races, this was a 27-year-old who had come from nowhere to emphatically beat them in the mountains. They weren't just disappointed. Some were disgusted. How could this 'unknown' rider from a lower-tier Pro Continental team beat guys from elite WorldTour teams? *L'Equipe's* reporter at these early season races inhaled the scepticism.

'Are we in the presence of a champion or a chimera? Tiernan-Locke can only be one or the other in order to win five races in a row [two stages and overall at Tour Méditerranéen, second stage and overall at Tour du Haut Var]? He's part of a team from the third division, a category where the riders don't have to submit to biological monitoring, via the blood passport programme of the Union Cycliste Internationale.

'What do his peers think? With the microphone on, not much. But with the tape recorder turned off, they express some deep doubts.'

L'Equipe wasn't the only refuge for those wishing to unload their suspicion. It could also be found on social media outlets. The rider himself was aware of what was being said. 'I've heard the rumours, and the suspicion,' he said in that March 2012 interview with *Cyclingnews*. 'I've heard it all. I don't know what to say other than I'll do whatever it takes to show people, so I'll be doing weekly, or bi-weekly, blood tests. Like I said, whatever it takes.

'I can't let things like that get to me. There were comments made but I think a lot of it is sour grapes but it still does piss me off.'

He went on to say that if he was guilty of anything it was that he had in the past engaged in the same rumour-mongering that he was now a victim of. 'In the past, I've been guilty of that. Laughing at performances when I don't know what's fact or not but when it happens to you ... It will make me look at other riders differently in the future and if I've learnt something it's that I wouldn't be as critical as other people.'

Finally, he reiterated his intention of undergoing voluntary blood-testing. 'Whether they're weekly or bi-weekly, I don't know yet. I just want to remove any doubt.'

General manager of the Endura team Brian Smith confirmed that when Tiernan-Locke's performances were questioned, the rider volunteered for blood tests. 'I am one hundred per cent certain he is clean,' said Smith. 'He was the one pushing me last year to get him on the biological passport when he heard there were rumours after he won a couple of big races.'

Of course, the UCI could not change their rules to accommodate Tiernan-Locke. He wasn't in the top league and so could not be part of the bio-passport scheme. But this wouldn't remain the case for long. WorldTour teams Garmin and Sky wanted him.

Wishing to have a closer look, Sky invited Tiernan-Locke to a training camp in Tenerife in early April. Before that, he had been down to Girona for blood and physiological testing with Team Garmin. Any rider being seriously considered by Garmin has to undergo blood and physiological testing before a deal can be done. Ideally the rider shows up the morning after he's ridden well in a race, so his prospective employers can see his blood values when on top form.

On 26 March Tiernan-Locke turned up at Garmin's European headquarters in Girona where he had a blood test, did an hour's intensive effort on a stationary bike and then had another blood test. The first blood test gives some basic values, the physical effort offers a reading of the rider's physiological capacity and the second blood test gives a value that will be skewed by dehydration.

If blood values rise sharply when dehydrated, it may be because the rider has taken saline solution to dilute their blood concentrations for the first test.

Tiernan-Locke's blood results from that day's testing were normal. His performance on the bike suggested good but not outstanding physiological capacity. A solid B-grade but not the A needed to win races on the WorldTour. The rider explained he felt run down and Garmin weren't put off. They wanted him back for a second round of testing and preferably when he was riding well and not run down.

A week later Tiernan-Locke went to Tenerife with Team Sky. They knew he'd been to Garmin for testing and that the American team was still interested in him. That meant there was nothing irregular about his test results. Both Brailsford and Rod Ellingworth knew Rapha's *DS* John Herety and Julien Winn who had worked with Tiernan-Locke at Endura. From conversations with both, they harboured no doubts about the rider's ethics.

Had Garmin manager Jonathan Vaughters been aware of the scepticism surrounding Tiernan-Locke after the Tour Méditerranéen he wouldn't have given it that much credence. He had been through this with Ramunas Navardauskas, the young Lithuanian whom Garmin wanted to sign in 2010. He had won so many U23 races in France that many of those he was beating, and others, muttered under their breath that they were sure he had to be doping. Even riders within his own team told Vaughters not to touch Navardauskas. Such is the fear and loathing in cycling post Lance.

Garmin's boss didn't go along with the consensus, so he did what he always does. He let the rider know he would be interested in having him on the team but a final decision would be made only after the team ran some blood and physiological testing. His blood values were entirely normal, and his physiological testing suggested he was an extremely talented bike rider.

Following the initial test results, Garmin waited for Navardauskas to perform well in a race and then arranged for him to travel immediately to Girona. The day is well planned. The rider is picked up at the airport and does the first blood test before he is taken to breakfast. While digesting his meal, the rider finds out what the contract might look like should everything run smoothly. Then, the power test.

At all times, there's someone from Garmin in his company and straight after the power test comes the second blood test. Results from the two blood tests are set against each other. Again, the results showed very normal blood values and extraordinary power output. Vaughters satisfied himself, as much as any team boss could, that Ramunas Navardauskas was both highly talented and clean. He signed him.

Vaughters wanted to get Tiernan-Locke back for a second round of testing, preferably on the day after he'd finished a race in which he'd performed well. They tried but always something cropped up. Tiernan-Locke kept winning, though, adding the midsummer Tour of Alsace to his early-season victories in the south of France. He remained on Garmin's radar.

If there's one thing worse for Team Sky than getting into a bidding war with Garmin, it is losing that war. Especially if the rider happens to be British. Team Sky detect a piety in Vaughters which gets under their collective skin. It is odd because both teams are among the white knights trying to rescue the sport, but they are natural rivals in their respective approaches. Vaughters passionately disagrees with Sky's policy of not allowing anyone with a doping past to work in their team.

Being Vaughters, being the affable JV, he couldn't stop himself leaking a little *Schadenfreude* at Sky's turmoil when Sean Yates, Steven de Jongh and Bobby Julich had to leave the team at the end of 2012. If Vaughters had applied his intellect to devising the best way to get under Brailsford's skin, he wouldn't have come up with anything more effective than the prodding at the misfortune of his rivals.

So Brailsford didn't want Tiernan-Locke joining Garmin, while Vaughters would not have beaten himself up with guilt about pinching a rider from Sky's domestic pastures. Andrew McQuaid, son of the former UCI president Pat and agent to many riders, did what everyone in his job does by playing one off against the other.

Then Tiernan-Locke, still riding with Endura, won the end-of-season Tour of Britain. Jackpot! He was a trophy signing now. Team Sky just had to have him. They offered a two-year contract on the kind of money that Tiernan-Locke wouldn't have dreamt of three years before. Garmin stayed interested but in the end, they couldn't compete. Like a Royal Canadian Mounted Policeman, Brailsford got his man.

Without wishing to sound arrogant, Team Sky would have thought, 'If he can win four stage-race victories with Endura, how many is he going to claim with us?' There was no telling how good Tiernan-Locke might become.

It never worked out.

He was often sick, couldn't seem to handle the training load and didn't ride to the level expected. From the twenty-seven riders on Sky's roster in 2013, his performances were the most disappointing. He blamed it on the training, which he considered too intense and made him feel run down and low on energy. Sky, and especially Kerrison, listen to what riders say and it is common for them to lighten the training load for those struggling to cope.

Before the end of the season Tiernan-Locke spoke with

Shane Stokes for an interview that appeared on the *Velonation* website and accepted some responsibility for what had been a terrible season. 'I guess some of what happened this year is my fault, in terms of not being more communicative with my coaches,' he said.

A month later, it was members of the UCI medical panel who were after his communication.

That Saturday telephone interview with Brailsford was difficult.

He'd had a tough week in Italy. In the days before the Cookson/McQuaid presidential contest, there was gossip about Team Sky and whispered talk about suspect bio passports that went beyond Tiernan-Locke. From people in Cookson's camp, he heard that people on the other side were saying Sky might not be as pure as the driven snow. Though assured that these deep 'off the record' mutterings were really attempts to hurt Cookson's candidature, Brailsford still worried.

And the letter to Tiernan-Locke wasn't a rumour.

The call from me was one he could have done without.

I believed there was a good chance Tiernan-Locke would be able to explain why his end-of-year blood values in 2012 seemed unnaturally elevated in relation to his 2013 values. Could it be that he was over-trained and constantly run down in 2013 and this had led to unnaturally low blood values through his season with Sky? In other words, the low blood values of 2013 were mistakenly presumed to be his baseline values.

The greater question, though, related to the very fact that there was such uncertainty haunting the team. Were Team

Sky's recruitment protocols sufficiently rigorous for a team with such high ethical standards? Especially after Leinders? Brailsford continually refused to answer questions related to Tiernan-Locke, but it became clear that he wasn't aware of the controversial report in *L'Equipe* after the Tour Méditerranéen victory. Fellow riders had all but openly accused Tiernan-Locke of cheating, but Team Sky hadn't been plugged into the grapevine.

'Dave, what did you think when you read that report in *L'Equipe* that virtually accused Jonathan of doping?'

'I'm not sure we saw that.'

'It appeared after his win in the Tour du Haut Var.'

'Don't know whether we talked about it, but we were confident about the information we had from John [Herety] and Julien [Winn].'

Team Sky was also reassured by the fact that Garmin had tested him and were still trying to sign him. But if that testing by Garmin was deemed to be helpful, shouldn't Sky have done its own testing on Tiernan-Locke when he trained with the team in Tenerife?

It was hard to see what exactly Sky had learned from the mistake of Geert Leinders, what new measures had been implemented to better protect the interests of the team. This is not to say that Tiernan-Locke had been involved in anything untoward, but given Sky's position on doping, for them to have not known about the accusations made in *L'Equipe* was very surprising.

Two aspects of the story bothered Brailsford. The overriding concern was that this story should not have been leaked and be in the public domain. Disappointment at this outcome wasn't lessened by the entire affair being a self-inflicted wound: the journalist that was going to undermine the UCI's process and cast a slur on the team's reputation was the one to whom Team Sky had opened its doors. Thanks, mate. But, of course, he couldn't say this.

The second was even harder to take. Tiernan-Locke's story showed Sky still wasn't getting its recruitment right. This wasn't to say he had ever been involved in anything unethical but the background checks should have been more thorough. They needed to have investigated the *L'Equipe* accusations. As for Sky's monitoring of riders' bio passports, neither was that where it needed to be. How could the UCI's medical panel have picked up an irregularity that the team had missed?

Brailsford and key personnel such as Kerrison and the lead doctor, Alan Farrell, spoke about what they could do. They discussed the possibility of setting up a panel of experts, working for the team but independent of Brailsford and his management colleagues, to oversee recruitment and monitor riders' bio passports. Chinks had been revealed in the team's anti-doping armour and, having failed to properly protect itself after the Leinders episode, Brailsford was determined to sort this out once and for all.

For example, it became clear from the Tiernan-Locke case that one of the dangers inherent in taking a rider from a Pro Continental team is that there is no available bio-passport data. Given this, wouldn't it be sensible for the team to have a policy of doing their own tests on riders who come to them from a Pro Continental team? Saying it knew Garmin tested Tiernan-Locke and being reassured by its rival being satisfied with the results was to apply a standard that Sky would not tolerate in any other area of its existence.

In the aftermath of the Tiernan-Locke story running in the *Sunday Times*, Sky issued a statement that sought to distance the team from the issue its rider had to address. 'Team Sky has been informed by Jonathan Tiernan-Locke that the UCI has notified him of a potential discrepancy in his biological passport data. He has withdrawn from racing whilst his response to the UCI is prepared then considered by the UCI. We have no doubts over his performance, behaviour or tests at Team Sky and understand any anomaly is in readings taken before he joined the team.

'Team Sky has tried to respect what should be a confidential process, allowing the rider to explain in private, without prejudice, and the anti-doping authorities to do their valuable job. At this stage in the ongoing process we will not add any further detail.'

Tiernan-Locke had twenty days to respond to the letter, but then sought and was granted an extension while he prepared his case to explain the anomaly.

Before running with the story, I called him, and left a message on his voicemail asking him to call back. He did not respond.

CHAPTER EIGHTEEN

I do not try to dance better than anyone else. I only try to dance better than myself.

Mikhail Baryshnikov

EPILOGUE

When the invitation came to travel with Team Sky in 2013 and experience the dips and swells of a season in a pro team, I was in two minds. If Team Sky was all that Dave Brailsford said it was, then the time spent with them would refresh the palate and flush the bad taste left by the Lance years. In truth, I was keen to fall in love with the sport again.

On the other hand there was the fear of disappointment. Finding or even suspecting that Brailsford was running the cycling equivalent of a speakeasy presented no journalistic difficulties, but personally to see the sport screwing its people all over again would have been too much. After all that has gone before, cycling more than any other sport needs to offer some hope, some proof of integrity.

I believe I found that. Everybody else can make up their own mind, but I believe that David Brailsford deserves a fair hearing first. I didn't find an organisation which always lives up to the billing it provides for itself, but Team Sky try. The nascent team's biggest achievements have been the Tours de France of 2012 and 2013. Yet those victories were bookended by the Leinders affair and by the Jonathan Tiernan-Locke business. For many, those bookends are all that can be seen.

The Jonathan Tiernan-Locke business gave me a few shivers of *déjà vu* when it arose. These are not pleasant things to write about at any time, and especially not after a summer in the sun. Suddenly I found myself back in those dark places, old sources ringing and talking science instead of sport. Life is too short to be starting a PhD in Haematology at age sixty.

The news for Tiernan-Locke and Team Sky seems mixed at the time of writing at the beginning of November 2013. Sources confirm that the problem is a single test from late 2012, a few months before he officially became a Sky rider. The case, should it go forward, will hinge on the rider's explanation for a very low percentage of reticulocytes in that test. Reticulocytes are immature red cells that circulate for a day in the body before developing into mature cells. They should comprise 0.5 percent to 1.5 percent of the total red cell population.

Abnormally low reticulocyte numbers can be caused by various conditions, mostly to do with anaemia, but they can also be triggered by a problem with erythropoietin production, which in turn could have related to use of synthetic or recombinant EPO. An uncommonly low reticulocyte count is not easily accounted for and Tiernan-Locke's fate will hinge on the credibility of his explanation.

The young rider could well have a satisfactory explanation, but Team Sky still needs to absorb the lessons of how they left themselves exposed once again to the jeers and catcalls of their detractors. A refreshing aspect of life within Team Sky is the willingness to absorb those lessons. Over the space of a few months, I found that I could put to Dave Brailsford the harshest of accusations about the failures of his protocols, and if he thought it reasonable he would take it on the chin and explain how he intended to deal with it. If doing the same thing over and over again but expecting different results suggests a sign of madness, Brailsford is eminently sane.

After the 2013 season, for instance, Team Sky had to look at the annual issue of freshening up the team. In retrospect, most around the team would quietly admit that simply having Googled Jonathan Tiernan-Locke's name would have revealed the suspicions (however fair or unfair) articulated about the rider in *L'Equipe*. They certainly would have revealed the need for a more rigorous examination of the rider's credentials than relying on the fact that Jonathan Vaughters' Garmin team had tested him once and found things satisfactory, but with the caveat that they wanted him back for more tests. Regardless of the outcome of Tiernan-Locke's eventual case (if any), the need for more improvement in the recruiting process is accepted.

For the 2014 season, the biggest of Team Sky's signings has been Mikel Nieve, a Spanish climber from the Euskaltel team, who has a proven Tour record.

What were the protocols this time?

First and foremost, clarity. Team Sky stressed relentlessly the importance of the rider understanding team policy in relation to drugs and where Team Sky are at the moment.

Next, the rider hands over his biological passport passwords. With these, Sky can mine and examine data that stretches back to 2009, when the rider first became part of a WorldTour team. Normally Sky would request this data set from the UCI. With permission the UCI will supply more information on the blood samples. If the team has questions, they can zoom in on particular values at particular times: was he training that day, was he racing or at what point of the season did that test take place?

The bio-passport data is then sent off to independent experts who have zero interest in whether Nieve or anyone else joins Team Sky, only that their bio-passport numbers stack up. Sky has a sort of ranking system with which to analyse the results.

Additionally they spoke to several people at great length about Nieve. Not just stakeholders in his career, but a contact they trusted who had worked with Nieve at Euskaltel. They went to their sources and looked as deep as they could for intelligence.

At the other end of the spectrum from Nieve was the signing of Nathan Earle, a well-respected young Australian making the same step up from Pro Continental level which brought Jonathan Tiernan-Locke to Team Sky's attention. Earle was tested to within an inch of his life.

Signing new riders is a competitive business, though. So what Sky have said is that in future they will commit to a rider only when the 'i's are dotted and the 't's crossed. That is, they have gathered the intelligence and satisfied themselves about the data. Until that moment, they will retain the right to release the rider without penalty.

For Sky, though, that is never enough. Correcting mistakes is one thing. Finding a better way forward is another. Brailsford and Kerrison have made a point of stepping down off the pedestal and engaging and speaking with cycling people with greater experience of doping. Their backgrounds, far from the doping heartland of the old continent, have been no help. To better make your way in a clean world, you need to know the terrain of the doper.

And they have taken apart the biological passport system for a forensic analysis.

Their conclusions on just how robust a tool the passport is will make interesting reading. There is a growing feeling within the world of drug testing that, with the best will in the world, authorities are trying to make this tool work at a level of sensitivity that it isn't designed for. If there are chances of a false positive, the entire system will be undermined.

As it stands the disciplinary panel look at data anomalies in isolation. They ask themselves how can this quirk be explained through the context of doping. Would microdosing fit the picture? Blood doping maybe. Then they ask the athlete to explain why the anomaly wouldn't be down to doping. Generally the athlete isn't equipped to know.

Much of the winter of 2013 was spent reviewing what had happened during the summer. Brailsford's feeling during 2013, successful though it had been, was that the ripples from the USADA report into Lance Armstrong and co had been so seismic that the team hadn't spent enough time the previous winter assessing and revising their own protocols. It had been a time to just get up on the roof and fix everything that might need fixing. A cruel and brutal time.

At the end of 2013, Brailsford intended to set aside the first week of December and dedicate it to reworking the core values of his team. He wanted to do a lot of work on the behavioural side of what Team Sky do. He is talking again about 'winning behaviours'.

He intended to ask the staff and riders what would stop them winning the Tour de France in 2014. What would stop them winning a longed-for classic. What might cause disharmony. From small groups answers would be fed back, a list of losing behaviours if you like. From there the task would be to find the winning behaviours. That is our way.

To many of his detractors that would sound like typical Dave Brailsford speak. Everything has a label as if being sold from a shelf, but speaking to him as he talks about his desire to keep winning and to be trusted he says things which challenge the usual rap against him.

He talks of needing even more openness and transparency. Maintaining the same level of performance is very important, but Team Sky will be looking to collaborate more openly with science community experts to provide more evidence and be more open. Blood data, power data, training regimes; he would hand them all to genuine experts in a heartbeat. Let them draw conclusions that would be beyond reproach.

Even the small things with the team are up for review. Through the long season that brought the second Tour de

France, Chris Froome, the star of the production had virtually his own personal *soigneur* (or carer) in David Rozman.
This helped Froome but it caused small ripples. Rozman was
occasionally unable to perform the other tasks that *soigneurs*
were asked to do. Someone had to cover for him. Lead carer
Mario Pafundi thought it wasn't right.

So Brailsford and Rod Ellingworth and Tim Kerrison
talked about it. David Rozman had worked hard and done a
good job, but he wasn't employed by Chris Froome, he
worked for Team Sky. Within the team's inner sanctum, any
move towards individual relationships is considered a slightly
dangerous thing. So Rozman was gently told he wouldn't be
doing Froome that much in 2014. Like Premiership footballers, Sky's carers will be rotated. In most teams, if the star
rider wanted to be rubbed down every evening by Scarlett
Johansson, someone would try to make it happen.

That is what keeps me interested. Team Sky are organic, a
work in progress. They get things wrong, of course they do,
but they plan and build in a post-nuclear winter. As such they
are pioneers.

No sport has ever laid waste to itself like cycling has. No
sport has had to vacate the winner's podium seven times in its
iconic event. No sport has records so liberally spangled with
asterisks cautioning us that the adventures within may be
entirely fictional. As Sandro Donati once said, the good thing
about the theatre is that the audience knows it's not for real.

Team Sky are yomping across territory which no team has
previously explored. And they have chosen to hobble themselves with their zero tolerance policy. When they make a
mistake, they go back and they stand at the drawing board

conscious that the air is filled with laughter and sneers and envy. In fact, even when they succeed they find their way back to that drawing board. They are always looking for ways to fail less and to succeed better.

They won the 2013 Tour de France but along the route to Corsica and the start of that race, they know they got so much wrong.

Dave Brailsford once said to me that his team's expedition through the wastelands of modern professional cycling was jeopardised by the fact that the people the team depended upon – Tim Kerrison, Rod Ellingworth, Alan Farrell and himself – had all come from the clean side of the tracks. I believed him. They don't think like cheats.

For the cynic – and the legacy of Lance has ensured cycling is littered with cynicism so potent it is only rivalled by his career – this is a hard line to digest. Many still believe that for Team Sky to succeed not only do they have to be cheating, but they have to be cheating better than anybody has ever cheated.

That is what I set out to examine when I went to live within the tent Brailsford has pitched. That is why this book concerns itself more with the hands who hold the reins than it does with the hands which grip the handlebars. For Team Sky to cheat on the levels which their detractors allege – and in social media those allegations come in blizzards of libel – they would have to be operating a cheating wing to the organisation which consumed as much time and energy as the actual cycling did.

I bow to no man when it comes to cynicism and scepticism about extraordinary achievements in cycling. But like the apostle Thomas, I need to put my finger on the scar left by the EPO needle. To speak to someone with more than just a gut feeling. I came to Team Sky after more than a decade fishing in the toxic world of Lance. I came with the stories of Tyler Hamilton and Floyd Landis in my bloodstream. The first thing that occurred to me was that no team operating like Lance's teams operated could ever afford to invite a journalist into the tent. Too much to keep hidden. Rozman put his finger on it: 'You will know,' he said, 'from the conversations that stop when you walk into the room.'

I met the people. With great respect to the man, the team doctor Alan Farrell is almost entirely tone deaf when it comes to the tragic opera of cheating. It's not his music, nor his world. If Team Sky are doping as alleged, there would have to be a medical team hiding behind the curtains. Nobody could spend five minutes speaking with Alan Farrell and then start dropping hints about needing a little Edgar Allan (as Lance's confederates called EPO). Farrell would need the request spelled out to him in large letters, delivered in triplicate with the correct documentation, and then there would be a good chance that he would convulse with anger before bringing the story to Brailsford.

Ellingworth? Central casting couldn't create a more old-style cycling man. You see the disappointment which almost smothers him like a smog when a rider does badly, when a rider quits or when a rider fails to appreciate what a wonderful hand of cards his career is. You see that and you know that Rod isn't designed for a world of lies and deceit. It would break him.

Tim Kerrison? To spend time with Kerrison is to encounter

a savant who sees and understands the world of sport differently. He can lose himself in long paragraphs expressing his shy enthusiasm about equations and figures and the science of performance. I spent many hours speaking to him or about him, looking for the darkness, wondering if he was the Svengali genius operating an enterprise which I just couldn't see. I found him to be a man so in love with and so convinced of the science of performance that the pollution of his mental database with fraudulent statistics would break his heart.

And Brailsford? There is no doubt that he is an operator. No man could build the empire that is Team Sky without knowing how to duck and dive a little. But he is astonishingly open. As a journalist I felt able to ask him just about anything. We had discussions which ranged from his life, to the world of cheating as he saw it, and on to the queries about Geert Leinders and Jonathan Tiernan-Locke. With respect to the privacy of some of the people we spoke about, there were things he couldn't or wouldn't say, but he is a man who puts his hands up when he makes a mistake (and he would allow you to enter several big mistakes on the balance sheet), and also a man fascinated by the challenge of doing things properly and being seen to do things properly. He isn't just the brains behind Team Sky, he is the heartbeat at the team's core.

He opened the doors to me and let me at it. He sat down with me and talked any time I needed him to. He picked up the phone, even when he knew what was coming and would have preferred not to. I put things to him which might have hurt him or offended him. I could feel him wince, but he never ducked, and never danced away. He took his shots and kept on.

People see the bespoke Volvo buses and the Jaguar team cars, they laugh at the obsession with detail and sneer at Brailsford's motivational buzz phrases. He knows that, but he believes in what he is doing. He believes that cycling has permitted its philosophy on performance to be entirely coloured by drugs down through the decades. He is in love with the idea that there is a different way and that he can be the man to chart that way. It's ego, it's the love of a challenge, it's obsession.

I never found evidence pointing to any conclusion other than that, for Dave Brailsford, cheating would diminish the fun and the sense of achievement. Had he reached the South Pole in a hot-air balloon, Roald Amundsen wouldn't have truly enjoyed his return to Norway. Brailsford cheating his way to the top would know the same emptiness.

For 2014 Team Sky's story will keep unfolding in interesting ways. It is a tall order for them to hope to become more successful and also more loved and trusted. Narrowing the fissure between Bradley Wiggins and Chris Froome just got a lot more interesting with the announcement of the route for the 2014 Tour de France. The second last stage is a 54km time trial, an immense test of riders after three weeks of hard riding. A guy like Wiggins will know that on his best form he could do a minute's worth of damage there. But as the penultimate stage, Wiggins could conceivably have his go at winning the Tour without even endangering the team. He could come along as a *domestique* and, as long as he were in touching distance coming into the time trial, could take his leadership rather than wait for it to be awarded. Will the thought tempt him, on the iciest days of winter, to slip on the earphones and churn out the wattage in that shed at the end of his garden? And will the thought that he might be help to determine how Froome spends his own winter?

Of the young riders in Team Sky's enviable roster, everybody will look forward to watching the progress of one or two. Josh Edmondson from Leeds impressed in 2013. His attitude, his application, his willingness to learn – those things and his natural climbing talent were commented on again and again. He trains a lot with Yorkshire's greatest heroes, the Brownlee boys, and if he can live with them . . .

The same with Joe Dombrowski, who improved no end as 2013 wore on. For a kid coming from America to settle in the south of France, a good first year was a big ask. Before the season began, we spoke in Mallorca and I didn't have to put my finger behind his ear to feel the wetness. So it took him time but by the end of the season, everyone knew. The kid could climb. If he hits the rising ground running in 2014, watch him soar.

Sky still yearn for credibility in the classics. Gabriel Rasch, a Norwegian, will ride the classics next year and ease into his apprenticeship as a *directeur sportif* with the team. Catch them young and they will fly. His compatriot Edvald Boasson Hagen will be looking to improve on 2013, a year which brought more curses than blessings. Everyone loves Eddy so much it's hard to tell him he should be doing better.

The story I tried to cover, it rolls onward like a long mountain stage; at times it will be gruelling, at times spectacular. With every steep incline, though, Team Sky will learn something and the higher the altitude the more interesting they will become. There will be those who doubt them and those who stand on the side of the road shouting abuse. There will be very few people, though, who won't watch with interest and, in time, I hope, with respect. You can't live and breathe with Team Sky on the road without knowing that something different this way comes.

I recall the team having a celebratory drink in Annecy the evening before the ceremonial final stage to Paris and Tim Kerrison mentioned he was on his way back to the team's base in Nice that night.

'You'll come to Paris tomorrow morning,' I said, 'to see the first night-time finish on the Champs-Elysées?'

'I'll come to Paris in the late afternoon,' he replied. 'Some of our other riders, guys who didn't make the Tour team, are doing a training ride up the Col de la Madone in the morning and I'd like to be with them for that.'

'Wow,' I thought.

That enthusiasm, that dedication, that madness will be enough to keep me watching and hoping that the team's influence in terms of integrity, openness and willingness to learn proves to be contagious in the bleak post-Lance winter.

Acknowledgements

On the fourth day of the 2013 Tour de France, Team Sky's *directeur sportif* Nico Portal drove the number one race car into Boulevard Jean Jaures in Nice. And then noticed he had a flat tyre. Front right. *Merde!* With the importance and imminence of the team time trial, Portal had much on his mind and hadn't bargained for having to change a wheel. The bike mechanics couldn't help. They were checking and re-checking nine time-trial bikes about to be used for the first time.

No one panicked.

Sky's performance manager Rod Ellingworth told Portal to just concentrate on the team's race against the clock. The puncture would be taken care of. Ellingworth has never worn sleeves that weren't rolled up, and in a flash the bus driver Claudio Lucchini saw what was needed and was at Ellingworth's side. They laughed as they got to work, cursing the law that makes it compulsory for the spare to be a uselessly thin wheel designed to take you no further than the next garage.

So they removed the punctured wheel, took a proper wheel off the nearby carers' car, put the short-term spare onto that vehicle and then bolted the good wheel onto Portal's car.

They worked like beavers, Ellingworth the performance manager and Lucchini the bus driver. Their twenty minutes of doubling up as mechanics reflected what it was that made being around Team Sky so much fun.

They dig in. They do the long hours. They don't complain. Team doctor Alan Farrell packs away the poles used to create the cordoned-off area for the riders by the bus. Operations manager Carsten Jeppesen stands by the roadside and hands out food and drink to the riders. More than that, they were okay about allowing a non-contributing stranger into their world and they made sure I didn't feel unwanted.

For their welcome and their company and their help, for helping me to believe again in professional cycling I thank each and every one of them.

In part this book is a tribute to their work.

There are others, too, that are entitled to feel a stake in this book. As has always been his way, my sports editor at the *Sunday Times*, Alex Butler, has been supportive. I know I'm running low on credit. And there's my remarkably patient editor at Simon & Schuster, Ian Marshall. We go back some way and I don't think it's stretching things to say that from me he's learnt patience. If you wait long enough, it arrives.

Speaking of patience, I am indebted to my family for whom, too often over the last twelve months, I have been a ship passing in the night. But whenever I get home, they are still there. Thank you. And the next twelve months will be better.

In the course of writing this book, I had the good fortune to begin a working relationship with Connor Schwartz, a close friend of our youngest son Conor. At first I asked if he could do some transcribing. Quick and accurate with his transcriptions, he was soon editing. Chapter after chapter, everything he touched he improved.

He's only a kid out of university, but I tell you the country's future is in good hands.